Negotiating Violence

Studies in Medieval and Reformation Traditions

Edited by

Andrew Colin Gow (*Edmonton, Alberta*)

In cooperation with

Founding Editor

Heiko A. Oberman †

VOLUME 213

The titles published in this series are listed at *brill.com/smrt*

Negotiating Violence

Papal Pardons and Everyday Life in East Central Europe (1450–1550)

By

Gabriella Erdélyi

TUTA SUB AEGIDE PALLAS · 1683 ·

BRILL

LEIDEN | BOSTON

Cover illustration: Niccolò dell'Arca, *Lamentation over the Dead Christ* (Compianto sul Cristo morto), Santa Maria della Vita, Bologna, completed either 1462–63 or c. 1485 (detail). Author's photo.

The Library of Congress Cataloging-in-Publication Data is available online at http://catalog.loc.gov

Names: Erdélyi, Gabriella, author.
Title: Negotiating violence : Papal pardons and everyday life in East Central Europe (1450–1550) / Gabriella Erdélyi.
Description: Boston : Brill, 2018. | Includes bibliographical references and index.
Identifiers: LCCN 2018016198 | ISBN 9789004361157 (alk. paper)
Subjects: LCSH: Catholic Church—Europe, Eastern—History. | Catholic Church—Europe, Central—History. | Pardon—Europe, Eastern—History. | Pardon—Europe, Central—History. | Europe, Eastern—Church history. | Europe, Central—Church history.
Classification: LCC BX1490.5 .E73 2018 | DDC 940.2/1—dc23
LC record available at https://lccn.loc.gov/2018016198

Typeface for the Latin, Greek, and Cyrillic scripts: "Brill." See and download: brill.com/brill-typeface.

ISSN 1573-4188
ISBN 978-90-04-36115-7 (hardback)
ISBN 978-90-04-36126-3 (e-book)

This book is printed on acid-free paper and produced in a sustainable manner.

Contents

Acknowledgements

The book is finished, and the end of the long and mazy road is reached with mixed feelings. There remains a particularly enjoyable duty, however: to thank all those friends and colleagues who assisted and accompanied me on the journey.

Everyday conversations with my colleagues at the Institute of History of the Research Centre for the Humanities of the Hungarian Academy of Sciences considerably shaped the book and made it a better one. I owe, as always, my greatest intellectual debt to Katalin Péter, with whom it has always been a pleasure to share ideas and thoughts on emerging research. I have also benefited a great deal from the conversations with several colleagues on different occasions, Gábor Sarbak, Klára Hegyi, Beatrix Romhányi, Kornél Szovák, Tamás Pálosvölgyi, Szabolcs Varga, Géza Pálffy, Zoltán Csepregi, Géza Hegyi, Tamás Fedeles, Ilona Kristóf and Tibor Neumann. I am also grateful for the comments on papers delivered at conferences and seminars. In particular I would like to acknowledge the suggestions and ideas of Judith Pollmann, Erika Kuijpers, Sarah Covington, Stephen Cummins, Laura Kounine, Taral Alberts, Stuart Carroll and Natasa Stefanec which they shared with me at the International Medieval Congress in Leeds, a Leiden workshop on early modern memories, a Cambridge workshop on conflict resolution and a Cluj-Napoca workshop on popular religion. I am grateful for their helpful advice and references.

The petitions of papal pardon, the basis for this book, are kept in the Archives of the Apostolic Penitentiary (Tribunale della Penitenzieria Apostolica, Archivio Storico) in Rome. I am sincerely grateful for the generous assistance of Alessandro Saracco and Ugo Tarraborelli, the archivists of this papal tribunal, which continues to serve the needs of penitent Christians in our own days. The head of the Penitentiary, the Penitenziere Maggiore Mauro Card. Piacenza, was kind enough to study the manuscript and provide his consent for publication.

The research and completion of this book were funded by a grant from the Gerda Henkel Foundation in Germany. The copy-editing of my first English text was supported by the National Bank of Hungary and the Hungarian Scientific Research Fund (OTKA-81435). Illustrations were collected and the scientific apparatus of the book prepared with the help of the Momentum Project of the Hungarian Academy of Sciences (LP2017-3/2017). I am very much indebted for their financial support.

I am grateful for the critical comments of two anonymous readers that strengthened this book, and I would like to thank Béla Nagy and Gabriella Kocsis who provided expert help in producing maps and illustrations. Sean

Lambert, József Litkei and and Monica MacFadzean played an indispensible role in the creation of the final text as my scrupulous copy editors. Last, but not least, the dedicated staff of my publisher and my editor Ivo Romein made the final and often stressful stages of production a pleasurable experience.

Acknowledgements often reflect family lineages, so what could be more proper than to express my ultimate gratitude to my family: my husband, Sándor, my mother, Ildikó, my mother-in-law, Tamara and my three children, Anna, Júlia and Ferenc, whose company lends me both cheerful diversion and unwavering love and support: I dedicate this book to all of them.

G.E., October 2017

List of Maps and Illustrations

Maps

Figures

CHAPTER 1

Introduction

At noon on Christmas Eve, 1499, thousands jostled onto St. Peter's Square in Rome to secure a prime spot for watching the magnificent ceremonies welcoming in the jubilee year. The hustle and bustle settled when the ceremonial procession, led by confessors dressed in black, set off toward St. Peter's Basilica. Pope Alexander VI took the holy hammer from the head cardinal of the office of the Apostolic Penitentiary to knock down the wall that blocked the holy door. As the pope pushed the giant doors open, symbolically granting free access to divine grace, the psalm "Open to me the gates of justice!" was sung. After the papal penitentiaries cleansed the threshold with holy water, the pontiff walked through with a lit candle as the sound of bells intermingled with that of gunfire.[1]

Pilgrims, many of whom had traveled from afar and spent an icy night under the sky, followed the pope into the church.[2] They had come to the Eternal City in order to gain plenary indulgence, exemption from the sufferings of purgatory and assistance for their afterlife journey to paradise. They also sought to acquire a share of the treasury of divine grace and justice by visiting the four basilicas, where they would confess their sins and be absolved through the sacrament of penance. They hoped that justice would be administered to them in the halls of papal courts, where the same papal confessors who heard confessions participated in legal procedures as minor penitentiaries.[3]

The splendid spectacles and the complex interconnected services of the papal curia had attracted Mihály Krausz of the remote town of Enyed (Aiud, Romania) in Transylvania. He traveled to Rome in the 1500 jubilee year and submitted a written petition composed in the third person to the papal court requesting clemency for killing a man:

> He had been staying in the house of Ágnes, the daughter of a local burgher named Mihály Szabó, when the woman's husband surprised them.

1 On the opening ceremonies, see Pastor, *Die Geschichte der Päpste*, vol. 3, 485.

2 On pilgrims sleeping by fires: Csukovits, *Középkori magyar zarándokok*, 146.

3 For an overview of the proceedings of evidence of ecclesiastical courts, see Brundage, *Medieval Canon Law*, 120–53. On papal confessors in the role of minor penitentiaries, officials of the lower office of the Apostolic Penitentiary, see Salonen and Schmugge, *A Sip From the "Well of Grace,"* 16.

 | DOI 10.1163/9789004361263_002

FIGURE 1 *The Pope opens the Holy Door during the Jubilee of 1675.*

> While escaping, he heard the husband threatening to kill his wife, whom he had caught in the act, so he turned back to save her [...]. The husband then released her and attacked him, and he killed the husband in self-defense. Ágnes was arrested and sentenced to death, but her release was procured and they clandestinely became betrothed; however, friends of the deceased husband, with whom Mihály was making a deal, made him swear that he would never marry her. As they hadn't intended to kill the husband for the sake of their marriage, Mihály viewed the vow as detrimental and intended to have it revoked in order to enter into marriage with Ágnes. He beseeched the pope to absolve him from the crime of homicide and Ágnes from fornication, and to annul his oath.[4]

Mihály formally addressed his petition to Pope Alexander VI, who of course could not personally read the dozens of petitions arriving at the papal offices each day.[5] This man in trouble turned specifically to the tribunal of

4 APA, vol. 48, fol. 475v–6r (Transylvanien. dioc.). Mihály asked for a declaration that would attest that they had been obliged to swear the oath under duress, and that breaking it should therefore not qualify as perjury, a very typical request at the Penitentiary. Salonen and Schmugge, *A Sip from the "Well of Grace,"* 39.

5 The Penitentiary at the time handled around ten cases per day (three thousand per year). Together with other curial offices such as the Chancery and Datary, the number amounted to forty per day, ten times more than the daily business of the imperial court. Schmugge, Hersperger and Wiggenhauser, *Die Supplikenregister*, 22; Frenz, *Die Kanzlei der Päpste*, 35, 80–83.

the Apostolic Penitentiary, which issued letters of pardon for severe crimes that only the pope could forgive. Ordinary people such as Mihály, as opposed to members of the secular and ecclesiastical elite, preferred to use the services of this papal office due to its lower fee and quick and smooth handling of affairs.[6]

Mihály had not traveled to Rome alone; his lover, Ágnes Szabó ("Tailor") accompanied him, which we know because three days following the approval of Mihály's petition, they enrolled together in the Confraternity of the Holy Spirit in Rome.[7] This was a rather fashionable, though costly investment, which promoted the public good by supporting the hospital of the Holy Spirit, an ancient and prestigious institution of Christian charity in the neighborhood of the papal palaces. It was also another device to earn plenary indulgence and secure individual salvation, which the faithful—ranging from kings to peasants and artisans—made use of in great numbers.[8] Their pilgrimage to Rome in the jubilee year served the same end, although the Transylvanian couple seems not to have voluntarily undertaken this great voyage for their salvation, but were probably ordered to do so. Urban magistrates often imposed a penitential pilgrimage as part of the penalty for homicide, since in this way the perpetrators, they thought, could intercede on behalf of the salvation of their victims. Additionally, the pilgrimage, similarly to banishment, entailed the temporary removal of the perpetrators, which helped restore communal harmony. The family of Ágnes, which had intervened and stood for her as guarantors, was able, under this condition, to save the life of the woman convicted of adultery and murder.[9]

6 On the character and workings of the office, the basic work remains Emil Göller, *Die Päpstliche Pönitentiarie*. More recent is Schmugge, Hersperger and Wiggenhauser, *Die Supplikenregister* and Salonen and Schmugge, *A Sip From the "Well of Grace."* On the fees of the administrative services of the office, see more below.

7 The list of members from Hungary collected from the enrollment book of the confraternity is published by Bunyitay, ed., *Liber confraternitatis S. Spiritus de Urbe*, 94 (*Michael Crauus cum uxore Agnese de Enneydt*).

8 On the Hospitaller order that ran the hospital in Rome as well as the confraternity founded in 1446 and its register book into which new members jotted their names and the entrance fee they paid (originally the substantial sum of three ducats), see Csukovits, *Középkori magyar zarándokok*, 168–89. In the jubilee year of 1500, more than 1,700 people from the Kingdom of Hungary enrolled.

9 On penitential pilgrimages and urban courts, see Csukovits, "Bűn és büntetés," 218–19.

Research Agenda

"Magnifying" extraordinary social practices and their representations renders more visible the otherwise obscure contours of social norms—norms that are under constant change. Narratives of norm violations, paradoxically, open a window onto norms that govern everyday behavior.[10] What kinds of tensions triggered the conflicts that often resulted in bloodshed between neighbors as well as between laymen and priests? How and why did skirmishes between town dwellers and local students develop? Why did certain family feasts, such as betrothals or religious rituals such as public processions, so often end in street scuffles? Why did friars become involved in fistfights before they permanently left their cloisters in great numbers prior to the Protestant Reformation? Why was it possible to graphically portray the 1514 public execution of the leader of the rebellious Hungarian peasants, while participants of the peasant war denied having killed anyone during battle? How did clergymen, simple priests and friars come to fight on the side of rebels? What made it possible during the ferocious Christian-Muslim military conflict in East Central Europe for individuals to voluntarily "turn Turk?" To answer these questions, this book travels to new areas of historical inquiry into the late medieval cultures of violence and conflict resolution, while also navigating some recent "turns" toward emotion, narrativity, identity and memory.

Pardon requests were craftily fabricated legal narratives and thus require their readers to apply several interpretive strategies. Petitions were written humbly and respectfully in order to solicit the benevolence of their audiences, and descriptions of past events had to be constructed compellingly to gain credibility within the legal procedure.[11] Pardon tales, as other judicial sources, were the products of a collaborative enterprise between the semiliterate and legal professionals. Curial proctors awaited their clients in rented offices around the four basilicas, then took the written petitions to the curia and ensured they got through the labyrinth of officials by using their expertise and contacts.[12] While

10 On the notion of the "exceptional normal" (*eccessionalmente normale*) coined by Italian microhistory to capture the dynamic between social practices and norms, see Grendi, "Micro-analisi e storia sociale," esp. 512. It has since been interpreted in diverse ways. The one preferred here is outlined by Ginzburg and Poni, "The Name and the Game," esp. 7–8.

11 On the constructedness and literary character of remission stories, see the authoritatively argued book by Davis, *Fiction in the Archives*.

12 On the professionalization of the trade, see Brundage, "Professional Canon Lawyers." The college of the proctors (*penitentiariae procurator*) of the Penitentiary was officially limited to 24 members, but proctors were needed and active. Schmugge, Hersperger and Wiggenhauser, *Die Supplikensregister*, 19–20, 48.

petitioners provided the original storylines in the vernacular, proctors had to respect a fixed legal protocol and produce *stilus curiae* documents in Latin. The resulting crime narratives followed a basic script, transforming the fragmentary and controversial events into coherent and credible stories crafted by literary tools of emplotment and necessary embellishment.[13] We get a clearer sense of how the legal agenda reduced muddled and long-held hostilities to isolated fistfights when we compare divergent petitions about the same event (as in chapter 7, where a single event is described by both a village priest and a chaplain, and in chapter 9, where we analyze two versions of a story by a woman wishing to remarry). Pardon tales represent a very unique kind of source since, compared to other judicial texts written by the elite, we get uninterrupted narratives (and, not infrequently, literal quotes and dialogues) from ordinary people.[14]

The story of Mihály and Ágnes must have seemed authentic to curial judges, who counterchecked their statements, since it was familiar: adultery was the most common of crimes, and adulterous and murderous husbands and wives—similarly to aberrant friars and priests—were the most commonplace figures in marriage trials at church courts as well as in everyday gossip and popular fiction. Bocaccio's tale of the secret lovers, Guiscardo and Sigismonda, found *in flagranti* and ending tragically, was retold in a variety of genres and languages in the years before and after 1500 and was widely read across Europe.[15] From everyday life they entered the pages of popular fiction and pardon tales in which fact and fiction blended into an inseparable whole.

Acknowledging the literary and legal character of petitions, we will read them "against the grain"[16] in order to gain access to the social realities from which they emerged. We will seek additional information from archives and secondary literature about the actors and the events to check the veracity of

13 For the distinction between historical truth versus narrative truth in judicial records and archives, see the classic work by Arlette Farge, *The Allure of the Archive*, for example 29–31. Royal or princely pardons deployed a hauntingly identical narrative pattern, described in Arnade and Prevenier, *Honor, Vengeance*, esp. 13–18.

14 See the pro and contra arguments for using judicial records as egodocuments (letters, autobiographies, diaries) in Fuchs and Schulze, eds, *Wahrheit, Wissen, Erinnerung.*

15 Bocaccio's love tale (Decameron IV, 1) entertained readers in vernacular verse, with adaptations of the Latin poem of the Italian humanist Filippo Beroaldo (Bologna, 1495). Its German rewritings were reprinted several times around 1500, warning readers of the dangers of erotic passion (Franz, *Deutscher Humanismus*, 1480–1520, vol. 1, 117–18, 327–28). It reached the Hungarian audience in a Protestant remake in the sixteenth century reloaded with the new moral message. Komlovszki, *Széphistóriák.*

16 On the method of reading against the grain, see Davis, *Fiction in the Archives*, 4.

the claims, but since such factual verification is only rarely possible, we will more generally strive to reconstruct the broader social context of a particular crime and appraise the verisimilitude of the pardon tale.

The protagonists of this book who emerge from the texts are not kings and cardinals, but ordinary people—villagers and small town inhabitants such as clerical students, poor priests and renegade friars. Poor clerics, who appeared on the social scene in ever growing numbers in the second part of the fifteenth century, were largely invisible in other sources. Here they come to the foreground as violators of canon law, negotiating their social status and identity at court. This book is not about the lower clergy, but is an exploration of religious culture and everyday life with a focus upon lay-clerical interactions. The evolving historical narrative will be framed within a story of runaway friars conceived as prototypical figures of their times, deeply engaged in the negotiation of lay-clerical relations. In order to attempt to understand why village youths entered and left religious orders en masse in the early sixteenth century, the chapters that follow examine their careers and roles in a variety of social contexts, starting with their socialization in school (chapter 4) and following them to the cloisters (chapter 2). We then glimpse them as unbeneficed clergymen in village communities (chapters 6 and 7) and focus on their relationships vis-à-vis the beneficed clergy (chapter 5). Finally, we will see them in the act of crossing several cultural and social boundaries; they will appear as rebels in the peasant army against the nobility (chapter 8), among the Ottoman Turks (chapter 9) and as the first preachers of the *evangelium* (conclusion).

Their routine crossing of the boundaries between the cloister and the world, I will argue, was a tactic to negotiate social status: they were seeking free education in religious houses (discussed in detail in chapter 3) and a gateway to the priesthood (chapter 5). Learning was a means of upward social mobility and, as I will demonstrate, the lower strata of society, often imagined as ignorant and passive, consciously and effectively used it as such. Ex-friars were symbolic figures of the era famously dubbed the "age of ambition,"[17] which witnessed an increasing lay demand for learning and mobility, as will be more extensively discussed in chapters 2, 3 and 4. The stories about the careers of renegade friars will paradoxically illuminate another aspect of sixteenth-century transition in which the motor of social and religious change was lay society rather than the clergy, as accepted wisdom would have us believe.[18] In

17 Du Boulay, *An Age of Ambition*.

18 A long history of traditional approaches starting with Leopold von Ranke is to be noted here; the clergy and church were viewed as the central agents of religious life, and placed center stage in narrations of stories of religious change, both crises and reform.

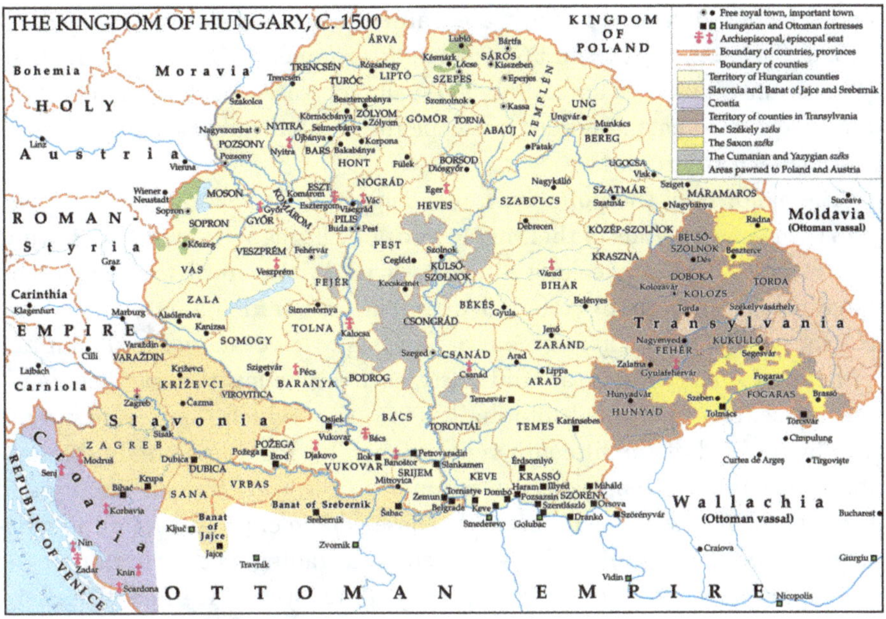

MAP 1 *The Kingdom of Hungary, c. 1500.*

more general terms, the question of how individuals seeking their destinies and livelihoods promoted the transformation of prevailing structures will be addressed in various contexts.

Although the variety of methodologies applied and issues raised renders this book a mosaic, the evolving historical narrative reads as the stages of life of renegade friars, spanning from family and school via cloister to secular clergy or lay literate professions. This multi-tiered story will play itself out in the geographical arena of the Kingdom of Hungary, one of the largest countries in late medieval Europe, which included the territories of modern-day Hungary and Croatia as well as Slovakia, Transylvania (Romania) and parts of Ukraine, Serbia and Austria (Burgenland). It was a composite region in terms of its political structure (the result of the union of two kingdoms, Hungary and Croatia, with separate metropolitan provinces and national diets sharing one king from the Hunyadi family, followed in 1490 by the Jagiellonian dynasty and, from 1526, the Habsburgs), and was noteworthy for its ethnic

Recently: Appold, *The Reformation*, 1–42. In the 1990s, attention turned toward the role of the laity, with a new focus on parish religion (for example Kümin, *The Shaping of a Community*) and "communal religion" (Mayes, *Communal Christianity*).

and religious diversity. Besides the Latin Christian majority (Hungarians, Croats, Slovenes, Slovaks and Germans), the number of Orthodox Christians (Romanians, Ruthenes and Serbs) gradually increased as the inhabitants of the Balkans fled north in order to escape the Ottoman advance and ceaseless Ottoman-Christian warfare.[19]

The majority of the population was comprised of peasant tenants (*iobagio*) living on the lands of their noble lords in villages and small towns, while the mostly German-speaking citizenry lived in the royal free cities, and large blocks of German (referred to as "Saxon") settlements were located in Transylvania and Spiš (in modern Slovakia). However, due to the limited number of such *civitates* (around thirty, each with a few thousand citizens), market centers developed into market towns, of which there were around 150 by the end of the fifteenth century, each having a few hundred inhabitants. A similar urban pattern was found in the Holy Roman Empire and other parts of East Central Europe.[20] These *oppida* enjoyed communal privileges in terms of municipal government and trading, and were in part the motor of the region's economic prosperity at the turn of the fifteenth and sixteenth centuries through large-scale exporting of cattle to the German States and Italy as well as wine production. Their non-privileged though economically thriving peasantry seized arms in order to fight for freedom or, in other words, for noble status[21] in the uprising of 1514, followed by a memory war for the right to legitimize violence and just war between rebels and rulers, as depicted in chapter 8.

Even if towns were small and had agrarian outlooks, they resembled their western counterparts with regard to the large number of ecclesiastical institutions. By 1500, the network of monasteries and friaries had become dense even by Western European standards, primarily due to the heavy presence of Franciscans and Paulines. Nevertheless, the rivalry of regular and secular clergy in this region (in contrast with the Continental West) seems to have ended with the latter's triumph in the context of parish religion (in other words, the center of parish religion remained the parish church), as is also suggested by the choices made by our protagonists, who opted for diocesan careers (chapter 5). Their career choices direct attention to the neglected portions of their elementary education: chapter 4 will show that an astonishingly dense network of

19 Kubinyi, "Die Bevölkerung des Königreichs Ungarns."

20 On the urban network, see Bácskai, "Small Towns in Eastern Central Europe."

21 The sharp divide between nobles and peasants lay in the perpetual right of property: peasants, even if enjoying personal freedoms, did not have property, but lived as tenants on the property of their landlords. Engel, *The Realm of St. Stephen*, 325–26.

parish schools was visited by the sons of commoners from the countryside and that taking the friar's habit for a while was a tactic to overcome the shortcomings of parish school education.

The late medieval structures of state and Church came under dramatic challenge via the Hungarian-Ottoman military conflict. A long period of Ottoman-Hungarian static warfare, signaled by peace treaties and military incursions, ended in 1521, when the most important fortress of the border defense system, Nándorfehérvár (Belgrade), fell to the Turks. In the years following, the army of the Hungarian King, Louis II Jagiello, lost a fatal battle at Mohács (1526), which opened the way for the Ottomans to take the capital city of Buda (1541), after which the medieval kingdom split into three parts (Habsburg territories, Turkish vilayets and a more or less independent principality in Transylvania).

Chapter 9 approaches the Hungarian-Ottoman conflict from a bottom-up perspective, rendering visible the rationalities of those who voluntarily crossed the Christian-Muslim boundary. While Catholic structures, high clergy and landed estates had fallen victim to the Ottoman conquest and all that came in its wake, the movement of religious reform emanating from German territories captivated the followers of the old Church as of the 1520s, starting with the German-speaking citizenry and the royal court-based aristocracy, and quickly enticed the rural population as well. The story of the life and learning of pre-Reformation lower clergy, a central theme of this book, will reflect relevant scholarly discourses regarding the Reformation. I will revisit the paradigm of the "clerical reformation," or the concept of the Reformation as an "educational revolution" (chapter 2), as well as the much-debated issue of how lay-clerical relations transformed (chapter 7). Unsurprisingly, seen from a late medieval perspective focused on monastic culture (chapter 3) and lay-clerical everyday exchanges (explored primarily in chapters 4, 6 and 7), lay society rather than clergy as the agent of religious and social change will emerge, just as continuity will appear to have been more powerful than change in the dynamic of sixteenth-century renewal and reform.

The Uses of Papal Pardon

Let us now turn back to our initial story about the murderous and adulterous lovers, Mihály Krausz and Ágnes Szabó, who described in exceptional detail not only their crime, but also the familial peacemaking procedures that followed, which helps us to discern what they expected from the Roman tribunal.

Under the impact of Mihály's request, the Major Penitentiary commissioned one of the papal confessors to examine the case, including the verification of his written statements as well as his sacramental confession and absolution.[22] The procedure accurately reflects how closely the role of the judge and the confessor, the legal and spiritual realms, were intertwined in late medieval (and early modern) judicial practice.[23] In canonical terminology, the two spheres were distinguished as the internal (or forum of conscience) and external forums, and their entangled natures were embodied in the operations of the Penitentiary, which Pope Leo X described as a place where "the correction of morals and the salvation of souls was daily business."[24]

The rise of the tribunal of the papal Penitentiary in the late twelfth century paralleled the rise of the papal *plenitudo potestatis*, in which temporal and spiritual powers intermingled, over the practices of Latin Christians. This was facilitated by the development of canon law, which regulated the daily lives of ordinary Christians. The Penitentiary's operations were fairly complex. It functioned partly as a supreme criminal court by granting papal pardons (absolutions from automatic excommunication) for severe crimes (typically homicide, violence against clerics, sacrilege and breaking marital and monastic vows) that, according to canon law, only the pope could forgive. It also acted as a court of appeal, overruling sentences of diocesan jurisdictions regarding the validity of marriages and priestly ordinations.[25] Papal clemency was exercised beyond the sacrament of penance as a non-sacramental act, similarly to the right and practice of the supreme jurisdiction of kings to pardon condemned criminals and sinners in exile. Overruling the "rigors of justice" by granting grace served as a political tool to promote the sovereignty of princes and popes by eliciting the loyalty of their "humble" petitioners.[26] By granting pardons, the pope not only subjugated competing authorities, but also imposed his will on his subjects, who became entangled in the process of

22 Cases could be examined in the curia when petitioners were present and could be cited in person at court. When the petitioner sent his request via mediators, the verification process was entrusted to the vicars (judges) of respective diocesan courts.

23 This phenomenon long misled the leaders of the Catholic Church, who wrongly thought that petitions contained information under the seal of confession and thus kept the historical material of the Apostolic Penitentiary locked away until 1983, when it was made accessible for research. On the debate regarding the opening of the archives, see Schmugge, Hersperger and Wiggenhauser, *Die Supplikenregister*, 5–8.

24 Wienfried Trusen, "Zur Bedeutung des geistlichen Forum internum und externum." The Bull *Pastoralis Cura* (1513) of Pope Leo X. ("in qua morum censura et animarum precipue salus vertitur") is quoted by Schmugge, Hersperger, Wiggenhauser, *Die Supplikenregister*, 9.

25 Furthermore, its widespread dispensation activity made it possible for people to live in "legal" marriages and clerical status even if they failed to satisfy canonical requirements.

26 On pardoning as a political tool of rulers, see Gauvard, "Le roi de France et l'opinion publique," 353–66; Millet, ed., *Suppliques et requêtes: gouvernement par la grâce.*

domination while designing their narratives. Even if people were wise enough to manipulate the regulations, they still became—by asking pardon—agents of the construction of sin and of the authority of the Church, albeit unconsciously. Therefore, I will also address the issue of how, by engaging in petitioning and pardoning, East Central European commoners and the Roman church officials mutually shaped one another's practices, expectations, values, notions and languages.

There is an extensive body of work trying to explain the marked rise of the central law courts in late medieval and early modern Europe. In the master narratives of modernity, the evolving state gradually monopolized violence, taming thus the violent tenor of the European Middle Ages, as

FIGURE 2 *Cardinal-judge conducting a court hearing.*

people learned to restrain their hot emotional responses.[27] More recently, however, this top-down model of repression has been replaced by bottom-up approaches, leading historians to the consensus that ordinary users of the courts contributed to the growth of state and courts.[28] Reflections, however, on what late medieval and early modern litigants expected from courts, are extremely varied. There seems to be a widespread assumption that people were eager to exchange the unpredictable violence and irrational modes of evidence of the outside world for the peaceful, rational proceedings of courts.[29] Charles Duggan, a leading historian of medieval justice, has argued that the massive use of papal appellate courts "was a reflection of a widespread desire to substitute lawful process for arbitrary judgment: to place authority of the law above that of the person. Appeals to the Roman curia offered a relief from oppression, irrationality, bias or illegality, whether real or imagined."[30] It has also been suggested that people gradually resorted to the use of courts not autonomously, but under the pressure of the state, which sought to monopolize legitimate violence.[31]

From the bottom-up perspective of legal anthropology and the cultural histories of social conflicts applied in this book, the binary division of violence and law appears to have been an uninterrupted process of conflict resolution. Although pardon tales were officially designed to regulate vertical social relations, I will examine the ways in which ordinary people used the central courts for disputing their private hostilities in the public sphere.[32] In doing so, we will gain vivid insights into the late medieval culture of honor that molded the patterns of actions and emotions of the parties engaged in hostilities using either the weapons of law or violence. As will be discussed at greater length

27 This thesis was most trenchantly formulated by the sociologist Norbert Elias during the interwar period, but only became more widely received in the late 1960s. Elias, *The Civilizing Process*. On the recent debate of his thesis, see Dinges, "Formenwandel der Gewalt in der Neuzeit."

28 Dinges, "Usi della giustizia"; Blockmans, Holenstein, Mathieu, eds., *Empowering interactions*.

29 Hyams, "Due Process versus the Maintenance of Order," esp. 76–78.

30 Duggan, "Papal Judges Delegate," esp. 194–95. See also Pennington, *The Prince and the Law*, 132–33.

31 Brunner, *Land and Lordship*, 29–30.

32 On the strategic use of courts, see most importantly Smail, *The Consumption of Justice*. On the performative nature of late medieval and early modern justice and their appropriation by ordinary litigants, see also Kuehn, *Law, Family and Women*; Cohen and Cohen, *Words and Deeds in Renaissance Rome*.

in chapters 6, 7 and 9, in the late medieval culture of honor, feuds, duels and disputes were performative acts staging rivalries for legitimacy.[33]

Mihály, who came from a small town in Transylvania, invested a considerable amount of time and money in acquiring a letter from the pope in order to triumph over his enemies. His voyage to the Eternal City must have cost him at least ten ducats, but a more comfortable trip could have cost him four times as much.[34] Mihály paid at least another four or five ducats for the services of the papal office.[35] Fifteen ducats was the price of a cow or a fairly good horse. He could also have bought a new set of clothes, a piece of land for viticulture or a tenant plot in pledge for that amount.[36] Obviously, he considered the letter of papal pardon to be worth the investment. Mihály anticipated that the papal document annulling his vow would make it possible for him to marry his lover. He did not seek security or calculable rules at the court in a world of extreme violence; on the contrary, he intended to violate the agreement made with his enemies, which had the power to place him in danger once again. Mihály asserted that he would pursue negotiation of the conflict *iustitia mediante*, by going to court, which might have further angered the family of the deceased husband, who refused to let the matter alone.

For me, the most striking aspect of this story is that ordinary people such as Mihály and Ágnes (we have no reason to regard them as exceptional) were able to navigate through the gaps of the overlapping system of legal pluralism with such acumen, and could smartly use the multiplicity of legal means for their own ends. Required to go to Rome to fulfill the prescribed penitential pilgrimage, they used the occasion to free themselves from the obligations that

33 From among the extensive literature, see the landmark volume edited by John Bossy, *Disputes and Settlements: Law and Human Relations in the West* (Cambridge, 1983). For a later overview of approaches, theories and themes, see Blauert and Schwerhoff (eds.), *Kriminalitätsgeschichte: Beiträge zur social- und Kulturgeschichte der Vormoderne*. More recently: Carroll, *Blood and Violence*.

34 In 1494–95 the chaplain of the city of Bártfa (Bardejov, Slovakia) spent thirty-six ducats on the journey alone (including ten ducats for lodgings in Rome for two weeks) and paid twelve ducats for the pope's bull issued at the Papal Chancery, where he distributed another two ducats to curial officials. For this and further details concerning the expenditures of pilgrims, see Csukovits, *Középkori Magyar zarándokok*, 95–98.

35 The four or five ducats were shared by the proctor who formulated and submitted the petition, the notary who wrote the papal letter and further legal specialists who participated in the procedure, such as auditors. The name of the proctor and the fee paid was registered as of 1510. For more detail, see Müller, "The Price of Papal Pardon."

36 This data comes from charters recording such transactions, such as MNL OL DL 14480 (anno 1451), DL 55333 (anno 1446), DF 106763 (anno 1509), DL 47392 (anno 1520), DL 46311 (anno 1495).

derived from the public vow they were compelled to swear. The papal absolution also served as a legal tool to prove, if challenged, the legal status of their marriage and future offspring. They acted very consciously, as signaled by the calculated tactic of Mihály in presenting his petition alone and suppressing the fact that he had already married Ágnes.

This capacity of the common man, labeled most recently by historians as "popular legalism,"[37] will be investigated in this book on a transnational level. Surely the most arresting feature of petitions to the pope was how ordinary men and women from remote places used their skills and determination to utilize such a distant, pan-European institution for their own ends. Obviously, this contradicts the historical platitude concerning the "profound ignorance" of the simple people at the time. In this book the ordinary men and women who maneuvered cleverly in the world around them will be portrayed as intelligent educated and cultured, even if many were illiterate. In doing so, I follow the notion of anthropologist Robert Redfield, who has argued that purposeful human action does not only reflect education, but presumes scientific thinking and a strong belief in reason.[38]

Mihály and Ágnes navigated smartly between the competing stages of conflict resolution: the formal judicial sentence passed by the town magistrate was brokered toward peacemaking by the communal system of reconciliation (via the mediation of arbiters) with monetary compensation for the murder victim's family. The costly travel to Rome and the request for the pope's pardon served as a legal strategy to break and supersede an out-of-court agreement, which Mihály and Ágnes felt to be unfair and imposed. They were obviously not guided by the diocesan vicar along this judicial route, but they knew—maybe from fellow townspeople—how to play the civil court, the communal deal and the papal bureaucracy against one other.

Some chapters of this book, those tracking the routes of late medieval litigants, will navigate through this judicial labyrinth—crossing national as well as secular and ecclesiastical boundaries—from remote little settlements to the capital of Latin Christendom. The story that evolves thus also reads as a travelogue. It will examine everyday interactions entailing the contesting and reshaping of governing norms and boundaries: boundaries between law and conscience, sacred and profane, legitimate and illegitimate (violence, marriage or change of identity), privileged and nonprivileged, learned and unlearned, laity and clergy. From this perspective, the careers of renegade friars and their routine crossovers will exemplify the permeability of social and cultural boundaries.

---

37 Blockmans, Holenstein and Mathieu, Introduction to *Empowering Interactions*, 23.

38 Redfield, *Peasant Society and Culture.*

CHAPTER 2

Negotiating Apostasy

In 1510 a black-cowled friar ascended the twenty-eight white marble steps of the *Scala Sancta* at the Lateran Palace in Rome on his knees while praying fervently for the absolution of his sins. This scene was not unusual; pilgrims by the thousands did the same each day.

This Augustinian friar, however, was none other than Martin Luther.

This image serves to introduce our inquiries in this chapter by asking why individuals assumed and abandoned their professed religious identities and how they negotiated the reshaping of their identities at the papal curia. The transformation of individual identity was a long and tedious process. The German reformer continued to sign letters as "Friar Martin Luther" until the end of 1520.[1] Like Luther, some of the other iconic figures of the intellectual and religious adventures of the first half of the sixteenth century, including Erasmus of Rotterdam, Martin Bucer and François Rabelais, spent their youths in religious houses, typically in mendicant cloisters. Leaving the orders often constituted a stage in their transition to adulthood.

And who might those unknown religious men have been, who had left their religious orders and appeared as petitioners at the Apostolic Penitentiary in increasing numbers at the beginning of the sixteenth century? Because they had abandoned cloistered religious life without permission and with no intention to return, they had, according to canon law, committed *apostasia a religione* and were therefore considered apostates by the Church. In the period between 1410 and 1500, only thirteen friars turned from the Kingdom of Hungary to the papal office asking to be absolved from the crime of apostasy. Then, however, contrary to the general trend of decrease in the number of petitioners after the jubilee of 1500, the number of apostate friars grew rapidly: between 1510 and 1533 a total of sixty-five apostate friars appealed for papal clemency. In other words, religious renegades submitted between four and six pardon requests per year. Considering that similar absolutions were granted by other ecclesiastical authorities and offices, and that only a minority of "sinners" ever felt the need to turn to one of them with a petition, one must presume the number of apostate religious in Hungary to have been many

1 Luther signed his letters as *Martinus Luther, Augustinianus* or *Frater Martinus Lutherus*. WA Briefwechsel, vols. 1–2, passim.

 | DOI 10.1163/9789004361263_003

FIGURE 3 *La Scala Santa at the Monastery San Benedetto near Subiaco.*

times higher during this period. The change that occurred in the 1510s and 1520s is even more conspicuous in light of the overall tendencies: the sudden "swarm" of previously scant religious to the papal office occurred during the same time that the number of cases produced by laymen and secular clergymen declined. As a result, two out of three cases at the Penitentiary were initiated by the religious during these decades. The "flight" from religious orders can be traced in records of the office until 1533, after which no more renegade religious from the Kingdom of Hungary sought to remedy their status there.

This chapter seeks to better understand the careers of this sizeable group of young men who entered but later left religious life in the early sixteenth century. While itinerant monks and friars moving between religious houses and orders are portrayed as characteristic of late medieval society in England,

FIGURE 4 *Posthumous portrait of Martin Luther as Augustinian friar.*

France, Germany and Italy, no similar increase of monastic apostasy has been registered by historical scholarship in other regions in the years directly preceding the religious upheaval and transformation triggered by the discontent of Luther, the Augustinian friar.[2] Who were these apostate friars in the territory of the late medieval Kingdom of Hungary and what attracted them in

2 Heinrich, "Klosterflucht"; Mayali, "Du vagabonde à l'apostasie"; Logan, *Runaway Religious*; Condorelli, *Clerigi peregrini;* and Svec Goetschi, *Klosterflucht*. The latter book is an analysis of papal pardon letters from fifteenth-century Germany.

such great numbers to a religious career in the early sixteenth century and prompted them to turn their backs on their cloisters? In order to better comprehend their potential and limitations as well as their intentions and options, I will first establish the historical and historiographical contexts of their actions. I will then look at how they maneuvered as best they could within the "structures" set by class, power and culture. More concretely, an analysis of their storytelling skills will show how they accounted for their motivations, and whether and how they crafted, from their winding career paths, conversions and subsequent de-conversions, coherent and thus acceptable storylines through judicial negotiation and individual identity formation.

Apostates and Evangelicals

Even though the phenomenon of large-scale apostasy from religious orders in Hungary can be dated to the time before the appearance and spread of evangelical ideas, the story of the apostate friars may serve to reveal the rather unexplored patterns of behavior of the lower clergy during the early Reformation period. Since a grand historical narrative may be structured upon the social backgrounds and behavioral models of its protagonists, the investigation of the everyday lives of the lower clergy may explain certain aspects of the history of the early Reformation in Hungary.[3]

It is well known that Lutheran ideas, which induced large numbers of religious to leave their monasteries in other European regions, appeared in the Kingdom of Hungary in the 1520s. In Germany, the exodus of monks and friars from religious houses under the impact of Luther's criticism of monasticism began in 1522.[4] Ex-friars who felt compelled to publicly account for their motives typically declared that they had been driven by the same impulse that had inspired them to join the orders in the first place: the quest to live a truly Christian life.[5] The runaway friars from East Central Europe examined here mentioned not a single word about Luther and his teachings, though one cannot exclude the possibility that those who left the orders in the second half of the 1520s and the early 1530s were acting under the influence of evangelical ideas. To be sure, the friar exchanging his monastic habit for a wife was a familiar figure of the time. The first instance that caused a public scandal occurred

3 With regard to the limitations of this approach, see Danto, "The Decline and Fall."

4 Rüttgardt, *Klosteraustritte*; and Moeller, "Die frühe Reformation," 85.

5 Schilling, *Gewesene Mönche.*

in the northern mining town of Körmöcbánya (Kremnica, Slovakia), where the apostate Dominican friar, Lénárt Körmöci ("from Körmöc"), married publicly in 1524.[6] That this was not a rare occurrence is suggested by the proposal of the bishop of Szerém (Syrmia), István Brodarics, to the pope in 1533 that clergy be allowed to marry because "the priests are openly taking wives."[7] In fact, members of the old clergy taking wives seems to have become a central theme of gossip and rumor.[8] Even though the act of clerical marriage was taken as a clear sign of Lutheran sympathies, in the 1530s it did not yet signal an intention to break from the old Church, as the case of the Provost of Székesfehérvár, Imre Bebek, suggests. According to contemporary authors who recorded the scandalous events, the high-born provost, on the one hand, corrected the celebrating priest's words during the wedding ceremony to explicitly indicate that he was marrying pursuant to evangelical precepts and not those of the Roman Church; on the other hand, the prelate requested a papal dispensation for his matrimony in 1533, which made sense only if he presumed that it might be possible for him to remain a priest within the Church despite his marriage.[9]

Apostate friars who turned to the papal office openly claimed that they would continue to serve the Church as secular clergymen, although they made no mention of marriage. Typical in this respect was the request of Bálint Körmöci, who wrote in 1527 that he had entered the Dominican cloister in Gölnic (Gelnica, Slovakia) and professed as an underage boy. Reaching the canonical age of majority, he protested against his vow—never confirmed—and as soon as he was able he returned to the secular world, where, he claimed, he wished to serve further as a secular priest. Finally, the ex-friar Körmöci requested that the Penitentiary issue a letter addressed to his diocesan bishop declaring that "based on that indicated he does not belong to the Dominican order, but can work as a secular priest, and [...] can receive a benefice."[10]

A brief survey of the better documented contemporary careers of the "famous" apostates and their attempts to justify their conversion from the cloister to the outside world might reveal some patterns of behavior they held in common with ordinary friars. Theology professor Martin Luther used very original arguments to justify his escape. He had at one time chosen to enter the Erfurt

6 ETE vol. 1, 177–78.

7 ETE vol. 2, 272–74.

8 This is reflected in correspondence between two aristocrats in 1532, in which the letter writer metaphorically describes the betrothal of the addressee as a conversion from the celibacy of the Roman clergy to Lutheran marriage. See Csepregi, *A reformáció nyelve*, 215–16.

9 On the events of the provost's marriage, see ibid., 212–14.

10 APA vol. 75, fol. 249r.

friary, believing that the prevailing spirit in the old *studium generale* of the Augustinians closely resembled that projected in the instruction of his favorite former teachers,[11] but after spending a decade and a half in the Augustinian cloisters in Erfurt and Wittenberg,[12] he did not simply abandon the order, but questioned the legitimacy of monasticism in general, thereby inducing its collapse. Writing in 1521, Luther rejected the traditional understanding of monastic vows and rules as being the perfect Christian path to salvation, calling upon fellow friars to abandon their cloistered lives.[13] He made his final decision in 1524, when he hung up his friar's habit and married.

Martin Bucer, who later became the leading figure of the evangelical movement in southern Germany, also spent fifteen years in a different mendicant community, the Dominican Order. He was attending university as a friar when, in 1520, he came under attack for espousing similar views to those of Erasmus and the Wittenberg friar. In the Heidelberg friary where he lived in the tense atmosphere evoked by Luther, conservatives gained the upper hand over the humanist reformers who followed Bucer. In order to avoid the imminent investigations against him, Bucer decided to forsake the Dominicans. In his petition to the pope to annul his monastic vows, Bucer asserted that he had joined the preaching friars under duress. Due to the intercession of his friends, Bucer quickly obtained the papal letter and left the Dominican *studium generale* and cloister in Heidelberg in the spring of 1521. Nevertheless, Bucer did not manage to avoid excommunication because, instead of serving the Church as a diocesan clergyman, he took a wife and began preaching the new religious tenets in Strasbourg.[14]

The model figure of Christian humanism, Erasmus of Rotterdam, spent a good part of his youth in religious houses as of the late 1480s, acquiring the foundations of his learning in cloister schools. Erasmus was ordained into the priesthood in 1492, becoming an Augustinian canon regular at the age of twenty-five. By the time he became a famous scholar throughout Europe in the 1500s, he was no longer leading a monastic life, working rather as an episcopal secretary or private tutor or attending lectures as a student at the University of Paris. However, he was doing so with the authorization of his Church superiors, wearing the Augustinian habit. He finally decided to request the annulment of his religious vows in a petition to Pope Leo X so that he could acquire a Church benefice in England, which he was granted in January 1517 despite his

11 Pilvousek, "Askese, Brüderlichkeit und Wissenschaft."

12 Lindner, "Martin Luther im Augustinerkloster"; and Brecht, *Martin Luther*.

13 "De votis monasticis iudicium." WA 8, 573–669.

14 Greschat, *Martin Bucer*, 33–34.

illegitimate birth. Erasmus abandoned the order definitively with permission from the bishop of Worcester—"at the command of the bishop" in his own overstated words—after the English prelate absolved him of his sins on April 9, 1517.[15] However, Erasmus never formally left the Roman Catholic Church, living the rest of his life as a humanist priest-scholar.

Finally, the French *enfant terrible* of Renaissance literature, François Rabelais, also joined the ranks of apostate friars in the first decades of the sixteenth century. Beginning in 1510, he lived as a Franciscan friar for two decades, pursuing wide-ranging studies amid the tranquility provided by monastic life until 1523. The spiritual upheavals triggered by Luther's protest disturbed his career as a scholar-friar: after the Franciscans prohibited the reading of Greek books, which the order deemed dangerous, he transferred to the Benedictine order with the permission of Pope Clement VII. Rabelais continued his studies at the Sorbonne's faculty of medicine until 1530, living at the Benedictine college during this period; however, after receiving his degree in medicine, Rabelais began to grow weary of the constraints of monastic life, eventually abandoning the order amid great scandal. He nevertheless thought it important to retroactively legitimize his flight from the Benedictine order, successfully petitioning Pope Paul III for absolution from the sin of apostasy. But not even Rabelais left the Church: with support from some liberal-minded prelates, he acquired benefices that made it possible for him to follow his medical and literary pursuits.[16]

The biographies of Luther, Bucer, Erasmus and Rabelais have several common features. Early in their lives, they were all priests and religious of the established Church armed with the entire repository of late medieval knowledge. One tends to forget that they all made the rather conventional decision to enter religious life in their youths and did not begin to express open contempt for monasticism until later in their lives. In spite of this, all four always thought in terms of renewing the established Church and became leading figures in the various factions attempting to achieve this objective—Rabelais and Erasmus as Renaissance humanist intellectuals, and Luther and Bucer as religious reformers whose work led to the foundation of new Churches. Did the runaway friars from the Kingdom of Hungary, in their own way, continue their careers as literate professionals or as pastors of the new Churches? A surprising similarity between the great men described above and the ordinary

15 Smith, *Erasmus*, 74–77; "Permissu atque adeo iussu epicopi ordinarii"—Erasmus is quoted by Febvre in *The Problem of Unbelief*, 311.

16 Plattard, *The Life of François Rabelais*, 1–33. His petition to Pope Paul III is quoted in Smith, *Rabelais*, 19.

renegade friars from Hungary is that the majority of them left the mendicant orders. In Hungary, the Dominicans sustained the greatest losses, followed by the Franciscans, the Paulines and the Augustinians.[17] The monastic orders suffered minimal losses in comparison to the mendicants.[18] Among Luther, Bucer, Rabelais and Erasmus, only the latter belonged to a monastic order—the Augustinian Canons Regular.

Cloisters and Learning

The exodus from the mendicant orders in Hungary is surprising since they held a growing appeal for lay society due to their pastoral profile and internal reforms.[19] Why did friars flee these prospering orders, for whom the faithful—primarily aristocrats and occasionally urban communities—founded several new houses in the early sixteenth century? The fact that the orders had little difficulty finding up to twenty-five friars to reside in these newly built cloisters suggests that young people found communal religious life to be inviting and that continuous recruitment ensured not only stability, but also an increase in the number of friars.[20] Lay donations also reflect their appeal: the continued flow of pious bequests facilitated the magnificent reconstructions of their cloisters.[21] This thriving monastic culture produced not only a rich body of vernacular religious writings for the use of nuns and the laity, but monastic

17 The Paulines, founded in Hungary, had eremitic traditions, but by this time placed as much emphasis on *vita apostolica*, the pastoral care of lay society, as mendicants. The order had seventy-four houses in Hungary at the beginning of the sixteenth century and their communities took root in Austria, Moravia-Bohemia, Poland, the German territories and Portugal as well. Sarbak, ed., *Der Paulinerorden;* Weinrich, *Hungarici monasterii;* Romhányi, "Kolostorhálózat," 25, 27.

18 There were thirty-two Dominicans, seventeen Franciscans, eleven Paulines, ten Augustianians, five Benedictines, two Cistercians and a single Premonstratensian among the apostate religious.

19 Several aspects of late medieval monastic revival, the so-called Observant movement and cloister reform in Hungary, are discussed in the following recently published series of books: Medgyesy-Schmikli and Őze, eds., *A ferences lelkiség;* Illés and Zágorhidy Czigány, eds., *A domonkos rend*; Sarbak, ed., *Decus solitudinis*. See also Romhányi, "A koldulóbarátok szerepe." On the impact and legacy of Observant reforms in a European context, see most recently Roest, ed., *Religious Orders*.

20 For a list of novices who entered the Dominican order in the 1520s and 1530s, see Romhányi, "Egy régi-új forrás," 243–45.

21 Lupescuné Makó, "A Domonkos Rend," passim.

FIGURE 5 *St. Anthony of Padua Taking the Habit of the Franciscan Order.*

historiographies that shaped the process of remaking the identities of the orders, while other literary genres born within the cloisters, such as mystery plays, songs and sermons, would be further developed by agents of the Protestant Reformation.[22]

In brief, there is no trace of internal crisis within the orders to explain the sudden "flight" of friars, while the decision of many young men to don the "black habit" around the turn of the fifteenth and sixteenth centuries can be attributed to the fertile monastic culture that prevailed at the time. This flourishing monastic culture, together with some shared episodes in the careers of the famous apostates, gives rise to the hypothesis that young men, often at the urging of their parents, opted to join the mendicant orders for the sake of the education provided by their cloister schools. Martin Bucer, son of a small town cooper in Alsace,[23] tried to alter his destiny by living and studying at the local Dominican cloister that was undergoing a renewal

22 Tarnai, *"A Magyar nyelvet írni kezdik,"* 74–154; Kovács, "Kolostori műveltség"; Lázs, *Apácaműveltség.*

23 On Bucer's childhood, years in the cloister and university studies and erudition, see Greschat, *Martin Bucer*, 10–23.

in terms of lifestyle and education. It was a good decision for a youth lacking both the means to finance his university studies and the social capital to gain a place among the beneficed clergy. A list of Bucer's books reveals that, in addition to scholastic theology and philosophy, he acquired a broad humanist education at the cloister school after taking his vows in 1508. While he subsequently studied theology at the famous Heidelberg University, he was not charged a fee for matriculation and enjoyed other privileges as a resident friar of the Dominican *studium generale*. After becoming a *baccalaureus biblicus*, Bucer's Dominican superiors supported him in pursuing doctoral studies in 1520. The son of the barrel maker was on his way to attaining the highest academic degree, one that qualified him for university professorship.

Erasmus was born an illegitimate and sickly son of a small-town priest in Holland and thus started his career in a much more difficult position than Bucer. When he became an orphan at the age of fifteen, the only viable educational option for him was to enter the Augustinian monastery in the nearby village of Stein, where he found the necessary conditions: tranquility, a huge library and financial security. He was still an Augustinian regular canon when he obtained his doctorate in theology.[24]

The early careers of the celebrated thinkers of the early sixteenth century support the assumption that fugitive friars in contemporary Hungary likewise entered the mendicant orders as a social strategy to overcome, through education, the disadvantages stemming from their meager social backgrounds.

The Ambitious Common Man

The conjectured connection between religious careers and education is based on two further presumptions: first, that studying was an effective means of attaining social advancement in Hungary during this period; and second, that simple people from villages and small towns were aware of this opportunity and acted accordingly. Speaking more generally, an intense desire and an active search for education characterized people from all segments of late medieval society down to the lowest social strata.

My hypothesis regarding the apostate friars and focus on the figure of the ambitious simple layman who sought social ascent through learning was certainly influenced by recent trends in historical scholarship. Some decades ago, historians argued that the old clergy represented the agent of the evangelical

24 Smith, *Erasmus*, 13–18, 103.

movement, pinpointing numerous priests and religious among this group in the first generation of reformers.[25] The historiographical function of the concept of clerical reformation was meant to supplant the former notion that the Reformation emerged as a reaction to the crisis of the late medieval Church. Instead, the new concept depicted the Reformation as a continuation of the late medieval reform movement.[26] Recently, however, attention has begun to focus on the broad masses of lay society, a shift that is undoubtedly connected to the impact of modern mass society and mass culture. As a result, social historians of the Protestant Reformation tend to claim that the agent of religious change was not the clergy, but lay society and they seek to better understand the role that common people played in initiating and realizing reforms.[27] My vision of the common man seeking to advance his social position via education by entering cloisters goes back to this general historical interest in lay society and the concept that the Reformation was the product of an active interaction between laity and clergy. Nevertheless, the character of the studying peasant in the late medieval period to this day seems somewhat startling or simply implausible. The portrayal of late medieval and early modern peasants as exploited and oppressed figures robbed of any and all initiative and therefore both intellectually and emotionally stunted is no less common in academic literature than it is in popular thinking.[28] This classic image has been modified only recently,[29] although even the latest approaches apply a top-down narrative of the peasant world, investigating the ways in which peasants and their resistance contributed to the making of the modern centralized state rather than seeking to understand their actions and thoughts.[30]

Peasants as active historical agents with the capacity to take independent action have appeared in Hungarian historical scholarship in the works of

25 Moeller, "Die frühe Reformation"; Péter, "A reformáció és a művelődés," 508–9; Szakály, *Mezőváros és reformáció*, 9–32.

26 Péter, "Il Rinnovamento Cattolico"; Schilling, "Reformation-Umbruch oder Gipfelpunkt."

27 Péter, *A reformáció*, above all 36–44, 62–69; the works of Robert Scribner and Peter Blickle are of particular interest. See Scribner, *Popular Culture*; and Blickle, *Gemeindereformation*.

28 Lawrence Stone, for instance, presents peasants as ignorant and submissive in his classic book. See Stone, *The Family, Sex and Marriage*. Peasants appear as passive victims of great historical processes, namely the rivalry between territorial states and landlords for control of the serfs in Evans, *The Making of the Habsburg Monarchy*, 88–91.

29 For an examination of the agency of peasants in Prussia, the archetypal region of peasant exploitation, see Eddie, *Freedom's Price*.

30 See the volume on peasant resistance within the project entitled "The Origins of the Modern State in Europe." Blickle, ed., *Resistance*; Blockmans, Holenstein and Mathieu, eds., *Empowering Interactions*.

Katalin Péter, who has presented the figure of the intelligent serf capable of eluding seigniorial duties and acquiring considerable wealth by leasing vineyards and conducting trade, while others strove to attain social advancement by moving from small villages to cities, seeking advantageous marriages or scraping together enough money to purchase titles of nobility.[31] Learning, as argued here, was another means of negotiating social status.[32] That study was a common strategy used to fulfill late medieval social aspirations is reinforced by the contemporary—albeit rather biased—observations of Luther. In 1524, he urged city magistrates to establish public schools and make education (which would serve spiritual salvation) compulsory for all, arguing that ordinary people had so far sent their children to cloister and cathedral schools to learn to make a living—in other words, to turn them into priests and friars. Since monasteries were declining, Luther continued and the privileged order of clergy had been challenged, they no longer cared about the education of their children.[33]

Furthermore, the traditional scholarly depiction of peasants as ignorant and apathetic (which differs from Luther's judgment of peasants being driven by worldly goals) has been closely intertwined with the notion of the Reformation as an educational revolution.[34] The essential point of departure for this familiar argument is the contention that at the time of the early Reformation, society was comprised primarily of illiterate and uneducated masses. With regard to the education of society at large, two significant changes have been identified that took place in the sixteenth century: the abrupt rise in literacy rates, and the ever greater accessibility of university studies for members of the lower social strata. Both academic disciplines and popular thinking have considered the democratization of education—as well as the general intellectual development in the early modern period that culminated in the scientific revolution—to be an achievement of the Reformation.[35] This train of thought is built upon the assumption that the Lutheran doctrine of vernacular Bible

31 Péter, "The Other Way"; Péter, "Társadalom és gazdálkodás."

32 The role of learning in social mobility has been recently acknowledged by medievalists in connection to university studies. See Gramsch, "Erfurter Juristen." This book, in turn, emphasizes the identical role of learning in village and town schools.

33 "An die Ratsherren aller Städte deutschen Lands." WA 15, 27–53, 29. In English: "To the Councilmen of all Cities in Germany that they establish and maintain Christian Schools."

34 For the grand-scale elaboration of this concept, see Stone, "The Educational Revolution."

35 For an analysis of the connection between cultural production and the Reformation in Hungary, see Péter, "Bibellesen"; Klaniczay, "A reformáció szerepe."

reading prompted reformers to delve enthusiastically into the field of popular education, while under their influence the previously passive and intellectually listless masses became aware of the importance of knowledge and literacy and happily took their places on school benches.

This interpretation rests on the presumption that abstract principles govern social action and that a narrow enlightened stratum of society leads passive masses incapable of independent action and thought. The figure of the autonomous peasant who independently decides to pursue an education hardly fits into this picture and could shatter many of the standard ideas regarding the origins of the Reformation. It would mean that the widespread aspiration for education was not a result of the efforts of the reformers, but just the opposite: it stemmed from an intensive social demand for change in the field of education that took place in the sixteenth century, including an increase in the availability of schools to broad strata of lay society, the modernization of curricula and a growing market for printed books. Apparently, however, the expansion of learning opportunities—the "educational revolution"—cannot be regarded as the achievement of the Reformation, since the same phenomenon occurred in other regions of Europe that resisted religious reform and remained loyal to the Roman Catholic Church.[36] The story of apostate friars evolving in this book illuminates another aspect of sixteenth-century transition in which the motor of change was lay society and not the clergy, as accepted wisdom would have us believe.

Storytelling Strategies

In 1523, Martin Bucer penned an apology entitled *Verantwortung* (Justification) in order to justify his apostasy in the face of accusations and to ask for the protection of the Strasbourg magistrate amidst tremendous religious upheaval. Sixteen years after the fact, he openly claimed that it had been his grandfather who had forced him to enter the cloister when he was in his mid-teens.[37] Erasmus likewise contended that his guardians had compelled him, an illegitimate orphan, to become a canon, portraying them in a vastly exaggerated role as quasi kidnappers. In a moment of great candor, he cited the enticement of a school friend as a factor that had impelled him to join the Augustinians, depicting his decision to enter the monastery as a

36 With regard to Spain and Italy, see: Kagan, *Students and Society*; Grendler, "Le scuola." See also Grendler, "Schooling in Western Europe," 818–24; Comerford, "Clerical Education."

37 Greschat, *Martin Bucer*, 14, 58.

mistake that "he immediately started to regret."[38] Obviously, we must read his apologetic interpretation of his monastic past carefully. As a young man living in the monastery, he wrote a hortatory epistle (*De Contemptu Mundi*) encouraging a young man to enter religious life by discussing the pleasant tranquility of monastic life fostering study and contemplation.[39] A closer look at the story-telling strategies of the petitioning apostate friars from Hungary will provide us with a glimpse of the ways in which they shaped their versions of events in order to fit the politics of the moment and to construct and maintain their personal identities.

Vagrant friars appear to have been characteristic figures of the fifteenth century. They left their cloisters for various reasons, most typically due to some internal conflict, but after having spent some time in the "world" they either returned to their original orders or asked permission to transfer to another one.[40] From the beginning of the 1510s, however, the figure of the apostate, who abandons the cloister forever, appears (sixty-five cases). How did they explain their apostasy to the judges who considered their cases? What could they freely speak of and what did they have to hide so that their broken careers and their acts of de-conversion could be presented as linear and coherent life stories? Since the religious vow bound one for life, just as the vow of marriage, only the validity of the circumstances under which it had been made could be negotiated.

One of the most commonly used arguments for annulling the religious vow, with reference to canonical regulations, was minority of age. Canon law defined the age of majority as fourteen, though some of the religious orders raised it to fifteen or sixteen for novices.[41] Ex-friars claimed to have entered cloisters in childhood (*in puerili etate*), at puberty (*infra annum pubertatis*), or as minors (*minor annis existens*). The youngest was Péter Üvsghewri, who joined the Dominicans at the age of seven, followed by János Futaki, said to

38 Smith, *Erasmus*, 75.

39 On the various interpretations of this early writing, see: Tracey, *Erasmus*. Accessed at: http://ark.cdlib.org/ark:/13030/ft5q2nb3vp/ (June 28, 2016).

40 A total of fifty-eight runaway religious petitioned for license (or absolution) to return to an order, or transfer (twenty-one cases) to another order. This clerical mobility intensified in the 1510s as well: during the thirty years after 1510, a total of thirty-three friars returned to the orders after leaving without permission, while only twenty-five had done so over the previous seventy years.

41 Friedberg, ed., *Corpus Iuris Canonici*, vol. 2, 572 (X 3.31.11). The Pauline age limit was fifteen years. Sarbak, ed., *Declarationes constitutionum*, Rubrica LXII, 297. Dominicans lowered the minimum age for entrance from eighteen to sixteen. Harsányi, *A domonkos rend*, 115.

MAP 2 *The Dioceses of the Kingdom of Hungary around 1500.*

have lived with the Franciscans in the Bács diocese from the time he was eight years old.[42]

By the late Middle Ages, however, the common practice of sending small children to monasteries had already declined and religious orders did not easily make concessions with regard to age limits for accepting novices.[43] Thus, the familiar topos of the levity and pliancy of youth (*ex quadam animi levitate*) served as a more plausible argument to support the acceptance of young children into cloisters.[44] This contradicted ecclesiastical expectations, which considered free and inner conviction as necessary prerequisites for true conversion.[45] Even those who had reached the canonical age of majority emphasized

42 A total of thirty-seven petitioners claimed that they had been minors when they entered the religious house. APA vol. 59, fol. 585v (1515, Agrien. dioc.); vol. 3, fol. 81r (1450).

43 This is reinforced by the fact that most Dominican novices had joined the order as clerics, not as laymen, as later indicated in their petitions to the pope. Romhányi, "Egy régi-új forrás," 243.

44 For example, APA vol. 3, fol. 81r; vol. 57, fol. 807r (Domokos Tamási at the age of twelve); vol. 63, fols 39rv; vol. 64, fols 57rv.

45 Fredriksen, "Paul and Augustine."

that they had been in their youth (*in iuvenili etate*) when they had converted from a worldly life to one of religion.[46] External pressure on hesitant young men came either from the local friary (*nonnullorum fratrum persuasionibus*) or family members.[47] Albert Pálfi asserted that he had been "tempted by the enticements" (*blanditiis allectus*) of friars describing the beauty and benefits of monastic life, leading him to enter the Observant Franciscan house in Szeged. The priest Gál Ötvös of Pest claimed that preaching friars who used to visit his paternal home had convinced him to join the order, while the priest Jakab Verőcei ("from Verőce") stated that he had become the sexton at the Cistercian Abbey in Gotó at the bidding of the abbot.[48] The urging of older family members, parents, brothers, relatives and friends was less frequently cited, though no less plausible.[49] The cleric Balázs Csitei specified that his main influence had been his brother, a friar himself, when he joined the Dominican community in the town of Székesfehérvár.[50]

János Asway showed himself to be an indecisive young man. First, he let some friars (either Dominicans or Franciscans) from the town of Győr persuade him to take the habit, which he soon regretted and then he left the friary. After contracting the plague, Asway promised God to return to the cloister if he recuperated, which he failed to do after regaining his health.[51] Stories of vows being sworn in the hope of recovery from an illness comprise portions of both ecclesiastical and popular written and oral tradition, and convey the

46 Pl. APA vol. 72, fols 1201v–2r (Bálint Gyulai). Bertalan Boldi, for example, joined the Franciscans at the age of fourteen, while Lőrinc Tapasztó of Szőlős asserted that he had been either fifteen or sixteen years old when he entered the Paulines in Budaszentlőrinc. APA vol. 66, fols 1193rv and vol. 64, fols 878rv.

47 Claimed by ten petitioners altogether. Moreover, the Dominican friars from Lábatlan persuaded Péter Üvsghewri to join the order (APA vol. 59, fol. 585v), while friars from Győr invited János Asway to enter the local friary (vol. 72, fol. 311v).

48 APA vol. 72, fol. 320v (Bachien. dioc.); vol. 48, fol. 358rv (Strigonien. archdioc.); vol. 20, fol. 130r (Zagrabien. dioc.).

49 Five petitioners made this claim, i.e., "persuasionibus nonnullorum parentum et consanguineorum suorum et aliorum inductus" (for example, the priest Gergely, son of the late Farkas Demeter of Tiszavarsány, APA vol. 57, fol. 404rv). Furthermore, Ibid., vol. 59, fol. 36r; vol. 59, fol. 64v; vol. 66, fol. 1192v–93r.

50 APA vol. 63, fol. 35rv (1518, Quinqueecclesien. dioc.). See also the case of András Machy of Eger, the apostate Augustinian friar, who, at the age of twelve, "in quadam gravi infirmitate constitutus aliquam religionem de approbatis ingredi proposuit seu vovit." APA vol. 64, fol. 131v (1519, Agrien. dioc.).

51 "Ipse, qui postmodum peste forsan correptus timore mortis periculo ad eundem ordinem, si convaleret, redire in animo proposuit." APA vol. 72, fol. 311r (1524, Jaurien. dioc.).

belief in God's power and providence. Such vows served to justify breaking the monastic vow on the grounds that the promise to enter the order had been induced "by the fear of imminent death" (*timore mortis periculo*). It was a convenient canonical argument, as the emotion of fear negated the possibility of free will and invalidated the vow.

The majority of petitioners did not fear death, but coercion and violence—or at least that is what they claimed.[52] Fear of physical force was the most effective argument and petitioners made frequent use of it, especially with regard to the profession of the vow, if not their earlier entrance to the cloister.[53] It must have seemed realistic to the judges that unwilling novices had been easy targets of headstrong superiors. According to the laconic account of György Accolos, he had "gone to the St. Nicholas house of the preaching friars, where he put on their customarily worn habit and performed their regular vow under compulsion (*compulsus per vim et metum*)."[54] Unsurprisingly, compulsion to take the vow stemmed not from family members, but from co-resident elder friars and superiors.[55] The priest Gál Ötvös ("Goldsmith") of Pest "often told his fellow friars that he would like to leave and tried with all his might to do so. The friars rightfully feared that he would depart before the end of his novitiate and watched over him carefully, then pretended that the time for his vow had arrived. They then forced him, through beatings and threats of imprisonment, to take the vow as he begged in vain for them to return his lay clothing."[56]

---

52 Canon law made the following stipulation (X 3.31.1): "Non potest quis ad religionem admitti, nisi volens et in aetate idoneus." See Friedberg, ed., *Corpus Juris Canonici*, 2, 569.

53 A total of thirty-nine petitioners claimed to have been forced to perform the monastic vow, while only two remembered having been forced to enter the cloister; the priest Berec, son of Márton, claimed that he had entered the Pauline house in Garics "under the influence of threats and fear." APA vol. 25, fol. 129r (1477, Zagrabien. dioc.). Another escaped Pauline friar maintained that his guardian, his brother-in-law, had forced him to join the order when he was twelve years old. APA vol. 73, fol. 625rv (1525, Quinqueecclesien. dioc).

54 APA vol. 62, fols 917v–18r (1518, Strigonien. archdioc.).

55 The Dominican "prior and his friends" in the town of Várad (Oradea, Romania) forced Péter Ács ("Carpenter") to take the vow in order to prevent him from leaving (ibid., vol. 81, fol. 607v–8r, 1533, Waradien. dioc.). When Pál Molnár ("Miller") "openly declared that he did not want to profess, the friars did not let him leave, but forced him to take the vow." Ibid., vol. 42, fol. 386v (1493, Wesprimien. dioc.).

56 APA vol. 48, fol. 358rv (1499, Strigonien. archdioc.). In principle, novices were free to return to the secular world before the expiration of their probationary year. X 3.31.20 (Friedberg 2, 577).

While the priest Gál Ötvös emphasized the element of force, István Helye depicted himself as the victim of deceit, claiming that in his youthful naiveté and ignorance he had not realized that he had taken the monastic vow at the Pauline headquarters in Budaszentlőrinc. Helye's petition included the following claim:

> After a period of six months, the friars, in order to prevent him from leaving before the end of his year of novitiate, led him to a place within the friary where they showed him a book, which may have contained the procedure for taking the vow. They then forced him to read from the book, by which he took the vow five months before the end of his probationary year, though at this moment he was not aware of what he was doing.[57]

The total ignorance of the young novices regarding the procedure of professing must have seemed credible to the judges of the petitions, since several supplicants portrayed themselves in that manner. Helye's story furthermore suggests that he was a literate man, but his Latin was not proficient enough to understand the written text of the vow.

Generally speaking, the arguments of escaped friars were fairly plausible, since the vow professed before the end of the probationary year, although canonically prohibited, was nevertheless considered valid and its enforcement could therefore have been effectively applied against "rebellious" novices.[58] The refusal to return secular clothing was not enough to deter the most determined novices from leaving the cloister: the priest László Rachws remembered that he "returned to the world wearing his habit due to his lack of lay clothing."[59] There were, of course, other methods of preventing escape, most significantly the transfer of disobedient friars to other houses, or incarceration. Both means of punishment carry credibility in pardon narratives in light of the fact that they were the most accepted tools in the hands of superiors to discipline unruly friars. The Pauline prior in Rome, Gergely Gyöngyösi (1513–20),[60] in his instructions for novices ordered, that cloister superiors should transfer dissolute young friars not to remote cloisters, but to well-disciplined houses and that superiors should be informed

---

57 APA vol. 46, fol. 217rv (1498, Wesprimien. dioc.).

58 X 3.31.16 (Friedberg, ed., *Corpus Juris Canonici*, 2, 574).

59 APA vol. 63, fol. 39rv, 1518, Agrien. dioc.

60 Gergely Gyöngyösi (1472–1531) was later elected prior general of the Paulines (1520–22), during which time he published his most important opus, the history of the order, entitled *Vitae Fratrum*. Sarbak, "Gyöngyösi, Gregor."

of their transgressions.[61] Gergely Farkas of Tiszavarsány related that he had been transferred from a Franciscan house in the diocese of Pécs in southern Hungary to a distant friary situated in the market town of Szombathely in the western part of the kingdom:

> He tried to escape on several occasions during the two weeks he spent in the friary he had entered. When the friars saw that he did not want to remain among them, they sent him to another friary [...], where he spent eight months amid the continual urging of the friars to take the vow, which he steadfastly refused. He packed his clothes and other belongings and prepared to leave. When the friars saw that they could not deter him from his decision in any other way, they locked him up in prison for three–four days, thus under the influence of constraint and out of fear he finally took his vow.[62]

Furthermore, two Dominican novices alleged unambiguously that they had been subjected to beatings,[63] while Máté Szabó ("Tailor") confessed that two weeks of confinement in the prison at the Benedictine monastery in Kapornak

61 See, for example, the Pauline prior Gergely Gyöngyösi's *Directorium singulorum fratrum officialium ordinis sancti Pauli primi heremite sub regula beati Augustini episcopi militantium* (printed in Rome between 1514 and 1520), which mentions among the duties of the vicars and the priors the following: "Procurent apud patrem de dissolutis, ne ponantur in conventum desolatum, sed ubi magis viget disciplina. Et bonum erit, quod prelati, cum quibus degunt, sciant eorum fragilitates. Et dum removeri faciunt tales dissolutos, ad viam assignent eis socium bene reformatum, qui quantocius portet ad loca." Capitulum V, p. 41. Edited and translated by Sarbak, Bellus and Weinrich, *Gyöngyösi Gergely*, 31–67 (*Directorium*). Accessible at: http://www.fragmenta.oszk.hu/docs/gyongyosi_epit_dir_lhg.pdf. With regard to the imprisonment of disobedient friars, see the minutes of the general assemblies of the Salvatorian Franciscans (1531–1536) in ETE vol. 2, 482, 488.

62 APA vol. 57, fols 404rv (1512, Strigonien. archdioc.). Lőrinc Tapasztó of Szőlős was transferred from the Pauline's central cloister in Budaszentlőrinc to Máriavölgy (Marianka, Slovakia), near Pozsony (Bratislava, Slovakia), while the Augustinian novice Bertalan Bachdal of Varbó was sent from the southern town of Pécs to Vác, just north of Buda, after refusing to take his monastic vows at the former location. APA vol. 64, fols 878rv (1520) and vol. 47, fols 431rv (1499), both from the archdiocese of Esztergom.

63 "Eiusdem monasterii superiores et fratres contra eundem oratorem indignati eundem dictum monasterium minime exire permiserunt, sed ipsum propterea castigarunt et interim eundem ad professionem per fratres eiusdem ordinis emitti solitum emittendum coegerunt." (Tamás Bejsa in the Fehérvár friary, ibid., vol. 59, fol. 36r; 1515, Wesprimien. dioc.). János from Pest in the town of Pécs: APA vol. 64, fol. 982rv (1520, Bachien. dioc.).

(Krplivnik, Slovenia) had convinced him to profess the vow.[64] While some forms of coercion were possible to resist, as some of the renegade stories suggest, no young friar was strong enough to defy physical violence.

There were some, although very few ex-friars who did not attempt to invalidate their monastic vows. Instead of employing the exonerating argument of having been victim to external pressure, they spoke about inner, spiritual motives that had driven them to cloisters, probably influenced by the narrative patterns of the hagiographic tradition.[65] Pál Molnár ("Miller") explained that religious zeal (*zelo devotionis accensus*) had impelled him to join the Paulines, because he had wanted to find out if he had enough discipline to keep their rule.[66] The motif of youthful individual challenge and religious commitment was also invested with considerable credibility and may have indeed motivated some of the later apostates.[67] This type of story routinely entailed the argument that they had been unable to endure the austerity of monastic life.[68] Lukács Szakcsi claimed that his experiment with religious life (*factam experientiam in religionem*) over a six-month period in a Pauline house had been enough to convince him that "monastic life is not for him."[69] Here again the story of youthful zeal followed by disappointment and a failed challenge did not simply follow literary patterns; the stress on the unexpected rigor of monasticism functioned as a weapon in the legal battle to negotiate the validity of the religious vow. Religious orders were obliged to provide potential novices with

---

64 "Dictus abbas eundem oratorem carceribus, in quibus spatio quindecim dierum vel circa stetit, et recludi fecit, a quibus, ut illos evaderet, professionem emittere velle asserans liberatus professionem per eosdem monachos emitti solitam, ad hoc vi et metu, qui in constantem cadere poterant, coactus emisit regularem." APA vol. 68, fol. 390v–91r (1521, Wesprimien. dioc.). Gergely, son of Imre Domiani, was also incarcerated at the Franciscan cloister in the town of Győr, vol. 72, fols 328v–29r (1524).

65 APA vol. 2, fol. 139r, (Simon Császtai, 1439, Wesprimien. dioc.); ibid., vol. 56, fol. 96v (Péter Nagyszentmiklósi, 1511, Quinqueecclesien. dioc.); ibid., vol. 68, fol. 336rv–7r (János Tüzér, 1521, Miklovien-Strigonien. dioc.); ibid., vol. 72, fol. 311r (János Asway, 1524, Jaurien. dioc.).

66 APA vol. 42, fol. 386v (1493, Wesprimien. dioc.).

67 Bertalan Bachdal of Varbó entered the Augustinian cloister in the diocesan town of Pécs "observantias regulares aliquantulum experiri" (APA vol. 47, fol. 431rv, 1499). Imre Deák of Bélc claimed: "Zelo quodam devotionis accensus habitum fratrum Sancti Pauli primi heremite, in quadam illarum domo, animo et intentione illum ad tempus deferendi susceperat." (ASV Arm. XXXII. vol. 61, fol. 387v–88r, Quinqueecclesien. dioc., 1522).

68 APA vol. 42, fol. 386v (Pál Molnár, 1493, Wesprimien. dioc.); ibid., vol. 48, fol. 358rv (Gál Ötvös of Pest, 1499, Strigonien. archdioc.), etc.

69 APA vol. 41, fol. 319rv (1492, Quinqueecclesien. dioc.).

detailed preliminary information regarding life in the cloister. In his commentary on the Pauline constitution, Prior Gyöngyösi declared that "the severity of religious life must be explained to those who enter the order, everything that pertains to eating, drinking, sleeping, the vigil and fasting, prayer and work, furthermore how they must adapt to the other friars, when and how they must dine, drink, sleep together, how they must stand and walk and so on." Prior Gyöngyösi noted that those who had not received the stipulated information regarding the "strictness of the rule and the hardship, work and misery of monastic life" could not be compelled to remain.[70] Renegade friars who claimed that "they did not know what the religious vows commanded from them" were claiming that, due to the absence of such preliminary information, the validity of their vows was doubtful.[71]

Gaps in the Narrative

A loudly pronounced and routinely repeated theme in the remission stories of the apostates was the explicit and steadfast opposition that they had expressed against taking the monastic vow; the fact that they had also been ordained remained an incidental subreference. Ambrus Bressi's story provides an example. According to Bressi's petition, he had taken his religious vow as a minor and remained in the Franciscan order against his will:

> He did not reaffirm upon reaching his majority, but protested against it and continued to protest all through the years, during which he remained in the order and was ordained a priest. He did not stay though with the intention of remaining a member of the order; thus he left the cloister at the first available opportunity and returned to the world, where he would like to live as a secular priest."[72]

Most supplicants did not mention that they had been ordained in the cloister, which can be deduced indirectly from their presentations of themselves as priests or from their requests for permission to continue to minister as secular priests.[73] Almost none of the petitioners claimed that they had been forced

70 Sarbak, ed., *Declarationes constitutionum*, Rubrica LXIIaa, 311.

71 "Ignorans quid professio regularis importaret." Pl. APA vol. 64, fol. 131v.

72 APA vol. 64, fol. 57rv (1519, Agrien. dioc.).

73 Pl. APA vol. 24, fol. 152r; vol. 56, fol. 96v; vol. 58, fol. 139r; vol. 59, fol. 36r, etc.

to join the priesthood.[74] Their stories suggest that they had no objection to becoming secular priests,[75] a consciously constructed marginal episode in their self-serving narratives. Interestingly, even those few who reported that they had managed to resist taking the monastic vow eventually left the cloisters, indicating that they had done so, incidentally, as ordained priests.[76]

Further signs or gaps and ruptures between narrative and reality can be inferred from their storylines, derived, as I argue, from the narrator's intention to marginalize or totally conceal his ordination in the cloister.[77] Ex-friars tended to omit information regarding the length of their "compulsory" monastic lives after they took their vows, although they often stressed that they had realized within a month or two after entering the cloister that they wanted to return to the secular world. The petition of Lőrinc Tapasztó of Szőlős is very typical in this respect, stating that he spent one month at the Pauline cloister in Budaszentlőrinc before being transferred to the Máriavölgy cloister, where he lived another four months before being forced to take his vows. He claimed that he had returned to the secular world at the first "given opportunity" (*captata opportunitate*) in order to become a secular priest.[78] It was only the priest László Rachws who randomly admitted that he had stayed in the cloister for many years after he had involuntarily taken his vow, during which time he had been consecrated a priest.[79]

---

74 Only two ex-friars spoke about their unwillingness to become ordained priests. One of them, Imre Deák of Bélc, took only the minor orders and lived as a layman after his escape. ASV Arm. XXXII. vol. 61, fols 387v–88r (1522). The other, Bertalan Bachdal of Varbó, became a priest (APA vol. 47. fol. 431rv, 1499).

75 Six petitioners took clerical orders, including the subdeaconry—the lowest sacred order which entailed the obligation of celibacy. Taking the seven clerical orders was officially a six-month process, at minimum. Friedberg, ed., *Corpus Iuris Canonici*, 2, 118–24. "De temporibus ordinationum et qualitate ordinandorum," Decretalia Gregorii IX pape, Liber I, Titulus XI.

76 Altogether seven petitioners were non-professed secular priests. The priest Bertalan Bachdal of Varbó claimed "to have worn the friars' habit for a year and a month, since out of fear he could not take it off earlier and he was ordained to the priesthood at the prior's insistence." He stood alone in claiming that he had been ordained under pressure. APA vol. 47, fols 431rv (1499, Strigonien. archdioc.).

77 Natalie Zemon Davis described the same phenomenon with regard to royal pardons. *Fiction in the Archives*, 47–48.

78 APA vol. 64, fols 878rv (1520, Strigonien. archdioc.).

79 "Vi et metu durantibus in ordine huiusmodi pluries annos permanendo ad omnes etiam sacros et presbyteratus ordines promotus fuit." APA vol. 63, fol. 39rv (1518, Agrien. dioc.).

Another telltale sign is that lay petitioners tended to be wordier, while clergymen divulged as little circumstantial evidence as possible (even though, in other situations, their remission stories were usually more detailed).[80] The layman Imre Deák (*Litteratus*) of Bélc, for example, dramatically described the two years he had spent at a Pauline cloister. Deák asserted that he had chosen to join the order "out of religious zeal," though he took his vow only after the friars had "deceitfully fooled" him, and that he had then been consecrated as an acolyte (the highest of the four minor clerical orders) to prevent him from escaping. Deák's petition stated that monastic life had driven him mad:

> He immediately regretted the vow and the consecration and continuously protested against them while dreading all the while that he would remain tied to the order. For this reason, he descended into such a state of madness that he had to leave the order and they dragged him bound to sacred places so that he could be delivered of his infirmity. When he recovered, they took him back to the cloister, where he was again submitted to the rigorous lifestyle, which caused madness to break out upon him once again.[81]

Deák's flight from the order apparently cured him of his recurring illness. Another lay petitioner was the nobleman Miklós Pestenyei, who stated that he had wed the daughter of fellow noble Fülöp Horváth, Dorottya, but then joined the Benedictines "without the knowledge and permission of his wife." As Pestenyei explained years later, he returned to his wife through the intervention of the concerned families after having attained the sacred order of subdeacon while at the monastery. At the time of his petition, Pestenyei had been living with his wife and appeared to be concerned that the validity of his marriage could be called into question as a result of his monastic past. He therefore requested an official inquiry in order to confirm the legitimacy of his matrimony, promising that he would return to the monastery if his wife died, lead an ascetic life and regularly recite the lesser Marian Hymns.[82]

As for the motivation of the petitioners, it served the very practical function of creating the legal conditions necessary for their lives outside the cloister. For laymen, the papal letter meant the legalization of their marriages and

80 See the pardon requests for homicide in chapter 7, for example.

81 ASV Arm. XXXII. vol. 61, 387v–88r (1522, Quinqueecclesien. dioc.).

82 APA vol. 66, fol. 1166r (1521, Zagrabien. dioc.).

offspring.[83] Clergymen sought to secure their right to acquire and maintain ecclesiastical benefices and offices.[84] The laborious and costly step of turning to the papal curia was undertaken by those who feared the possibility of being sued or who had already been taken to court by their "enemies and foes," as the requests referred to actual or potential accusers. Litigants could either be religious superiors trying to win back their disobedient subordinate, envious clergymen claiming the ineptitude of their rivals for benefices at diocesan courts,[85] or kinsmen unwilling to share the family inheritance.[86] The fact that almost half of the renegade friars went to Rome in person to handle their affairs[87] reflects their attempt to flee local conflict and prosecution.[88]

Even though the purpose of petitions was to legalize their functions and offices as secular clergymen, renegade friars conspicuously kept silent about how they had become clergymen. The legal jargon of their requests adapted to the expectations of their audiences shrouded their actual intentions and circumstances, which became clearer only in exceptional moments of spontaneous storytelling. The request narrative of Péter Ferriani, dated 1466, diverged from the standardized line of argumentation:

---

83 The petition of György Accolos reveals that he had left the order years previously, married and even had a child. APA vol. 62, fols 917v–18r (1518, Strigonien. archdioc.).

84 According to the recurring formula of petitions: "Supplicatur igitur etc. quatenus si canonice constiterit de assertis prefatum oratorem propter premissa religioni huiusmodi, in quem vel in specie minime obligari et ad regularem observantiam non teneri, sed eisdem premissis non obstantibus in seculo ut secularis presbyter remanere et quecunque beneficia ecclesiastica compatibilia sibi in futurum canonice conferenda recipere et retinere libere et licite posse aliaque sibi canonice ministrari declarari mandare dignemini." APA vol. 59, fol. 585v.

85 See the recurrent legal formula: "Super premissis vel eorum occasione per loci ordinarium vel eius in spiritualibus vicarium seu officialem generalem, aut dicti ordinis generalem, custodes, guardianos, reformatores et alios religiosos vel quoscunque alios [iudices vel dominos tam] ecclesiasticos quam seculares molestari." APA vol. 72, fols 345rv.

86 See the less frequently advanced claim: "In bonis paternis et maternis succedere libere et licite posse." APA vol. 66, fols 1167rv.

87 In thirty-five cases, the petitions of ex-friars were delegated for further examination to curial prelates instead of their diocesan bishops, indicating their presence in Rome at the time of petitioning. Priest Bertalan Bachdal of Varbó petitioned through intermediaries, since his case had been assigned to the bishop of Vác "because the monastery that he left is in the town of Vác." APA vol. 47, fols 431rv.

88 Curial investigations entailed the hearing of curial attorneys of religious orders ("si vocato procuratore generali dicti ordinis iudicibus infrascriptis canonice constiterit de assertis"), while diocesan vicars heard the priors of the cloister ("si vocato priore dicte domus iudicibus infrascriptis canonice constiterit de assertis").

> He was a subdeacon and wanted to have himself consecrated into the holy orders; however, when he appeared before the bishop, the latter was not willing to ordinate him. Seeing this, he entered the friary of the Augustinians in Buda and donned the habit, then after the passing of six months, in the prescribed period of time, he was consecrated deacon and priest. [...] Then without taking the vow, he escaped from the cloister and returned to the world.[89]

Ferriani served as a priest in the diocese of Pécs, distant from the cloister in Buda, when he submitted his petition to Rome. Even though we can only make vague guesses about why he was able to submit a more straightforward account (perhaps his different perspective was due to his presumed Italian origin), his words reinforce the hypothesis that mendicant cloisters were generally used as byways to the priesthood. Ferriani did not reveal the reasons for which the bishop refused to consecrate him, though he did refer to the three-day examination he had undergone during which the bishop probed his "knowledge, morals and status."[90] The latter term referred to the respectable livelihood provided to working priests: the prelate celebrating ordination was personally responsible for ensuring that newly consecrated clerics received an office or benefice (*titulus* in canon law terminology) that would enable them to live a lifestyle worthy of a minister of the Church.[91] In the absence of such an office and income, which occurred with increasing frequency as a result of the rising number of priests in the later Middle Ages, mendicant cloisters provided an alternative solution. As their pardon requests reveal, the ordination of mendicant friars into the priesthood was a routine affair, since the explicit mission of these orders—as opposed to their monastic counterparts—was the pastoral care of the laity. In the Dominican order, all friars, with the exception of the *conversi* i.e. lay brothers who performed physical work, were clerics,[92] while Franciscans were typically classified as either "peasant friars" or "officiating friars."[93] Mendicant communal life and the vow of poverty made the holding of a benefice at ordination unnecessary.[94] In England, where the number of

89 APA vol. 15, fol. 76v (1466, Quinqueecclesien. dioc.).

90 Békefi, *A káptalani iskolák*, 298–300, 451–53.

91 Plöchl, *Geschichte des Kirchenrechts*, 2, 264–65.

92 Harsányi, *A domonkos rend*, 116.

93 Szmollény, *A középkori Szeged műveltsége*, 72–74 and 192–93.

94 In some English dioceses, mendicant friars were not included in ordination records, as Virginia Davis assumes, since they were exempt from the requirement of having a *titulus*, ensuring a decent living at their ordination. See Davis, "Rivals for Ministry?," esp. 105.

unbeneficed clergymen had drastically increased by the early sixteenth century, ordination often entailed *titulus* at the nearest monastic house in the vicinity in which the clerics served throughout their lives.[95] Poor young men in Hungary applied a similar trick by entering the orders and leaving them as ordained priests.

Another exceptional moment of spontaneous storytelling appears to support the presumption that many petitioning fugitive friars had been poor clerics who had had trouble acquiring a *titulus*. Lőrinc Baktan was the only one to openly state that "since he could not escape poverty in any other way, he remained within the Augustinian order for many years" and assumed the holy orders even after being forced to take his vows and spend time in prison following an unsuccessful attempt to flee.[96] Obviously it was necessity, not compulsion, that prompted him and many other clerics to remain in the cloisters. The "first opportunity to leave" may not have arisen as a result of "the cessation of force and fear" (*vi et metu huiusmodi cessante*) as supplicants claimed, but may rather have been the possibility of acquiring a benefice, just as Erasmus became inclined to petition to Pope Leo X to release him from his monastic vow after he had been offered a decent ecclesiastical benefice in England.

Mátyás Besztercei composed a completely standard piece: he took his vows under coercion after unsuccessfully attempting to flee from the Dominican cloister in Beszterce (Bistrița, Romania) before the expiration of his probationary year; he remained in the friary for years thereafter, during which time he was ordained a priest. After finally escaping, he wanted to serve as a secular priest and hold an ecclesiastical benefice. What is exceptional about this Transylvanian friar's case is that he had been a doctor of theology at the time he submitted his request. He had presumably spent his cloistered years in study, even attending a university, probably in Italy. As the Dominican vicar general recorded in 1521, Besztercei concluded his Italian studies with a successful exam, thus earning a master of theology degree that earned him the

95 Cooper, *The Last Generation*, 19–27. This may have been legal fiction, that is, plain trickery. Cooper, however, considers it possible that some secure source of subsistence (such as family wealth or the support of a patron), if not a benefice, was a necessary prerequisite for obtaining a monastic *titulus*. This simplified the procedure for the consecrating bishop, who only had to examine the knowledge and morals of the cleric.

96 "Quod percipiens prefatus orator nec alias rationem paupertatis sue aufugere valens, in eodem ordine per pluries annos non tamen animo nec intentione inibi obligari debere permansit." APA vol. 63, fols 203rv (1518, Agrien. dioc.).

title of "doctor."[97] However, he did not request the pope's annulment of his vows until five years later, in 1526. Besztercei's decision to join the Dominicans was ostensibly based on the fact that this order offered its friars the highest level of training and education.[98] Moreover, he had the good fortune to come from a town in which the Dominicans operated a *studium particulare*, preparing young friars for university level theological studies through instruction in the liberal arts.[99]

Martin Bucer resorted to the same legal repertoire in his 1521 request, identical in form and content to the petitions of apostate friars from the Kingdom of Hungary. The reformer and successor of Huldrych Zwingli declared that he had joined the Dominican order at the age of fifteen, claiming, as did so many of his fellow petitioners, that he had been forced to take the vows, which he never confirmed and that with the passing of this constraint he wished to return to the secular world. The German reformer asked the pope to help him leave the cloister "without inconvenience to his reputation and status" and, similarly to the ordinary friars from Hungary, he wished to continue his service as a secular priest.[100] In another instance, when Bucer sought to vindicate himself before a lay audience two years later, he claimed to have been forced to enter the Dominican order not by the friars, but by his grandfather. Bucer maintained that he had had no desire to join the Dominicans because they were less concerned with study than others,[101] illuminating his storytelling strategies more than actual circumstances.

Conclusion

It was primarily the exceptional remission stories, invested with some illuminating circumstantial truth added to the schematic legal program of nullifying

97 Veress, *Olasz egyetemeken*, 259. See also Harsányi, *A domonkos rend*, 121–23. Beatrix Romhányi presumes that the Mátyás Besztercei who attended an Italian university was the organist Mátyás who lived in Segesvár (Sighişoara, Romania) in 1529 and was also the prior at Beszterce (Bistriţa, Romania). Romhányi, "Egy régi-új forrás," 240.

98 The highest academic degree was the master or doctor of theology. Harsányi, *A domonkos rend*, 121.

99 Luspescuné, "Domonkos iskoláztatás," 847.

100 See the bull of Pope Leo X to the bishop of Speyer, April 29, 1521. Rott, ed., *Correspondance de Martin Bucer*, vol. 1, 21–26, 155–57. Since the pope himself responded to the appeal (and not the Major Penitentiary), it follows that Bucer submitted his petition to the Apostolic Dataria.

101 Greschat, *Martin Bucer*, 14.

religious vows, that help us identify some shared episodes in the life stories of apostate friars. These friars came from the lower social ranks that considered mendicant orders to be attractive religious institutions that could be used for social advancement through study, and act as gateways to the priesthood. In the following chapter, I will explore how and why cloisters and the possibility of learning overlapped in the careers of poor but ambitious young men. The meaning of "poor" will be defined through a brief survey of the social origins of the friars, after which I will map the cloisters and the type of schools they tended to prefer and outline the nature of the knowledge they sought.

CHAPTER 3

The Gates of Upward Social Mobility

The great humanist scholar Cardinal Basilios Bessarion wrote in 1460 that the following adage had gained widespread use within the royal court of Buda: "There is nobody as ignorant as a monk."[1] One century later, the Lutheran pastor Gáspár Heltai remarked in a work castigating the monks and monasteries of the age, that "at first the cloisters" were schools "in which there lived learned masters and humble pupils from among whom eminent and scholarly teachers were taken."[2] Who should we believe? Were the religious ignorant or learned? The adage from Buda was one of the expressions of derision used among members of the humanist circles at the royal court. Whom might their scorn have been targeting? Intellectual rivals? Scholastic theologians and their obsolete knowledge? Or perhaps the ignorance of a typical friar?

The first generation of Reformation preachers, who rose in opposition to the monastic culture that was still in full force at the beginning of the sixteenth century, talked about the religious houses of their age in a completely different voice. In 1524, Luther wrote: "It is true that, rather than have the universities and monasteries continue as before, with no other place for youth to study and live, I should wish no boy ever to study nor to be able to speak; for it is my earnest intention, prayer and desire, that those ass stables and devil's schools should either sink into the abyss or be converted into Christian schools."[3] Luther harshly criticized the schools of his age as un-Christian and irrelevant because they taught useless knowledge instead of the Bible. At the same time, Luther—just as Heltai—regarded the cloisters, along with the universities, to be centers of education and scholarship. I shall examine the identity of those who studied at the cloister schools and the body of knowledge that Luther, in retrospect, characterized as pointless, though it drew both him and the clerics of his youth into the mendicant

1 This quote appears in Kovács, *Eszmetörténet*, 214. Cardinal Bessarion stayed in Vienna in 1460 in order to arbitrate a peace agreement between Frederick III, Holy Roman Emperor and Matthias Hunyadi, King of Hungary, in preparation for a planned crusade against the Ottoman-Turks. Bessarion likely derived his information regarding the royal court in Buda from his humanist friends there. Ritoókné Szalay, *"Nympha Super Ripam Danubii,"* 6.

2 Heltai, *Krónika*, 470.

3 Luther, "To the Councilmen of all Cities," 79.

© KONINKLIJKE BRILL NV, LEIDEN, 2018 | DOI 10.1163/9789004361263_004 cloisters. Furthermore, we will explore the dynamic between the ideals of the religious elite regarding the objectives of learning and social demands that shaped the curricula of cloister schools.

The Social Origin of the Friars

We can determine the social standing of the friars who entered the friaries in the Kingdom of Hungary through an examination of their names. The only one to mark his social position was *nobilis* Miklós Pestenyei, a member of the Slavonian lesser nobility who had been married when he joined the Benedictine order and eventually returned to his wife following the annulment of his religious vows.[4] Trade names used as family names indicate occupations.[5] The religious novices examined here most often had family names referring to simple trades, such as tailor, carpenter, shoemaker, mason, baker and smith, denoting both rural and urban artisans.[6] People with such names included three laymen, who presumably continued to practice their vocations in the cloister as lay brothers. Designations such as "Lukács Varga, smith" may have indicated that the person in question worked as a smith at the cloister, while his father or another ancestor had been a shoemaker (*varga* in Hungarian).[7] Interestingly, these simple artisans were ordained to the priesthood in the same manner as the large majority of novices, reflecting the low social origin of friars in general.[8] The occupation of goldsmith was usually regarded as a more distinguished urban trade, as confirmed in the case of Gál Ötvös ("goldsmith"), a burgher of Pest who joined the Dominicans.[9]

4 *Nobilis vir Nicolaus de Presteneg*, APA vol. 66, fol. 1166r (1521). The Slavonian Pestenyei family included two men named Miklós, one the son of Péter and the other the son of László Weres (MNL OL DL 94324).

5 The fundamental work regarding the use of names during this period: Mező, *Várdai-birtokok jobbágynevei*. See also Szabó, "A jobbágynevek kialakulása."

6 There were eight such names among those examined, including two masons.

7 Pá Molnár ("Miller"), Pauline friar (APA vol. 42, fol. 386v, 1493); Lukács Varga "Shoemaker", smith, Dominican friar (ibid., vol. 66, fol. 44rv, 1520); and Péter Ács "Carpenter", another Dominican (ibid., vol. 81, fol. 607v–8r, 1533).

8 For the sake of comparison, the artisans active in the Dominican cloisters in Transylvania (cook, smith, carpenter, miller, butcher, cooper) were usually lay brothers. See Romhányi, "Egy régi-új forrás," 240–41.

9 APA vol. 48, fol. 358rv (1499).

Names could also refer to place of origin, as did almost half of those examined in the present case.[10] Among those whose place of origin could be identified, seven were from cities, nine from market towns and seventeen from villages.[11] Due to the relative ease with which it is possible to identify landowning nobles, we can state with certainty that runaway friars did not come from this social category, but had been serfs or members of the lesser nobility. This conforms to our previous understanding that Paulines and mendicants typically originated from the non-noble strata of society: burghers (urban middle and lower strata rather than the elite) and villagers, many of whom inhabited market towns.[12] Without exception, those who chose to enter cloisters in their cities of origin joined the Dominicans or Augustinians even though Franciscans were also present in Pest, Eger, Székesfehérvár, Újlak (Ilok, Croatia) and Beszterce (Bistrița, Romania). Only László Temesvári had no apparent choice of orders to join in his native town, since only the Dominicans were active in Temesvár (Timișoara, Romania). Bálint Körmöci left his home in Körmöcbánya (Kremnica, Slovakia), a town with no cloister, to join the preaching friars in another mining town in northern Hungary, Gölnic (Gelnica, Slovakia).[13] The case of Péter Lippai suggests that he made a conscious choice between mendicant orders. Although he could have entered the Franciscan or Augustinian friary in his southern hometown of Lippa (Lipova, Romania), he instead traveled as far as the town of Beregszász (Berehovo, Ukraine) in northeastern Hungary to join the Dominicans. When internal conflicts at this location later prompted Lippai to return to his hometown, he joined the Augustinians rather than the Franciscans.[14] During the late fifteenth and early sixteenth centuries, the number of Franciscan cloisters and friars rose significantly in Hungary as a result of their appeal to lay society ranging from commoners to aristocratic patrons due to the successful reform of the order.[15] Thus, those who elected to join the Dominican and Augustine orders in contrast to the prevailing trend did so, we

10 Geographical designations did not appear in thirty-four examined names, while the location to which such designations referred could not be identified in a few other cases.

11 The seven cities in question were Pest, Székesfehérvár, Eger, Körmöcbánya (Kremnica, Slovakia), Beszterce (Bistrița, Romania), Temesvár (Timișoara, Romania) and Szalánkemén (Stari Slankamen, Serbia). The nine market towns were Gyula, Pestújlak, Szakcs, Szepetnek, Varsány, Verőce (Virovitica, Croatia), Futak (Futog, Serbia), Szabadka (Subotica, Serbia) and Pétervárad (Petrovaradin, Serbia).

12 See Szakály, *Mezőváros és reformáció*, 26–28; Kubinyi, "Magyarország és a pálosok," 50–51.

13 APA vol. 75, fol. 249r (1527).

14 APA vol. 72, fol. 339v–40r (1524, Waradien. dioc.).

15 For a summary examination of this phenomenon, see Erdélyi, *Cloister on Trial*, 49–50.

may presume, very consciously, following individual motives. Primary among these considerations, as I will argue below, was the aspiration to find the best possible education.

Among inhabitants of market towns, the balance seemed to tip toward the Franciscans. Residents of such towns tended to enter local cloisters if possible.[16] Such was the case with János Futaki and Lőrinc Gyulai, who joined the Observant Franciscans in their hometowns of Futak (Futog, Serbia) and Gyula, respectively and Dénes Péterváradi, who joined the Cistercian order in his hometown of Pétervárad (Petrovaradin, Serbia).[17] Jakab Verőcei was the exception to this rule, electing to leave Verőce (Virovitica, Croatia) in order to enter the Gotó Cistercian Abbey in nearby Pozsega County even though there were Franciscan and Dominican houses in his hometown. Jakab Verőcei presumably decided to take up residence at the Cistercian monastery after the abbot repeatedly invited him to serve as its sexton and servant.[18] The case of Jakab Verőcei is unique, as he did not relocate to a distant larger town in order to join the Franciscans. Gergely Szepetneki moved from the market town of Szepetnek in Zala County in western Hungary to Csanád County in the central part of the kingdom, while Ferenc Szabadkai moved from the market town of Szabadka (Subotica, Serbia) in the southern regions to enter a Franciscan house in the town of Székesfehérvár (where Dominican and Augustine cloisters also operated) and Gergely, the son of Farkas Demeter of Tiszavarsány, left Tiszavarsány in the northern Great Hungarian Plain to enter a Franciscan friary located in the diocese of Pécs in the south.[19]

I expected to confirm what others have already observed—that the Franciscans were exceptionally popular among villagers due to the fact that they continued to adhere strictly to the vow of poverty.[20] However, among the friars I examined, most of those of rural origin chose to enter the Dominican or Augustine orders.[21] This again suggests that young men sought to join orders that offered the best possible education and training and to enter larger

16 Among the friars from market towns were five Franciscans, two Cistercians, one Dominican and one Pauline.

17 Sources regarding Futaki, Gyulai and Péterváradi, respectively: APA vol. 3, fol. 181r (1450); vol. 72, fol. 345rv (1524); and vol. 66, fol. 1167rv (1521).

18 APA vol. 20, fol. 13 or (1472, Zagrabien. dioc).

19 Sources regarding Szepetneki, Szabadkai and Tiszavarsányi, respectively: APA vol. 74, fol. 557v (1526); vol. 64, fol. 69v–70r (1519); and vol. 57, fol. 404rv (1512).

20 Fazekas, *Szerzetesrendek*, 73.

21 The religious from villages included nine Dominicans, five Augustinians, four Paulines, three Franciscans and two Benedictines.

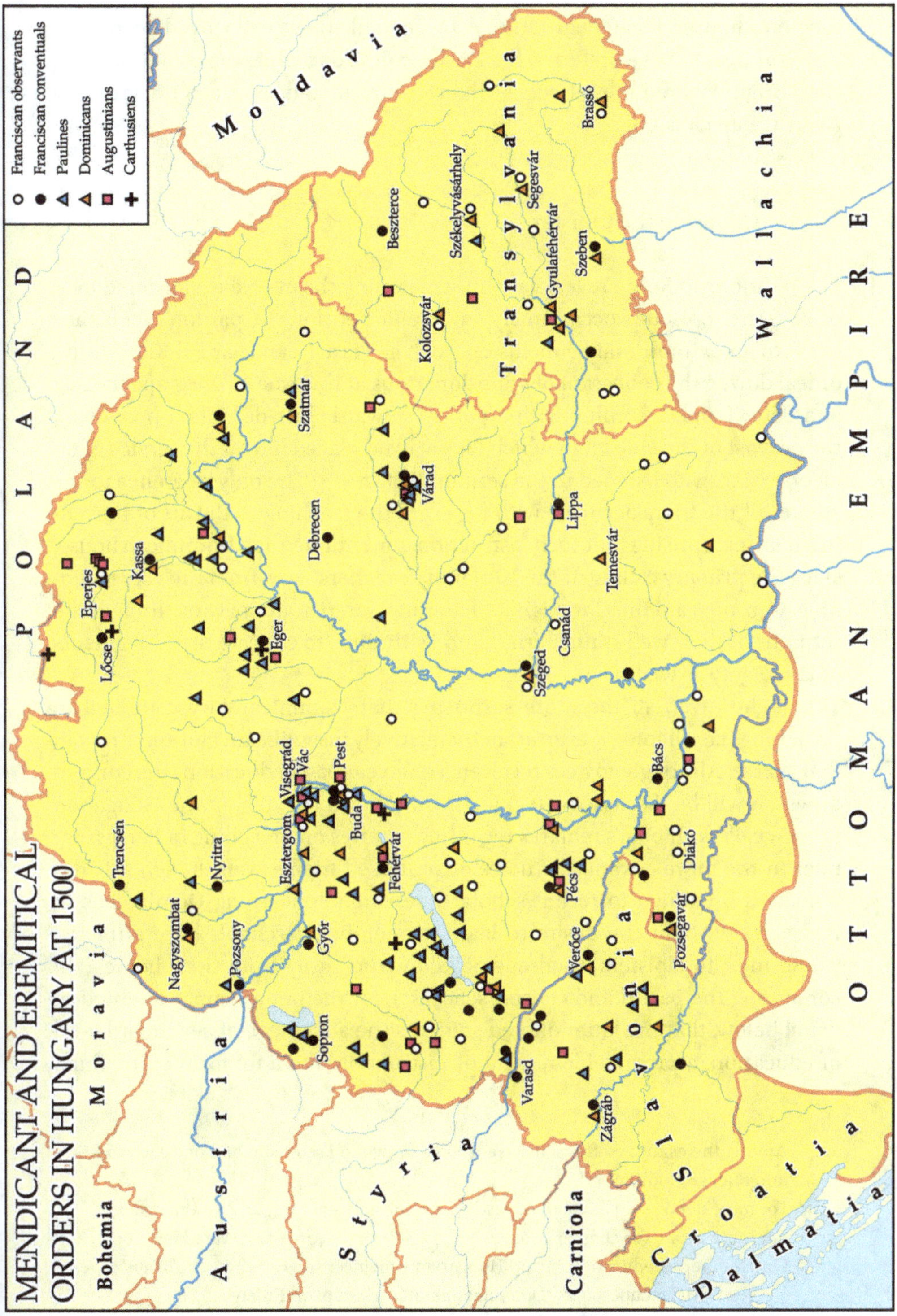

MAP 3 *Mendicant and Eremitical Orders in Hungary at 1500.*

religious houses located in cities.[22] In general, those who lived in market towns appear to have preferred the Franciscan Order, while those of urban and rural origin favored the schools of the Dominican and, to a lesser degree, the Augustinian cloisters.

Choosing the Cloister

The petitions to Rome reveal very little regarding the everyday cloistered lives of ex-friars. Episodes occasionally surface in petitions of pardon when they came to an extraordinary conclusion, such as Franciscan friar Pál Kaproncai's ordeal during the collection of wine donations at the time of the grape harvest and Péter Lippai's conflict with a pantry steward.[23] As described previously, the provost of the cloister in which Lippai lived placed him at the service of an elderly friar "who listened to the sermon-lectures."[24] The only reference to the studies of the friars occurred with regard to the teaching of the art of preaching. It is unsurprising that such instruction is mentioned at a Dominican house, since the primary calling of the "Order of Preachers" was, from the very beginning, to propagate the Christian faith among heretics and pagans through the sermons of their well-trained friars and, with time, to educate broad segments of lay society as well.

It is, however, all the more surprising that Dominicans were trained in preaching (i.e., theology) even at such a relatively insignificant cloister—that in Beregszász. Although novices received a one-year basic education (the content of which will be discussed later) in all Dominican cloisters in the Hungarian province, Péter Lippai's remarks regarding lectures on preaching in Beregszász refer to the more advanced studies of professed friars (even though this has remained unknown to recent scholarly research concerning Dominicans in Hungary).[25] Might the desire to learn at mendicant schools have attracted young men to cloisters hundreds of kilometers away from their homes? In comparing the parish and cloister schools, I got the impression, presented in detail below, that the latter offered students the advantage of a standard level of education, a predictable quality of instruction and a uniform curriculum,

22 Among the examined friars, five went to Pécs, two to Esztergom and one each to Kőrös and Budaszentlőrinc.

23 For more detail, see chapter two. APA vol. 72, fol. 338v–39r (1524, Zagrabien. dioc.).

24 For more detail, see chapter two. APA vol. 72, fol. 339v–40r (1524, Waradien. dioc).

25 On Dominican education in the Hungarian province, see Harsányi, *A domonkos rend,* 113–301; Makó Lupescuné, "Domonkos oktatás a középkori Erdélyben," 844–53.

even at a basic level. This integrated educational system was the product of the centralized organization of the mendicant orders. Although modern historiographies of learning and education tend to depict late medieval and early modern parish and municipal schools as components of a unified system, thus projecting the modern Western educational system into the past, the level of training and interest of any given teacher determined the quality of education. Education during this period was thus random and chaotic in terms of both content and quality regardless of whether it took place in urban or rural areas, as I will describe below.[26]

Returning to our point of departure, the majority of runaway friars who petitioned the Roman curia were Dominicans. This is interesting, because among all religious orders, Paulines most commonly turned to the curia with regard to other matters, while the Dominicans rarely did so, yet the number of apostates remained much lower among Paulines than Dominicans.[27] In light of the well-known facts that Dominicans placed a great emphasis on the education of their friars while Paulines explicitly rejected education due to their eremitic traditions, one may draw the self-evident conclusion that the phenomenon of apostasy was closely related to the issue of education.[28] The petitions to the pope reveal that those who joined the Dominicans tended to choose to enter cloisters that offered basic and advanced level education.[29] Only one runaway friar chose to live at the cloister of St. Michael in Buda, the *studium generale*, which provided the highest level of instruction in the entire

26 On the diversity of schools and the chaotic nature of the educational landscape in the Late Middle Ages as opposed to the systematic *Bildungswesen* projected back by German literature to medieval times, see also Sheffley, *Schools and Schooling*, 1–4.

27 There was a total of thirty-one Dominican apostates, while only twelve friars from the order turned to the Roman Curia concerning other issues. Among the Paulines, there were only eleven apostates, while friars submitted twenty petitions to the Curia regarding different cases.

28 For an overview of the system of education in late medieval mendicant houses, see Sheffley, *Schools and Schooling*, 117–30. With regard to Dominican education, see: Hasebrink, "Latinität als Bildungsfundamen"; and Frank, *Hausstudium und Universitätsstudium*.

29 The cloisters in which friars had lived before they left the order can be identified in twenty-two cases (of a total of thirty-one apostate Dominicans). In Dominican cloisters, a *lector* was designated to conduct the teaching of novices (*studium conventuale*). Of the Dominican apostates, nine entered cloisters that offered such basic education—those in Pest, Várad, Temesvár, etc.—while twelve went to locations where both *studium conventuale* as well as more advanced level education (*studium particulare*) were offered—four to Pécs, three to Székesfehérvár, two to Segesvár (Sighișoara, Romania) and one each to Szeged, Kassa (Košice, Slovakia) and Beszterce.

Kingdom of Hungary, which at the time had no university. Therefore, we are not dealing here with fledgling scholars who aspired to obtain a university diploma in order to become theologians or law professors, but intelligent and ambitious young men who wanted to acquire the best possible training in a practical profession.

Although there is only scattered information available regarding Franciscan schools, it is nevertheless clear that friars sought to enter cloisters that offered advanced studies.[30] As a result of the innovative spirit and reforms of Gergely Gyöngyösi in the early 1520s, education gained acceptance among the Paulines, who had opposed the scholarly learning of the friars. The cloister in Budaszentlőrinc housed the order's central school, which was entered and then deserted by all the Pauline apostate friars during the early 1520s.[31]

Researchers have deduced from data regarding the studies of individual Augustinian friars at foreign universities that their order maintained a high level of education in Hungary. This conclusion is convincing, since homeland monastic schools prepared friars to pursue university studies; however, aside from the *studium generale* in Esztergom and Pécs, the locations of the other schools are uncertain or unknown.[32] I suspect that schools may have operated in the northeastern episcopal town of Eger and the market town of Újlak in the south, since several brothers fled from the order after years spent in these places.[33]

Learning in the Cloister Schools

What kind of knowledge did the young men who aspired to attain education and success receive in these monastic schools? Comparison of the Pauline and Dominican educational systems, both of which can be reconstructed in relative

30 Two friars went to each of the friaries in Pécs, Székesfehérvár and Győr at which advanced learning (*studium particulare*) was available, while one went to the cloister in Szeged, the large library of which indicates that training of some sort took place there. See Bálint, *Szeged Városa*, 24–25. One friar chose to enter each of the cloisters in the towns of Csanád and Gyula, where evidence (the working of a *lector* and the production of a codex) suggests that advanced level schools operated. ETE vol. 2, 492, 496; Bálint, *Szeged*, 37.

31 A total of three friars, in 1520, 1522 and 1523.

32 Schools were presumably located in Buda, Bátmonostor, Kaza (Košeca, Slovakia), Torda (Turda, Romania) and Kusaly (Coșeiu, Romania). See Romhányi, "A koldulóbarátok szerepe," 37. Among these cloisters, one apostate came from each of those in Buda, Pécs and Esztergom.

33 APA vol. 63, fol. 203rv; vol. 64, fol. 131v; ASV Arm XXXII. vol. 61, fol. 109v–10r; vol. 72, fol. 326r.

detail, highlights the two extremes. The Pauline superior Gergely Gyöngyösi provided a comprehensive description of his ideas regarding the training of novices in the course of his explanation of the constitutions of his order. He suggested that the task of teaching novices should be assigned to elderly friars rather than to those with doctoral or magister degrees. During the probationary year, such teachers were expected to instill in novices the morals and habits worthy of a religious, such as deference, obedience and poverty as well as rules for everyday comportment, such as walking with downcast eyes, drinking while seated, talking only at appropriate times and praying silently. Learning the components of religious and spiritual life represented the other important domain of education, with particular emphasis placed on regular auricular confession and the requisite dogmatic knowledge (the Ten Commandments, the seven deadly sins, the four cardinal virtues), as well as ways of celebrating church services according to Pauline manners. In order to complete this training, novices had to be thoroughly familiar with the rules and constitution of the order and had to know how to sing and read; writing was unnecessary. Diligent study of the Bible was an important criterion in the constitution of the order, though surprisingly not in the provincial's appended explanations.[34] Gergely Gyöngyösi's list of ten recommended readings for novices included the instruction that "The novice should read often useful and simple texts rather than subtleties [*subtilia*] for nourishing the soul and the love for God."[35] Novices first had to learn the system of rules surrounding everyday behavior and religious practice in order to request to take their vows as part of a ceremony in which the prior "examined his life and morals" before the community of friars.[36] However, the training of novices went beyond this, at least at larger cloisters, in which friars were instructed by a *magister* in the "simple sciences" (*in primitivis scientiis*),[37] which were composed of the subjects of the trivium—grammar, rhetoric and logic.[38] Gyöngyösi's other writings reveal, however, that he continued to explicitly reject the notion of high level philosophical theological education for friars because he was trying to steer the order in the

34 Sarbak, ed., *Declarationes constitutionum*, Rubrica LXIII: Qualis debeat esse magister noviciorum, et de quibus ipsi novicii instruantur, 317.

35 Sarbak, Bellus and Weinrich, eds., *Gyöngyösi Gergely* OSPPE*: Epitoma és Directorium*, 49.

36 Sarbak, ed., *Declarationes constitutionum*, Rubrica LXIIII: De modo professionis faciende tam a fratribus presbiteris, quam conversis, 321.

37 "In singulis ipsorum monasteriis, quibus ad hoc suppetunt facultates, idoneus teneatur magister, qui eos in primitivis scientiis instruat diligenter." Sarbak, ed., *Declarationes constitutionum*, Rubrica LXIII, 317.

38 Mezey, *Deákság és Európa*, 184–85.

direction of mystical devotion in which friars would develop their religious personalities through meditation and individual prayer.[39] The following commentary, which Gyöngyösi appended to the Pauline constitution, reflects this ambition: "If the cleric still knows little and wants to become a priest, we recommend to him that he study outside the order. If he still wants to join, then he should be a lay brother [*conversus*], though he should not trouble us with cultivation of the sciences [*de studio litterarum*], because then we will not even admit him."[40] The Pauline order thus attempted to establish a unique profile and spirituality that required a completely different kind of training than was necessary for ordination as a priest during the era in question. Gyöngyösi essentially repudiated the idea of using the Pauline order as an institution for training priests. In other words, Gyöngyösi's comments suggest that many young men, among them the runaway friars in focus here, attempted to obtain such training in religious orders, including the Pauline order. Gyöngyösi's reasoning and the ordinary friars' choice is more understandable if one is familiar with the training conditions of the lesser clergy in the late Middle Ages, the level of which, it seems, was surmounted even in the Pauline order. First, however, we should consider why the Dominicans attracted the largest number of ambitious young men eager to study.

The uniform standard of the Dominican educational system differentiated itself from other religious orders. Basic level education took place at all larger Dominican houses and all friars were required to study some degree of theology in order to provide them with the religious foundations necessary for preaching.[41] The fact that even the lecturers (*lectors*) who guided basic level teaching were university-trained friars—contrary to their simple and elderly Pauline counterparts—serves to underscore the order's much higher standard of education. In addition to their lectures, trained assistants conducted individual exercises in Latin grammar, primarily through the reading of biblical passages. One can gain detailed information regarding this teaching method in the manual designed for the instruction of young friars of the vicar general, who was entrusted to introduce observant reforms in the cloisters of the Hungarian Dominican province.[42] This

39 See mention of Thomas à Kempis, best known for his connection with *Devotio Moderna*, on the list of readings for novices. Cf. Mályusz, "A pálosrend," 45–53. More recently see Sarbak, "Die 'devotio moderna' in Ungarn," 249–64.

40 Sarbak, ed., *Declarationes constitutionum*, Rubrica LXI, 296.

41 Mályusz, *Egyházi társadalom*, 262–65.

42 Kiss, "Latin és népnyelv."

work also reveals that the learning of the clerics and laymen who entered Dominican cloisters was very diverse: some did not know Latin at all; "less-educated clerics" (*clerici minus docti*) possessed a passive, ritualized familiarity with the language and could recite learned texts; others had reached a level of knowledge that enabled them to conjugate Latin verbs; and those who were the most proficient in Latin could explain the language's grammar, thus attaining the *ars grammatica* level. It is very exciting to gain a glimpse into the common activities of laymen and clerics, such as their collective meals at which clerics explained Latin biblical extracts in the vernacular for the purpose of practicing its use as well as for the interest of illiterate laymen. As a result of this close coexistence, the line between laymen and clergymen was not impermeable: young men, laymen and clerics alike, who entered Dominican cloisters with little education were offered the possibility, contrary to Pauline policy, to study basic to advanced levels of education and to become priests and friars. The superior, who had himself become a Dominican and a *doctor theologiae*, encouraged his associates to pursue such education and careers.[43]

Dominicans—again contrary to Paulines—stipulated that clerics had to be able to write at the time of taking the religious vow. Furthermore, they expected their priests to both speak and write Latin perfectly and to master Latin grammar. The friar who completed Dominican basic training thus acquired a much higher level of learning than members of the secular lesser clergy who had, at best, studied at parish schools. Those runaway friars who had first chosen and then left cloisters that offered advanced training—the *studium particulare*—were able, in addition to attending grammar lectures, to also study the subjects of the *quadrivium*—arithmetic, geometry, music and astronomy—and could even attend some theological-philosophical courses that represented the calling of the order. After completing these studies, those who wished to attain the highest degree of learning were able to move on to the *studium generale* in Buda, the capital city, at which students from Hungary and abroad attended university level courses in grammar, logic and theology taught by professors from Germany, Italy and France.[44] This is where Mátyás Besztercei presumably attained his magister degree before being sent to an Italian university to obtain his doctorate in theology. It is thus not coincidental that among the doctors who submitted

43 On the existence of grammar schools in Dominican cloisters elsewhere, see for example the case of the Province of Aragon: Vargas, *Taming a Brood of Vipers*, 181.

44 Mulchahey and Noone, "Religious Orders," 45–50.

petitions to the papal curia, we find two Dominicans in addition to canons and an urban parish priest.[45]

In light of the well-known erudition of the Dominicans with regard to preaching and polemical skills, it is surprising that active opposition to the evangelical ideas in Hungary beginning in the 1520s emerged primarily not among the preaching friars, but among the Franciscans. This is clearly reflected in the fact that Dominicans in Hungary produced no polemical writings as opposed to their peers from other European countries. The earliest religious disputes were performed by Franciscans.[46] Our surprise increases if we read the letter that the Franciscan Provincial, Balázs Dézsi, sent to the Italian superior general in May 1514: "We do not so much need to exercise our friars in hairsplitting and argumentations as we do in pious writings and grammatical studies, and they especially need the expertise necessary for administering holy confession."[47] The Hungarian Observant Franciscan superior wrote the letter to explain to his colleagues in Italy why he had sent the Italian *lector* back to his homeland after he had spent two years in the Hungarian province to develop the *studia litterarum*. The letter is interesting because it provides insight into the various concepts regarding the training of friars during this period. How should we interpret the words of the Hungarian provincial?

The letter of Dézsi reminds one of the previously cited words of the Pauline Gergely Gyöngyösi, who advocated the initial grammatical-rhetorical instruction of the seven liberal arts and rejected the study of advanced philosophical-theological subjects. The expression "subtleties and argumentations" seems to refer to the advanced theological training that Gyöngyösi openly disclaimed, which they both considered to be

45 One of the Dominicans who had obtained a doctoral degree was the above-mentioned Mátyás Besztercei, while the other was János Temesvári, who requested permission to receive his doctor of theology in 1536. APA vol. 91, fol. 125v–26rv. Temesvári studied in Bologna in 1506. Harsányi, *A domonkos rend*, 263.

46 The only Dominican friar remembered by evangelical reformers as their opponent in religious debates is Friar Józsa, who arrived from Padua in 1552 to become a parish priest in the market town of Tolna in Ottoman Hungary, where he took turns preaching in the parish church with the Lutheran pastor of the town. Ács, "Katolikus irodalom és kultúra." On the first disputes, see also Horváth, *A reformáció jegyében*, 162–163, 181. Reizner, *Szeged története*, 115–17; Kathona, Fejezetek, 105.

47 "Non tam opus esse nobis ad exercendum nostros in subtilibus et argumentationibus, quam ad studendum in devotis scripturis et planis scientiis, maxime in casibus scientie rebus utpote plus indigent." Quoted in Cevins, *Les Franciscains Observants*, 522–23.

scholastic "hairsplitting" self-serving disputations. The Franciscan provincial contrasted such superfluous hairsplitting with reading the Bible and the theological knowledge necessary for administering Confession, that is, with the foundations of pastoral activity. Dézsi continued his letter as follows: "We also have teachers in the province who are able to lecture and teach the friars the knowledge necessary for hearing confessions and similar simple sciences (*tales casus et scientias*); thus at our present assembly we ordered the *lectors* to continue the *studia* according to our own concept."[48] The detailed regulation adopted at the 1515 provincial assembly regarding the curriculum at the schools in Buda and Esztergom—which called for three *lectors* to teach subjects related to the seven liberal arts, the fundamentals of theology and hearing confession at each school—serves to substantiate Dézsi's words.[49]

Lectors were active at the Observant Franciscan cloisters in Várad (Oradea, Romania), Csanád, Sárospatak and Pápa even during the "turmoil" of the 1530s and 1540s. Eleven novices and clerics were sent to study in Szakolca (Skalica, Slovakia) in 1565.[50] At the beginning of the sixteenth century, the objectives underlying the education of friars continued to remain within the framework that had been formulated and implemented with great success during previous generations. At the center of this framework was preaching, specifically the new genre of mass preaching aimed at the broadest segments of society. Experiences acquired among the people, not books, provided the basic material for such sermons. This type of preaching explicitly aimed to increase lay literacy, which mattered more for its moral value than for the religious; learning elevated morality, which in turn helped to reduce social conflicts and promote peaceful coexistence among various social strata.[51] Saint Bernardino of Siena—the mentor of John of Capistrano, who preached the crusade against the Ottoman Turks at Nándorfehérvár (Belgrade) in 1456, claimed that all sin was rooted in ignorance; therefore, it was the obligation of all to study.[52] The ultimate goal, then, of learning and preaching was the suppression of violence and the promotion of peaceful coexistence.

48 Cevins, *Les Franciscains Observants*, 523.

49 Batthyany, ed., *Leges ecclesiasticae* vol. 3, 669.

50 See the published minutes of the Franciscan assemblies (1531–67), ETE vol. 2, 469, 474, 479, 485, 487, 492, 530.

51 Elm, "Die Franziskanerobservanz," 207–11.

52 Elm quotes Saint Bernardino, ibid., 210.

The Observant Franciscan preacher Pelbárt Temesvári (*Pelbartus de Temeswar*) was the leading figure in Hungary representing the ideas emerging from Italy at the end of the fifteenth century. Pelbárt's advice regarding Holy Week sermons clearly reflects thoughts on the nature of mass sermons:

> The preacher should first show his audience the bloody cross in order to get their hearts pumping, meanwhile he should say a prayer. [...] Then during the narration of the gospel, when he reaches moving episodes, such as Christ taking leave of his mother and his apostles, his flagellation or the ecce homo, he should display images depicting them. In the meantime, he should explain theological disputes and questions for the benefit of the literate and educated people in the audience.[53]

Popular sermons did not address the people with the theological tools of scholars or the literary devices of humanists,[54] but successfully reached ordinary audiences via an arsenal of words, images, music and gestures. The story of Máté Balinci from the year 1439 demonstrates the impact that Franciscan sermons exercised on simple people. Balinci, from the southern region of the kingdom, was in his early twenties when "he heard an Observant Franciscan friar preaching and, understanding the sweet words of God, he decided that he would join the order and serve God."[55] Máté subsequently violated his vow and did not enter the order, for which he asked the pope for forgiveness.[56] This did not, however, alter the fact that—as Balinci's case demonstrates—the preaching of the Franciscans managed to speak to

53 Szilády, *Temesvári Pelbárt*, 22–23.

54 The spirituality of the order's mainstream remained conservative in the sense that the ideology of the *Devotio Moderna* had no impact on their preaching and pastoral activities, as opposed to the Pauline mentality of the early sixteenth century. Sarbak, "Die 'Devotio moderna' in Ungarn." The young generation of Observant friars rebelled against the Observant leadership under the impact of medieval Franciscan spiritualistic ideas. See Szűcs, "Die Ideologie des Bauernkrieges."

55 "Audiens predicationem verbi dei a quodam fratre ordinis minorum de observantia et intelligens dulcea verba dei intra se ipsum deliberavit et simpliciter intentionem intra se habuit dictum ordinem intrare et deo ipso servire." APA vol. 2, fol. 18v (Chanadien. dioc., village of Balinc is to be found in Temes County [settlements will be identified by Engel's Database]).

56 Vows taken in sickness or captivity and cases of their violations also reflect the popularity of the Franciscans: seven petitioners vowed to enter the Franciscan order, compared to two Dominicans, two Paulines and one Augustinian hermit between 1439 and 1497.

ordinary men and women and impel them to action. Máté had been born in a remote little village and, as he acknowledged in his petition to Rome, was *litterarum ignarus*.

The training of friars had to be restructured in the interest of successful popular preaching. Bernardino of Siena established studies of moral theology at the cloister in Perugia in Italy, while Jacobo de Marchia—who had acted as inquisitor in Hungary—advocated for the introduction of studies in law and the humanities (the liberal arts) on the grounds that these subjects would enable friars to transmit all that which served "human and physical as well as spiritual and eternal welfare."[57] With the exception of law, such training was already taking place at the schools in Buda and Esztergom: basic theological knowledge needed for popular preaching, and the humanities and casuistry, which formed part of moral theology, figured in the curriculum.

Seen from this perspective, it was no coincidence that the Franciscan order survived the initial and subsequent waves of the Reformation and the Ottoman conquest. The continued vitality of the Franciscans was manifested in their propaganda in opposition to preachers of the new teachings and in the fact that some of their cloisters operated without interruption.[58] In other words, they continued to appeal to the faithful. The survival of the Paulines amid the religious and military upheavals of the time was possibly facilitated by their insistence that friars should be able to compose and deliver *sermones populares* designed for ordinary audiences.[59]

The simultaneous disappearance of the Dominicans in Hungary can perhaps be connected to the fact that they maintained different ideas with regard to education and learning, which distanced the members of the order from laypeople. Moreover, as a result of the Reformation, the Dominicans lost their traditional social base. Contrary to the Franciscans, whose activities were concentrated in market towns and villages, Dominican friaries were located in cities, largely German-speaking burghers which became Lutheran during

57 Elm, *Franziskanerobservanz*, 212. On the Franciscan curriculum—from grammar to logic and theology—in the thirteenth and fourteenth centuries, see Szabó, *A ferences skolasztika*.

58 During the second half of the fifteenth century the Conventual Franciscans also adopted Observant reforms.

59 Gyöngyösi asserted that some learned Paulines published collections of sample popular sermons for their fellow friars at the end of the fifteenth century. See Mályusz, "A pálosrend," 31. For Gyöngyösi's instructions to preachers, see Sarbak, Bellus and Weinrich, eds., *Gyöngyösi Gergely*, Directorium: Capitulum XI, 53–55. On the five to six surviving Pauline cloisters, see Kisbán, *A magyar pálosrend története*, 1938, 187–93; and Romhányi, *Kolostorok és társaskáptalanok*, 11, 45.

FIGURE 6 *Martin Luther preaches to the crowd from the pulpit in a church.*

the initial surge of the Reformation in Hungary.[60] All in all, one can detect differences in the characters and mentalities of the cloisters and schools of the various mendicant orders. Dominicans and Augustinians gave preference to elite, scholarly training, whereas Franciscans and Paulines insisted on their preachers being accessible to ordinary people. However, all four orders had the common traits of maintaining trained lecturers to instruct young members and of requiring all friars to complete basic education. This dependability seems to have made their cloisters attractive gateways for the sons of serfs and poor noblemen who aspired to attain social advancement through learning.

60 The large majority of Dominicans were of German origin in Transylvania as well. See Romhányi, *Egy régi-új forrás*, 244.

Learning in the Parish Schools

Mátyás, son of Egyed, went to school, though, according to his account, not in preparation for the priesthood, but for marriage: he had asked for the hand of Dorottya, the fifteen-year-old daughter of György Csezi. However, he then changed his mind, deciding that he wanted to become a priest and asked the Apostolic Penitentiary to annul his previous promise of marriage.[61] This unexceptional story provides a clear example of the choice that young men had to make between marriage and the priesthood as well as the fluidity of lay and clerical identity and the routine movement between the two careers. Clerics lived in close coexistence within religious houses, and some who attended parish schools became priests while others married and pursued lay careers.

One of the functions of parish schools operating in villages and market towns was to provide elementary education (reading, singing, catechism, writing and basic counting) to local children and clerical students. Parish priests or their auxiliary clergymen were able to serve as teachers, in many instances training their own relatives, typically their nephews, to be their successors.[62] This happened, for example, in the village of Zámor in central Hungary, where the incumbent Péter, son of Bálint, "corrected" one of his students with a whip and a switch because he had forgotten the Lord's Prayer and the Apostles' Creed.[63] Another parish priest beat one of his adolescent pupils, to whom he taught "grammar and good morals," because he failed to complete his prescribed lessons.[64] These stories demonstrate that physical discipline did not violate ecclesiastical or social norms, although extreme corporal punishment was not a part of the everyday life of schoolchildren. In the extraordinary instance that physical discipline resulted in the death of a student, the responsible priest had to

61 APA vol. 3, fol. 161r (1450, diocese of Pécs; Chez, presumably Csezfalva in Valkó County in modern-day Croatia).

62 For examples of parish priests who taught their nephews, see vol. 2, fol. 123rv; vol. 16, fol. 126r; vol. 29, fol. 187v; vol. 53, fol. 321r; vol. 54, fol. 261v; vol. 57, fol. 225r; vol. 70, fol. 656rv; vol. 72, fol. 304rv. Cf. chapter 7.

63 "Iuvenem quendam eius scolarem, quem … orationem dominicam et simbolum docuerat, ex eo, quod simbolum ipsum oblivioni tradiderat, tribus vicibus cum quodam flagello de corio correxit eumque cum palmatorio ligneo in manibus percussit…." APA vol. 16, fol. 126r (1467, Wesprimien. dioc.).

64 "Ipse olim tenens pro eius servitio quendam familiarem et quendam alium adolescentem, quem in grammatica et aliis bonis moribus instruebat dictusque adolescens lectionem sibi per exponentem ordinatam negligeret, ipsum adolescentem dictus exponens cum certis virgulis, prout in similibus convenit, verberavit."APA vol. 14, fol. 144v (1466, Agrien. dioc.).

obtain absolution from the pope.[65] If there were several schoolboys, a separate teacher was hired by the parish priest. Schoolmasters did not, however, pursue their profession as a career. Teaching represented only a temporary livelihood during their years of study, chaplain service and their first benefice.[66] The story about the conflict between Gergely, son of Bertalan, a schoolmaster of the parish school of Rádóc in western Hungary, and the parish priest in another nearby village, Lőrinc Szergény, demonstrates the tension that existed between teachers and the beneficed lower clergymen. Gergely stopped at a village tavern to have lunch while on his way home one day. Soon Lőrinc and another village incumbent from the area joined him. After Gergely told the priests that he had gone to the diocesan vicar to handle an affair, Lőrinc accused him of conspiring with the vicar in order to get his hands on his parish benefice. Lőrinc's response to this accusation is revealing: "That is not true, he never wanted to get hold of his benefice [...] though he knows that Lőrinc is so ignorant that he cannot even baptize and is incapable of properly administering other sacraments as well and because of this he had been driven out of a parish before."[67] Apparently the schoolmaster was a brazen benefice hunter and the parish priest lacked the competence to fill his office, according to how Lőrinc and Gergely depicted one another, which surely reveals more about the stereotypes of the time than about the individuals involved. Portrayals of unscrupulous schoolmasters eager to obtain a small village benefice and ignorant parish priests were likely familiar to contemporary audiences.

The following incident illustrates the great differences that existed between various village schools and regions. The episode took place in the Saxon Lands of Transylvania, one of the most economically developed, urbanized regions of Hungary that produced the greatest number of university students in the kingdom in the fifteenth and sixteenth centuries. In 1520, the student István Eceli wrote:

> When he was around 12 years old, he went over to his fellow students, Antal Mártontelki and Péter Seglares, who were holding a grammatical

65 For more examples of violent disciplining of *scolares*, see Esch, *Die Lebenswelt*, 71–72.

66 Körmend was a mid-sized market town in the western part of Transdanubia at the beginning of the sixteenth century. On the local parish clergy, schoolmasters and students, see Erdélyi, *A Cloister on Trial*, 127–29. Cf. Valter, *Falusi és mezővárosi iskolák*, 63 (examples of schoolmasters also serving as lawyers, and parish chaplains who become teachers). See, for more details, Chapter 7. For a European overview, see Kintzinger, "A profession but not a career?" On schoolmasters in late medieval England, see Moran, *The Growth of English Schooling*, 71–82.

67 APA vol. 14, fols 134rv (1466, Jaurien. dioc.).

> debate in the cemetery of the village of Baromlaka as young people customarily did. As he listened to the others, he playfully also asked a question, namely "Might Péter's father be the devil?" This made the students standing there in a circle begin to mock Péter, over which [...] Péter became extremely angry, grabbed a rock and threw it at student Antal, mortally injuring him.[68]

This event took place in the 400-inhabitant Transylvanian Saxon village of Baromlaka ("Wurmloch" in German; "Valea Viilor" in Romanian) during a student meeting convened to practice the material that had been presented in lectures through Latin conversation or debate.[69] The cemetery near the church and the school served as an obvious and pleasant venue for such outdoor gatherings. The participants of this grammatical-rhetorical exercise were perhaps students at the village parish school in Baromlaka, although some of them may have also come from the schools in surrounding Saxon villages such as Ecel ("Heczeldorf" in German, "Aţel" in Romanian) and Mártontelke ("Motisdorf" in German, "Motiş" in Romanian). The schools operating in Baromlaka, Ecel and Mártontelke were probably quite good, because these Saxon villages sent their seemingly talented sons to foreign universities to earn degrees in canon law so that they could serve as parish priests in their native villages.[70] Legal expertise was necessary because parish priests active in Saxon villages enjoyed a privileged status (*exemptus*) and higher income and arbitrated with archdeans in low-level ecclesiastical proceedings. They also functioned as public notaries, issuing charters in cases of civil law.[71] When István Eceli recounted the fatal incident that took place at the cemetery in Baromlaka, the parish priest in nearby Ecel had likely been Lázár, a man of noble origin who had attained a

68 APA vol. 66, fols 32v–33r (1520).

69 Such student gatherings are mentioned also in the school regulations in the German-speaking city of Bártfa ("Bartfeld" in German, "Bardejov" in Slovak) in northern Hungary. Mészáros, *XVI. századi városi iskoláink*, 154 (3rd article).

70 Three schoolboys from Baromlaka registered at the University of Kraków in 1504, while a total of seven students from the village had registered at this university by 1526. Nine pupils from the populous village of Ecel and one student from the village of Mártontelke went to the university of Vienna. Tonk, *Erdélyiek egyetemjárása*, 276, 350, 355; Csepregi, "Magyarországi iskolázás," 53.

71 The parish priests of Ecel also served as the heads of the decanate of Medgyes (Mediaş, Romania), the decanates being the free associations of regional parish incumbents exercising administrative and legal authority.

doctoral degree.[72] Lázár and other learned men certainly did not engage uneducated schoolmasters, whom the local community would not have tolerated. If students from Baromlaka, Ecel and Mártonlaka were unable to adequately prepare for university studies at the local schools operating in their home villages, they could always seek a higher level of education at the school run by the Saxon town of Medgyes (Mediaș, Romania) located just a few kilometers away.[73]

In conclusion, the evolving image of the network of parish schools in villages and market towns is multifaceted and contradictory. In contrast to the centrally organized mendicant school system with trained instructors, coordinated curricula and uniform educational standards, the level of education and subjects of study at parish schools depended primarily on the skills, interests and talents of the teacher; thus, differences between such schools could vary immensely from village to village.[74] This unpredictability meant that even advanced instruction could take place not only in cities, but also in many small towns and villages that had demanded and engaged the services of highly qualified teachers. The multitude of itinerant students carried the reputation of good schoolmasters far and wide, thus prompting some students to travel several hundred kilometers from their native villages in order to receive instruction in another village or small town schools.[75] Because schools had become important venues of communal identity formation and self-fashioning beginning in the late fifteenth century, competition emerged between various cities, towns and villages to acquire the services of the most capable and renowned schoolmasters. Therefore, teachers in the countryside of the region ranged from school rectors with university diplomas, sometimes even doctorates, to pupils and successors of simple parish priests.[76]

---

72 Lázár is mentioned between the years 1523 and 1526 as parish priest of Ecel (*venerabilis dominus Lazarus decretorum doctor plebanus de Eczelj decanus generalis*) MNL OL, DF 292020, 246290, 246292. The learned parish incumbents were also recruited from among local artisans, as indicated by the name of the parish priest in Ecel, *Johannes Sartoris de Birthalom* ("Johannes Tailor from Berethalom"). APA vol. 44, fol. 415r (1495). For other university-trained parish priests in the area, see DF 246291 (1525).

73 A total of forty-nine students from Medgyes registered for university before 1526. Tonk, *Erdélyiek egyetemjárása*, 364.

74 The centrality of the character of the schoolmaster, who motivated transregional student mobility and created strong personal bonds between students and teachers, has also been highlighted with regard to city schools in Germany around 1500. Kintzinger, *Wissen wird Macht*, 140–41.

75 See more on the mobility of students and the practice of "study-away" in Chapter 4.

76 György Szász from Enyed, who served as the parish priest in the town of Szászsebes (Mühlbach in German, modern-day Sebeș, Romania) in the culturally developed Saxon

The Costs of Learning

It is not possible to make a general statement regarding the subjects that the more advanced schoolboys in villages and small towns studied. According to a contemporary intellectual, the evangelical preacher Máté Skaricza, only grammar was taught at the beginning of the sixteenth century, even at the best schools in Hungary.[77] By contrast, modern histories of schooling maintain that more advanced students were able to study not only grammar, but the entire spectrum of liberal arts as well, and could also begin theology.[78] At any rate, it is certain that homeland schools provided students with the knowledge necessary for university studies abroad. Ambitious young men in the countryside could theoretically attend schools operating at cathedral chapters. Although chapter schools, located next to episcopal sees, were intended to train new generations of educated middle clergy, not all of their students became priests; some pursued secular professions and livelihoods.[79] Some of the schools, in order to satisfy the need for legal professionals of diocesan courts, provided courses on canon law in addition to *artes* and theology lectures, and students could also obtain experience issuing charters, a traditional function of cathedral chapters. Since legal professionals in Hungary most often acquired their expertise via practical experience, chapter school students of canon law who later found employment in royal and county offices and courts or acted as professional lawyers, were better trained and had better career prospects.[80]

Lands of Transylvania, received a doctoral degree in canon law following studies at the universities of Bologna and Padua from 1439 to 1448. Tonk, *Erdélyiek egyetemjárása*, 234; Békefi, *A népoktatás története*, 30, 120, 148. In 1455, he submitted a request to the Apostolic Penitentiary to be granted privileges with regard to absolving reserved sins: APA vol. 5, fol. 64r; Békefi, *Népoktatás*, 30, 120, 148; For further examples of graduated schoolmasters active in market town parish schools, primarily in northeastern Hungary, see Valter, *Falusi és mezővárosi iskolák*, 63. The cleric Gergely, son of István, served as the school rector in the market town of Túr in central Hungary with his laureate diploma in the liberal arts (APA vol. 16, fol. 141rv).

77 The life of István Szegedi by the Hungarian author Máté Skaricza, published in Kathona, *Fejezetek*, 118.

78 Mészáros, *XVI. századi városi iskoláink*, 13, passim.

79 Békefi, *A káptalani iskolák*, 276–77.

80 On the curriculum in chapter schools in general, see Békefi, *A káptalani iskolák*, 245–76. On the training of legal experts at chapter schools, see Fedeles, Sarbak and Sümegi, eds., *A középkor évszázadai*, 569. The content of chapter school libraries also indicates that legal training took place there. See Solymosi, "A veszprémi székesegyházi könvvtár." On the exclusive practical expertise of lay legal experts, see Bónis, "Men Learned in the Law."

However, these town and chapter schools that taught advanced levels using up-to-date curricula were inaccessible to the young men whose petitions to the papal court placed them in my purview.[81] In my opinion, these people represented the stratum of society that entertained the modest objective of exchanging the peasant lifestyle for that of rural lower clergy or lay clerks. Even if they desired a better career, their economic, social and cultural capital was insufficient. The communities from which they emerged were incapable of financing their studies and only the most fortunate ones had a canon relative able to pay for their education at chapter schools or secure a place for them among other poor students eligible for free schooling. Chances were also slim that somebody would provide them with a prebend to finance their studies, as so many canons did.[82]

Only the brightest boys managed to find an aristocratic or prelate patron willing to pay for the cost of their education, a circumstance that occurred primarily during the reign of King Matthias (1458–1490) when such patronage propelled some people of humble origin into the highest ranks of society.[83] The fortunes of Antal Kajári, for example, who figured among the petitioners to the Penitentiary, were unattainable for our runaway friars. This sharp-witted, industrious serf boy was supported by a local landowner, the abbot of Bakonybél; moreover, his father had attended university, so he was upholding a family tradition. In all probability, Kajári completed his university education and obtained his first positions as chapter notary and town notary public as well as a chapter prebend with support from the abbot. In 1521, Kajári asked the Apostolic Penitentiary for authorization to use the income from his

81 The humanist mentality had an impact on both types of school at the beginning of the sixteenth century due to their teachers having been trained at Western European universities. Mészáros, *XVI. századi városi iskoláink*, 14, 41–42.

82 On "poor students" who subsisted on alms and were typically the nephews of canons: "Et ipse sublector tenetur gratis informare pauperes scolares, et nepotes dominorum, sive sint eorum consanguinei, sive quos tenent propter Deum." Kollányi, "*Visitatio Capituli,*" 292. Békefi, *A káptalani iskolák*, 276–77. Both of the laymen mentioned by Békefi who had attended chapter schools were nobles possessing landed estates (ibid., 94–95). In 1500, László Zilhap, a canon at Gyulafehérvár (Alba Iulia, Romania), asked the Apostolic Penitentiary for permission to study law for seven years while continuing to receive his altar benefice (APA vol. 48, fol. 498v). On *scolares pauperes* in chapter schools in German territories, see Kintzinger, *Wissen Wird Macht*, 170–71.

83 On the career, university studies and patrons of bishops of peasant origin, see Fügedi, "A XV. századi magyar püspökök," 95–96. Canons of peasant origin amounted to around 10 to 15 percent of all canons. Kristóf, *Egyházi középréteg*, 41; Köblös, *Egyházi középréteg*, 29–30.

prebend to pay for his university studies, and eventually returned home with a doctorate in canon law. Kajári later obtained numerous chapter benefices, using his legal expertise to gain employment with the Esztergom court, first as a clerk and later as a vicar.[84]

Those of our runaway friars who came from more unfavorable backgrounds and had perhaps been endowed with less talent had been unable to attend chapter and town schools and were therefore forced to choose mendicant schools at which they could study at no cost. Mendicant schools not only provided students with tuition-free education, they also paid for room, board and textbooks. The religious order also covered most of the expenses related to subsequent university studies, although friars sometimes needed to supplement such funding through the collection of alms in order to pay for books and clothing.[85] Everyday life in the cloisters followed a strictly regulated routine in the spirit of moderation, though it did not demand the type of unbearable self-restraint that could serve to deter young men from joining the order.[86] Parishioners provided the friars with donations in the form of both movable property (clothing, chalices, etc.), immovable property (vineyards, agricultural land and urban houses) and money that essentially guaranteed their material well-being; thus they must have found it difficult to observe their vow of simplicity and poverty. The large-scale construction that took place at cloisters at the beginning of the sixteenth century and the amenities that were connected to them (bathhouses, bake houses and fish ponds) also serve to suggest that friars enjoyed rather comfortable lives during this period.[87] By the early sixteenth century, not only had the mendicant orders—with the exception of the Observant Franciscans—become wealthy and begun to manage landholdings, it also appears that friars had become eligible to receive individual benefices. The Augustinian friar Ferenc Szabó, previously a Pauline, turned to Rome in 1510, requesting that he be permitted to receive a benefice as an Augustinian.[88] Secular clerics, by contrast, were obliged to support themselves

84 APA vol. 66. 1162v–3r; Köblös, *Az egyházi középréteg*, 396–97.

85 On Dominican friars collecting alms to finance their university studies, see Harsányi, *A domonkos rend*, 246–58.

86 See Gergely Gyöngyösi's lines below with regard to the regulation of the friar's daily conduct on page 88, footnotes 81–86.

87 Cf. Majorossy, "Church in Town," passim. Lupescuné, "Két erdélyi domonkos kolostor." Gyöngyösi's instructions to the members of the religious community, from the novices to the prior, reflect such minute regulation, at least at the level of written norms. Sarbak, ed., *Gyöngyösi Gergely*, 31–67.

88 APA vol. 55, fol. 146v (1510, Strigonien. archdioc.).

until they could obtain a benefice. The case of Urbán Pásztor is revealing. Pásztor attended the parish school in the market town of Paks and worked as a sexton. Since Paks was not his hometown, he had to rent a room from a widow named Katalin.[89]

The Protean Literacy of the Lesser Clergy

There are only sporadic sources regarding the actual knowledge base of priests active in the sixteenth century. Guidelines adopted at diocesan councils stipulated minimum general requirements. These specifications indicate that the ability to carry out liturgical services according to the prescribed norms was the most important requirement.[90] Reports of archdeacons who traveled throughout the dioceses to inspect the conditions of parsonages reinforce this impression. Although the reports partially reflect official expectations because the visitors asked prescribed questions during these inspections, they still offer insight into everyday religious practice. At the beginning of the 1560s, Miklós Oláh, archbishop of Esztergom, ordered the visitation of all the parishes in the archdiocese as part of the preparations for a national Church council. The visiting prelates primarily recorded whether the church buildings and devotional objects used to conduct liturgical rites were properly stored and maintained and whether parish priests correctly conferred the sacraments. The Church undoubtedly placed heightened emphasis on the prescribed upkeep of devotional objects and the administration of the sacraments because they represented evidence of the loyalty of the parish priest at the time of the spread of Lutheranism. It was much simpler to compile written reports regarding the outfitting of altars than the theological beliefs of parish priests, who were often absent during the visitations and, if present, could not be relied upon to provide frank answers to theological questions.

These reports leave the modern reader feeling that the examination of external forms and appearances dominated the visitations. The accounts refer much more frequently to whether the priest wore a tonsure or was clean-shaven (a full head of hair and beard were signs of "heresy") than they do to whether he was educated (*doctus*) or uneducated (*simplex*).[91] The visiting superiors inquired much more frequently about the lifestyle of the priest (whether he

89 APA vol. 69, fol. 111v–12r (1522, Quinqueecclesien. dioc.).

90 Mályusz, *Egyházi társadalom*, 132–33; Solymosi, *A veszprémi egyház*, 72–73.

91 Bucko, ed., *Reformné hnutie*,198.

was prone to drunkenness, etc.) than about his preaching habits. Out of more than a thousand examined cases, I came across only five short references to whether the priest delivered sermons on Sundays and feast days and whether he did so from Catholic or "heretical" books.[92]

Of course, we might also speculate that the visiting archdeacons geared their questions to the expectations of the parishioners in the hope that this would make them more willing to talk openly. However, a comparison of the reports suggests that the topics of the investigations conformed to long-standing tradition and that the visitors exercised only a small influence over the formulation of the questions posed. The visitation records produced during the fifteenth century concerning the Esztergom cathedral chapter, during which only the canon members of the chapter were questioned, reveal that inquiries also focused on external forms and appearance. One suggested question regarding the theological knowledge of the Esztergom parish priest was the only exception to the rule, although it is difficult to determine the objective: "Have them ask the parish priest about the words attending the transubstantiation."[93] Was the interviewer trying to determine whether the parish priest knew the Latin text, commonly recited during Mass at the time of transubstantiation, by heart?[94] Or did Church superiors simply expect him to be aware of the theological interpretation of the words of Christ ("take this and eat it, for this is my body, which is given for you") that serve as the foundation of the doctrine of transubstantiation? The response of the canons supports the latter hypothesis. The canons uniformly responded that the Esztergom parish priest did not have a problem with the interpretation of transubstantiation because he kept company with many educated men, though it would have been better to question village priests in this regard.

The words of Márton Ratt, a German-speaking pastoral priest from the market town of Rohonc (Rechnitz, Austria), show that the disparaging opinion of the Esztergom canons regarding the theological-liturgical qualifications of their rural colleagues was, in certain instances, totally unfounded. Ratt asked to be absolved for committing multiple crimes, including homicide, heresy and apostasy. During the armed defense of his church, he had killed a man and

92 Bucko, ed., *Reformné hnutie*, 141 (*concionator ex postillis catholicorum scriptorum*, Dévény), 196 (Egres), 197 (Holida), 203 (*libros habet hereticorum*, Opatov).

93 "*Interrogetur parrochialis presbyter de verbis transsubstantialibus.*" Kollányi, "Visitatio capituli," 78 and 253. C. Tóth, *Az esztergomi székeskáptalan*, 8 (forthcoming vol. 3 revisits the dating of the published visitation records).

94 Texts beginning with the words *Qui pridie* and *Simili modo.*

caused the death of several others, actions he had concealed at his ordination; moreover, he had celebrated Mass during interdict. All this caused Ratt to suffer a grievous spiritual and bodily crisis:

> Afterward, his reason being reduced, he consecrated the host for administering the sacrament to the faithful; and more than that, he told some other priests that because of his manifold sins he did not believe that transubstantiation had taken place. Being shaken by that fear, he fell so severely ill and reached such a state of madness that one day, wanting to die, he tried to hang himself and put a rope around his neck, as a result of which he harmed his throat and fell under excommunication.[95]

In his petition aimed at establishing his credibility, Ratt revealed that he had discussed the issue of transubstantiation with his fellow rural priests. The theological issue of *transsubstantiatio* not only represented a source of conflict between Catholics and religious reformers a few decades later, but the confessions that emerged as a result of the Reformation held various opinions about this doctrine. It is not surprising that transubstantiation became one of the most significant points of contention within the theological debates that took place during the Reformation, because the issue appears to have truly engaged the attention of many people. Ratt's words reflect sound theological erudition. He was aware, for instance, that the Church regarded rejection of the efficacy of the sacrament to be heretical. During the sixteenth century, many priests and laymen were of this opinion, since they assumed that the sacred was influenced by the physical and moral world, an assumption that was incompatible with the official concept that "the sacrament is not perfected by the righteousness of the minister or of the recipient … but by the power of God."[96] It seems that, due to his heretical thoughts and words which questioned the redeeming power of Christ's death, he had to publicly ask for forgiveness (*hereticales articulos insuper publice abiuraverit*). Ratt's excessive anxiety and his ensuing illness and desperate actions also indicate that he perceived a serious issue touching upon the essence of belief to be at hand. That he was an educated man is further proved by the fact that he registered at the University of Vienna in 1451, where he may have studied not only the liberal arts, but theology as well.[97]

---

95 APA vol. 37, fol. 217v–18r. (1487, Jaurien. dioc.).

96 Aquinas, *Summa Theologiae*, Pars III, question 68, article 8.

97 Tüskés, *Magyarországi diákok*, 187 (no. 3564).

Ratt was still a layman at the time of his university studies, likely financially supported by either his family or a patron. Ratt was certainly not the only rural priest capable of understanding and debating the important theological issues of the day; however, if we think of how important the salvation of the soul was to people who lived during the Middle Ages, their interest in theological matters so tightly connected to this subject is not at all surprising.

Conclusion

All things considered, it appears that although Church superiors did not expect the pastoral clergy serving in the countryside to be endowed with theological learning, their erudition varied greatly beyond their own spiritual interests according to the needs and possibilities of the communities from which they emerged. Education at countryside parish schools was of uneven quality and was based on inconsistent curricula that depended largely on the qualifications of the schoolmaster, while the training provided by mendicant schools was of a more uniform quality and was based on a standardized curriculum. Moreover, the monastic lifestyle in which runaway friars lived was connected to regulated times and common activities that had the possibility of transforming their modes of behavior, gestures and everyday habits.[98] The characteristics of this disciplined, civilized conduct, which differed from the more relaxed manner of clerics socialized in the ecclesiastic family of the parsonage, will be the subject of the next chapter. The experience of monastic lifestyle represented a significant advantage for friars in the acquisition of ecclesiastical positions in courts, since everyday life in the royal and aristocratic courts took place under strictly regulated conditions. At the same time, their "otherness" may have more closely conformed to the changing expectations of simple parishioners toward priests.[99] In this way the sons of serfs could attain a sound education and learn how to lead orderly lives. They elected to take a detour through the mendicant orders in order to acquire the literacy necessary for advancement, since the gates of schools and society opened more widely to the laity during the course of the sixteenth century.

98 See Chapter 4 on the civilized manners expected of friars.

99 This will be examined in greater detail in Chapter 7.

CHAPTER 4

From Savage to Civilized: Village Schools and Student Life

One day a new student arrived at a school located in a small village in the southern part of the Hungarian lowlands. Two other pupils, Márton and Máté Khebele, celebrated the arrival of their new schoolmate in a tavern next to the parsonage. Something in their behavior angered the locals, who, according to Márton's account, began to harass them. A fight broke out, in the course of which a man was killed.[1] If one gives credence to Márton, who claimed that the youths had been indulging in little more than "quiet tippling," the locals must have been upset by the arrival of a newcomer in their village or, simply, angered by the loud and boisterous behavior of the youths.

Tavern brawls between local people and newcomers are hardly extraordinary events, yet how did the disputes between students and village people at the end of the Middle Ages differ from conflicts of earlier and later periods? In other words, how were the students themselves different from local society? At the time, learning was regarded as closely tied to morality. Unruliness was explained by lack of education. Rabelais contended that he was only able to restrain his fiery urges through study and work.[2] In the metaphoric language of initiation rituals of late medieval universities, filthy and sinful beasts became rational, self-controlled, moderate men through learning.[3] Students were therefore expected to be able to master their errant impulses.

Curial petitions narrate events, both ordinary and festive, the protagonists of which are very often students. In terms of numbers, roughly a tenth of all petitioners from the Kingdom of Hungary identified themselves as students (*scolaris*). Additionally, many petitioning priests wrote of the misdeeds they had once committed as students.[4] The high proportion is further enhanced

1 APA, vol. 66, fol. 47rv–48r (1520, Zagrabien. dioc.).

2 On Rabelais: Davis, "Women on Top," 125. A century later, the Transylvanian Reformed theologian and scholar János Apáczai Csere also attributed the increase in crime and the degradation of morals to the lack of schools. Apáczai, "*De summa scholarum necessitate*," 180.

3 Karras, *From Boys to Men*, 100–108.

4 "[…] alias eo tunc litteris operam dante ac sub cura et correctione magistri scolarium existente" – wrote the incumbent of Helmec in 1521 (APA, vol. 66, fols 1203rv, Agrien. diocesis). The parish priest of Pátroha, János Nyíregyházi, also related a story from his school years

 | DOI 10.1163/9789004361263_005

when one considers that many self-identified clerics (*clericus*) were actually students, teachers or both.[5]

The present chapter offers a glimpse into the everyday lives of students in villages and small towns in the decades leading up to the Protestant Reformation. How did students spend their free time? What influence did their school years have on their careers and how did the knowledge they acquired at school affect the local communities from which they came or in which they settled? I will investigate how young people were socialized in schools, and the individual and social consequences of this socialization.

The Interactions of Students and Locals

Stories related to the pope offer a vivid picture of village and small-town student life and sociability in the first decades of the sixteenth century. Students most frequently appeared on the scene in groups. Máté Száti, a student in a village in the south, was sharing dinner in a tavern with three of his fellow students when a man entered to purchase wine—thus begins the account of an evening which ended in bloodshed.[6] If four students were sitting together in the tavern, it seems reasonable to presume that a school was located either in the settlement or nearby, even if we take into account the high mobility of students. Kelemen Balog and three fellow students were on the road together when they stopped one night to sleep in a meadow. One of his companions awoke to find that their weapons had been stolen. The four drowsy students pursued the thieves to "peacefully" retrieve their arms; however, one of the thieves was, rather unsurprisingly, killed during the course of this "peaceful" enterprise.[7]

(Ibid., vol. 14, fol. 178r, 1466). Altogether around ten priests and twenty-two clerics narrated acts of mischief from their years at school.

5 Students describing themselves as clerics: APA vol. 8, fols 207rv; vol. 8, fols 210v–211r; vol. 9, fols 229rv; vol. 12, fols 110v–11r; vol. 40, fols 367v–68r; vol. 17, fol. 210v, etc. Petitioners in the lower ranks of clerical orders identifying themselves as clerics: APA, vol. 5, fol. 187v; vol. 7, fol. 272v. During his years of study, Gál Madarász of Pogány also worked as a schoolmaster "in villa Akan" (APA vol. 24, fol. 144v, 1475, Quinqueecclesien. dioc.). Balázs Lippai had earlier been a schoolmaster in his hometown of Lippa and was a student elsewhere at the time he submitted his petition. APA, vol. 66, fols 45rv (1520, Chanadien. dioc.).

6 APA vol. 46, fol. 262v–63r (1498, Bachien. dioc.).

7 APA vol. 70, fol. 316v–17r (1523, Waradien. dioc.).

Social historians took an early interest in the culture of youths, young, unmarried men who had left their parental homes to acquire a trade or an education. They were described in contemporary sources as *adolescens*, a term meant to include both teenagers and men in their early twenties. "Adolescents" were considered to be "wild and wanton" young men who had not yet assumed a profession or become independent heads of households.[8] These young men were among the loudest and unruliest members of society and often figured in the records of judicial proceedings. They spent the better part of their time on the streets or in semi-public spaces, such as taverns, so their behavior was less restricted than it would have been had they been living at home. At first glance, their distinctive habits might appear as violent acts of rebellion, explaining why their "boisterousness" has been interpreted as a matter of generational conflict between young and old;[9] however, closer scrutiny has unveiled the social and cultural functions of their practices; for instance, they exercised control over the local marriage market and contributed to the preservation of popular customs. Rituals and other carnivalesque forms of ridicule that served to humiliate people who had violated the marital and sexual norms of the community were organized by the youths, who dubbed themselves "guardians of disorder" or "lords of the night." These rites included charivari that targeted women who had cheated on or beaten their husbands, and placing old maids in a yoke or in the stocks. This type of tolerated mischief must have been the product of a consensus among old and young. Members of the older generation clearly did not mind if youths resolved conflicts among themselves, which the elderly could passively observe and occasionally enjoy. In short, the distinctive rituals of the youths, notwithstanding their seemingly disruptive nature, ultimately served to both enforce social norms and prepare adolescents for the assumption of adult roles.[10] This system of rituals and institutions characteristic of youthful culture has been observed across the continent and documented by historical ethnography in early modern Hungary.[11]

---

8 Karras, *From Boys to Men*, 12–15.; Eisenbichler, ed., *The Premodern Teenager.*

9 Cf. Muchembled, "Les jeunes," 563–79.

10 Schindler, "Guardians of Disorder," 240–82; Schindler, *Rebellion*, 93–235; and Davis, "The Reasons of Misrule."

11 Dömötör, "Erscheinungsformen des Charivari." The young men from the town of Eger celebrated the Feast of Fools at the end of the Carnival season in 1518 by staging a mock tournament. Lodovico Bagno's description is quoted by Endrei, *Társasjáték*, 150. With regard to early modern England, the limitations of the notion of a separate youth culture have been stressed by Ben-Amos, *Adolescence and Youth*, 183–207.

Modern historical and anthropological approaches present an idyllic image of intergenerational relations based on cooperation and consensus rather than conflict during the period prior to the "disciplinary frenzy" which, by the eighteenth century, had reached the countryside. If this was indeed the case, then the events discussed below constitute "functional disorders" in an otherwise smoothly operating system, particularly the times and places in which the forms of recreation chosen by young men explicitly perturbed and provoked villagers or townspeople.[12] One account describes four students who had been eating dinner in a tavern in a village in southern Transdanubia when their singing provoked the ire of a cantankerous nobleman at a neighboring table.[13] It is not surprising that at times people were intolerant of the occasionally infantile carousing of students. Even a schoolmaster reacted aggressively when one of his fourteen-year-old students chased him along a highway, swiped his hat and ran off with it.[14] László Egresi was dining in Szentmiklós, a neighboring village, with a fellow student. On the way home, he decided to play a prank on a stranger coming from the opposite direction and pretended to chase him, but the man misunderstood the joke and attacked him and his companion.[15] Mihály Kadosi's story, according to which a man walking alone began to mock and insult three students coming the other way, does not seem entirely plausible. It is difficult to imagine that one man would be foolhardy enough to confront three, especially on a highway at night; it seems considerably more likely that the three students had harassed him. They had been walking home from a gathering in the cemetery in the town of Brassó ("Kronstadt" in German, now Brașov, Romania) and had the clear advantage in terms of numbers.[16] Students were no doubt emboldened by the fact that they tended to come and go in groups, and in all likelihood groups of blustering students provoked the ire of respectable citizens.

The playful good spirits of students might have been a product of their youth and "strength in numbers," but may also have been the result of drinking.

---

12 On the tense relations and frequent violent clashes between citizens and students in late medieval Paris, derived from features of student lifestyle, see Geremek, *On the Margins of Society*, 151–53.

13 "Alias ipse cum tribus sociis scolaribus in quodam hospitio pacifice existeret, et unus scolarium ipsorum illaritatis causa cantare cepisset...." Tamás Székely, *scolaris*, APA vol. 70, fol. 315v–16r (1523, Quinqueecclesien. dioc.).

14 "Capellum de capite ludendo abstulit." APA vol. 14, fol. 109r (1466, Agrien. dioc.).

15 APA vol. 66, fol. 45v–46r (1520, Chanadien. dioc.). Szentmiklós is a village in Békés County.

16 APA vol. 66, fol. 33v–34r (1520, Transylvanien. dioc.).

Perhaps it was the wine he had consumed that gave one student the "courage" to take a stick from a guest who had entered the tavern in Keresztúr. Fortunately, Máté Száti, one of his three companions, was more clear-headed and immediately intervened to cool tempers. The stick was returned to its owner, who apparently swallowed his pride and left. The student must have continued to drink because, when the man unexpectedly returned, he resumed his impertinent joking; he wanted to take the man's sword, "lest he accidentally wound someone." The failure of the student to carry out the act was perhaps another sign of inebriation; he only managed to grab the sheath, allowing the man to wound one of the students with his sword. This caused tempers to flare and several people were wounded and one killed in the fight that broke out between students and laypeople.[17]

These cases exemplify, similarly to the stories designed to elicit the clemency of French or Burgundian rulers, how the recreation and sociability of young men in the countryside, fueled by alcohol, could quickly turn violent. Their festivals and tavern brawls, in the course of which social boundaries and norms were blurred and suspended, tended to produce spontaneous violence unlike the planned violence of vengeance between adults embedded in networks of kin, neighbors and friends.[18] Another characteristic of disputes between students and locals, similar to student rivalries, was that their rhetoric was regulated by honor codes that came into effect at the slightest hint of male humiliation, which could not be left unaddressed.[19]

Laypeople were perhaps even more angered when, in the course of their carousing, students went so far as to injure not only personal honor, but also material property. Students in the town of Székesfehérvár killed a piglet, whose owners incriminated one of them, István Babocsai, before the parish priest. Although the accused managed to clear his name, the owners were not to be appeased and they took compensation for their loss in a side street.[20] The tranquility of the village of Cirkvena in Slavonia (modern-day Croatia) was stirred by a prank committed by two students, who had stolen eggs from their

---

17 APA vol. 46, fol. 262v–63r (1498, Bachien. dioc.).

18 With regard to the narrative timeframe of rural festivities that ended in bloodshed, see Davis, *Fiction in the Archives*, 29–30. See also Arnaude and Prevenier, *Honor, Vengeance*, 82–87; Gauvard, "*De grace especial*," vol. 2, 504. The role of honor codes in channeling and debating disputes will also be discussed in Chapters 6 and 7.

19 For the role of the concept of honor in incidents involving young men, see Arnade and Prevenier, *Honor*, *Vengeance*, 87–89. See also Chapters 6 and 7.

20 Archivio Segreto Vaticano, Armadio XXXII, vol. 61, fol. 248rv (1522, Wesprimien. dioc.).

schoolmaster. The minor theft ended in a bloody confrontation between the students and their local superiors, the schoolmaster and the parish priest.

Quite paradoxically, because students had a lot of free time and wandered the streets at leisure, they witnessed a great deal and thus not only "disturbed" the peace, but also helped to "keep" it, for instance by seizing trespassers. Thus, they played an important social function as guardians of the peace. András Nagy and one of his fellow students were on their way to a well when they saw a thief climbing into a garden. They reported what they had seen to the school rector and then set out to catch the thief.[21] In Terebes (Trebišov, Slovakia), the town judge sent a group of students to catch a thief, while another school rector commanded his students to flog a prostitute.[22]

The Dense Network of Parish Schools in the Countryside

Unfortunately, our sources do not allow us to establish the number of students attending a particular school; however, if mention is made of a group of four or five students, as is often the case, one may presume the existence of a local school. The stories undoubtedly involved only a fraction of the actual student body. One account portrays an event in which all of the local students gathered to celebrate the visit of their former assistant cantor with the usual eating and drinking, although the account does not indicate how many students were present.[23] We encounter the largest number of students—twelve—in the town of Esztergom, which is not surprising, since they were students at the chapter school located in the archiepiscopal see rather than in a remote village. The chapter school in Esztergom was the largest school in Hungary at the time and—alongside the highest schools of the mendicants—the best in the country.[24] According to some estimates, by the end of the fifteenth century

21 "Ipse olim quadam die unacum quodam socio suo extra scolas ad quendam fontem pro aqua iret et a casu prope quendam ortum quendam [...] laicum, qui ortum prefatum intrare volens reperiret, eundem laicum coram magistro scolarum accusavit, ipse vero magister nonnullos ex scolaribus suis pro capiendo dictum laicum misit." APA vol. 17, fol. 210v (1469, Quinqueecclesien. dioc.).

22 APA vol. 3, fol. 85v (1450, Agrien. dioc.); ibid., vol. 9, fol. 229rv (1461, Quinqueecclesien. dioc.).

23 APA vol. 37, fol. 150r (1487, Strigonien. archdioc.).

24 To see how the number of students was estimated to be 117, deduced from the number of canons: Körmendy, "Literátusok,"182. With regard to the curriculum at the school in Esztergom, see: Madas, "Esztergomi iskoláskönyv." For details regarding the location of the school within the town of Esztergom, see Cevins, *Az egyház*, 66 and 196 (map).

there may well have been over a hundred students in Esztergom, but there must have been a student body of considerable size as early as 1464, when the tumult and commotion they caused aroused the ire of town residents. That year the students clashed with some noblemen and their clients (*familiares*) in front of the New Town (*Újváros*) gate located below the citadel. Since one nobleman perished in the fight, the case was probably transferred from the county magistrate to the royal court. In any event, it stirred up considerable controversy. Four pardon letters were sent to Rome in the space of five years: the students who had participated in the skirmish were requesting absolution for murder.[25] To summarize the incident, a few noblemen had beaten and robbed the young students, who had been making their usual rounds collecting alms. The noblemen had attacked the students as they were coming down into the town from the citadel where the school was located, next to the cathedral and the archbishop's palace). The frightened youths (one was only fourteen years old) had run back to the school, and told the others what had befallen them. The teachers and the older students attacked the noblemen to ensure that they would never again display such brazen audacity. A final battle erupted outside the school when the noblemen, who had taken flight, returned to besiege the students. The noblemen were not inhabitants of the town, and were presumably

For the purpose of comparison one may reasonably conclude that there were approximately twenty students at the chapter school in the town of Pécs in southern Hungary. See Fedeles, Sarbak and Sümegi, *A pécsi egyházmegye*, 179.

25 Among the students we find a local citizen (Pál Újvárosi, later canon in Esztergom), a lesser nobleman (András Henyei from Zala County, who later became a canon in Győr), as well as several others of peasant origin. As to their geographical distribution, some came to the centrally located archiepiscopal see from the nearby diocese of Vác (Máté Dömsödi and János Sarlói, later canon in Esztergom-Szentistván), while the clerics Kelemen Szabó of Vaska and János Haragys arrived from the more distant southern diocese of Zagreb. APA vol. 13, fol. 377v (1464); vol. 15, fol. 163v. (1467). The incidents were related by Haragys, the sole young student among older ones, as follows: "Cum olim nonnulli pauperes scolares ipsius exponentis socii, qui in scolis Strigoniensis unacum exponente ipso grammatica studebant et ex mendicitate vivebant, de quodam castro cum certis victualibus ex mendicitate per eos quesitis venientes per quosdam armigeros iuxta morem illius patrie clientes nuncupatos dictis victualibus vel aliis helemosinis et aliis spoliati et percussi usque ad sanguinis effusionem fuissent, dicti scolares spoliati er percussi facta huiusmodi nunciarunt superioribus suis, qui unacum ipso exponente tunc in fine sue etatis anno quartadecimo vel circa constituto, qui cum arma aliqua, nisi defensalia, non habebat, ut bona huiusmodi recuperarent, contra dictos armigeros seu clientes exierunt et contra illos certare ceperunt ac mutuo se percusserunt adeo, quod unus ex armigeris seu clientibus huiusmodi in dicto certamine percussus extitit et vulneratus." APA, vol. 17, fol. 230v–31r (1469).

motivated by the desire to make off with a bit of ill-gotten loot; however the students, who came from all over the country, also seem to have perturbed the burghers.[26]

On another occasion in the late 1450s, two students entering the New Town quarter of Esztergom to tend to their affairs ended up in a dispute with the locals not far from the parish church. The clash seems to have followed roughly the same script as the incident set out above. The two students fled from the townspeople and took refuge in the school from where fellow students launched an armed counterattack.[27] The arrival of assistance strengthened solidarity among the students, demonstrating their sense of camaraderie.[28]

Two images of students emerge. On the one hand, they resembled childish pranksters who often relied on others for protection. On the other hand, they seemed like independent figures who drank in the company of adults and were capable of defending themselves and their fellow students, with arms if necessary. The Latin term *scolaris* referred both to a seven-year-old child who had been sent to school and to a student who was attending school at the age of twenty. In other words, the students can be divided into at least two groups: those between the ages of seven and fifteen, sometimes referred to as "child students" or "young students" (as in the case of the aforementioned students in Esztergom); and those between the ages of sixteen and their early twenties, the so-called "big students" who were pursuing advanced studies.[29] The great age range was due to the fact that the school was divided into grades

26 The comings and goings of the 120 students who attended the chapter school located below the castle in the New Town of Esztergom must have been palpable to the district's residents, who could not have numbered more than a thousand. See Gerevich, ed., *Towns in Medieval Hungary*, 29–30.

27 A cleric named Tamás was the first person in the school to notice the noise coming from outside, and he spurred his colleagues to action: "Quadam die certi laici cum quibusdam scolaribus inibi residentibus diversis verbis scandalosis prope dictam scolam rixantes et scolares ipsos graviter percussentes, idem exponens existens in eisdem scolis rumores huiusmodi audivit et de dictis scolis exivit et vidit unum ex dictis scolaribus in medio dictorum laicorum quasi interreptum, quo visu facta alta voce clamavit ad alios adad vel cwca cwca, quia statim laici unum ex scolaribus interficerent et arripiens duos lapides in medio rixantium proiecisset…." APA, vol. 8, fol. 207rv (1460, Zagrabien. dioc.). See also vol. 7, fol. 298v–99rv, 1459.

28 On the importance of collective honor among youth, see Muchembled, "Die Jugend," esp. 41–42.

29 *Iuvenis scolaris* or *puer scolaris* were the younger students, while *scolaris maior* or *studens* were the older students. One of the students participating in the dispute in the Baromlaka cemetery was twelve years old. APA, vol. 66, fol. 32v–33r (1520, Transylvanien. dioc.).

according to curriculum rather than age.[30] Mixing children with adults was nothing extraordinary at a time when age was not a universal life marker, and studies, and work were not broken down into divided periods and spaces in an individual life course. Younger students learned the rudiments of Latin grammar from the "big students," for whom they acted as servants during daily activities.[31] The schoolmaster, himself an advanced student, would also make the younger students tend to various chores or errands; for example, when the schoolmaster had had enough of Lent and invited his students to a feast, he sent a younger student to the tavern for wine.[32]

The accounts contain mention of dozens of village schools, which suggests that by the end of the Middle Ages schools had become common elements in the Hungarian countryside just as they had in regions of northwestern and southern Europe.[33] The papal petitions thus reveal a dense network of village schools that had previously been invisible. This is important to emphasize because the work of rural parish schools embodied and expressed the aspirations of villagers, who were willing and able to employ and maintain not only a parish priest, but also a schoolmaster.[34] Although clerical school rectors were

30 Ariès, *Centuries of Childhood*, 189–240 (age of students). On how modern, compulsory schooling made the standardization of students and their classification according to age in school possible and necessary, see Stephen Lassonde, "Age, Schooling and Development."

31 APA vol. 8, fol. 211rv (cleric Mihály Kemzechi, 1460, Quinqueecclesien. dioc.).

32 "Petrus Dionisii Wkomich de Bela clericus Zagrabiensis diocesis, quod alias quadam die tempore carnisprivii quidam rector scolarium, in cuius scola exponens moram trahebat et habitabat, congregatis suis scolaribus et nonnulllis etiam laicis invitatis simul convenirent et conversarent, et dictus scolasticus quendam puerum scolarem suum ad afferendum vinum de taberna misisset." APA vol. 40, fols 367v–68r (1491).

33 The first historical account of schooling in medieval Hungary noted the prevalence of parish schools in the countryside, listing fifty, to which the Penitentiary petitions add another twenty-five. Békefi, *A népoktatás*, 52–53. Ariès, *Centuries of Childhood*, 137–54 and 286–314. In Italy, France, Germany and Spain a gradual expansion of elementary and grammar schools in the fourteenth and fifteenth centuries has been observed. Kintzinger, "A profession but not a career?" The most thoroughly studied and documented country in this respect is England, which seems to have most resembled the situation in Hungary with its sudden explosion of elementary and grammar schools in the early sixteenth century in the context of parish clergy and religion. Cf. Moran, *The Growth of English Schooling*, 221–22; Orme, *Education and Society*.

34 In rural England, schools were often founded at the initiative of well-to-do parishioners associated with chantries, chantry priests being prescribed by their patron the duty of teaching beyond the celebration of Masses. Orme, *Medieval Schools*, 228–29, 236–38. On

hired by the laity to perform liturgical services,[35] the importance of schools in villages was a clear indication of rising social ambitions. Villagers increasingly sent their sons to school in the late fifteenth and early sixteenth centuries to facilitate their economic and social advancement rather than for the sake of learning and knowledge, as Luther so bitterly lamented a few years later.[36]

The scholarly assumption that village schools were attended by the sons of local serfs and lesser nobles seems reasonable; it would mean that those communities maintained a school for which there was a significant demand due to the large number of local children and adolescents.[37] However, I have observed that there was another trend, which could be named "study-away."[38] The examined accounts clearly demonstrate that students often pursued studies or were hired as schoolmasters at locations outside their home communities. Some went to neighboring counties fifty or one hundred kilometers away,[39] while others went as far as one or two hundred kilometers, though they remained in the same greater region.[40] Even more surprisingly, some students decided to travel from one corner of Hungary to the other to pursue studies.[41] Indeed, people from northern counties even crossed the border into Moravia and Silesia to pursue more advanced studies, facilitated by the fact that the

---

the growth and forms of lay interest and investment in local schools in late medieval England, see Moran, *The Growth of English Schooling*, 150–84, 223.

35 On the role of rural small communities in the maintenance of a growing number of parochial assistant clergy (chantry priests) in the early sixteenth century, see Chapter 5 below and Erdélyi, *A Cloister on Trial*, 129–30, 214–19. The rural schoolmasters in Hungary were typically clerics, not ordained priests.

36 The notion that social mobility through learning was possible in the late Middle Ages and especially in the early sixteenth century has been repeatedly claimed (for example by Anna Bellavitis, "Education," 108). I stress here the agency of the lower classes and their strategic learning. See Luther's view in Chapter 2.

37 On the early modern marriage market, Katalin Péter argued from the opposite direction: where we have evidence of a school, there must have been a larger local age group that attended. Péter, *Házasság*, 74–75.

38 There is ample evidence regarding middle and lower-class schoolboys boarding away from home in early modern England. Ben-Amos, *Adolescence and Youth*, 55–58.

39 Such as from Tiszadob in Szabolcs County some one hundred kilometers to Hosszúpályi in Bihar County, for example (APA vol. 20, fol. 99v–100r), or from Egres in Csanád County to Szentmiklós in Békés County (APA, vol. 66, fol. 45v).

40 Such as from Besenyőd in Szabolcs County to Adfalva in Middle Szolnok County (APA vol. 57, fol. 257rv).

41 Such as from Obedszentkereszt in Slavonia to pursue studies in Halas in Keve County (in modern-day Serbia). APA vol. 63, fol. 206v–7r, or from the southern diocese of Pécs to the northeastern market town of Szatmár (Satu Mare, Romania). APA, vol. 72, fol. 320v–21r.

same Slavic languages and German dialects were spoken on both sides of the frontier.[42] One can clearly distinguish the students who moved from villages to cities[43] from those who traveled several hundred kilometers to attend another village school other than their local school. It may be difficult to understand why someone would have done this, but it must have happened, since in the sources one finds mention of students from a series of dioceses (such as Vác, Várad, Bács and Csanád) in one single rural school.[44] Why did István Pintér decide to take his seven-year-old son Gáspár from Bács diocese to the neighboring diocese of Csanád to pursue studies at a village school there, rather than sending him to the local school?[45] Older itinerant students, as we saw in the previous chapter, traveled great distances in order to find good teachers whose reputations had reached them from far away, but the practice of sending little children to "study-away" may have been inspired by the aim of having them live separately from their families so that they could learn to stand on their own feet. Children of the aristocracy were expected to learn independence at Italian universities or in the course of a grand tour of Europe in the company of a private preceptor. Gáspár Pintér, who was born to a family of more modest means, was able to venture only as far as a different village. Matters of scale notwithstanding, travel, physical distance and learning served similar goals. Difficult as it is to reconstruct personal motivations, the high occurrance of student mobility is apparent. Apparently landlords in Hungary did not demand fees from the boys of their serfs even if they chose to study away,

42 For instance, Bertalan Lichtner, a cleric in the diocese of Eger, wrote in 1521: "De certo opido Bohemie, ubi studii literati gratia moram fecerant" (APA vol. 66, fol. 1197v–98r). Archdiocese of Esztergom resident Boldizsár Elczi vowed while ill that if he recovered he would become a priest "causa studendi ad quandam regionem, in qua fideles catolici et etiam heretici iunxtim habitabant [presumably to Hussite Moravia] se transtulit" (ibid., vol. 15, fol. 209v, 1467). With regard to the parallel mobility patterns of sixteenth-century Lutheran *peregrinatio scolastica*, see Csepregi, "A magyarországi iskolázás."

43 Such as from Szentágota (Agnita, Romania)—a Saxon village in Transylvania—to the school in the city of Brassó (APA vol. 62, fol. 914rv, 1518); or from Babocsa, a market town in southern Transdanubia, to the town of Székesfehérvár (ASV Arm. XXXII. vol. 61, fol. 248rv, 1522).

44 According to the petition of Antal Bakó, a cleric from the diocese of Vác, he was sleeping in his room when a fellow student from the diocese of Várad awakened him and told him to come along with him, because Mihály and Pál, two students from the diocese of Csanád, wanted to kill a student named Gergely Karomi from the diocese of Bács (APA vol. 57, fol. 225rv, 1512).

45 APA vol. 57, fol. 225r (1512, Bachien. dioc.).

which facilitated student mobility.[46] It is also important to note that being separated from parents in the pre-modern age, when many children across all social strata lost one or both of their parents, and child-rearing was a shared enterprise between parents, kin, friends and strangers, was not—contrary to the present day—an exceptional experience for children and teenagers.[47]

Leaving the natal home, either out of necessity or personal choice, was an important step in a child's socialization. He found himself in a group of peers in which he had to assert his independence and solve conflicts on his own. Furthermore, in school he was assessed on the basis of his individual merits.[48] Distanced from parental care and control, students had to assume and master adult roles, for instance in the course of festive practices (as will be discussed in the following chapter) or carnivalesque rituals. As the nobility perceived, however, students did more than participate in rituals of symbolic violence, manifesting openly rebellious attitudes and behavior toward the established power structure. Repressive laws passed by the lords at the diet following the bloody suppression of the peasant uprising of 1514 mention among the seditious not only peasants and *hajduks*, but also "unbeneficed priests and students living in the schools," who were forbidden from bearing arms in the future.[49] These laws significantly refer to "those who live in schools," not merely to "those who attend schools" or "school students." This suggests that the lords considered the young clerics who had left their birthplaces and the guardianship of their parents to be the true troublemakers.

Pieces of circumstantial evidence in the pardon letters suggest that students who did not rent private lodgings all lived together in one building.[50] Demeter Jakószerdahelyi explained that "one night, when he stayed in the building of the school, certain laymen [...] battered the walls of the house with stones and other unidentifiable objects and the supplicant went outside with some of his

46 On the personal freedom of serfs, including their free movement in Hungary, see Péter, "The Other Way." On seigneurial restraints with regard to attending schools of serfs in England, see Moran, *The Growth of English Schooling*, 175–76.

47 On the roles of fostering, step-parenting and the practice of child circulation, see Laslett, *Family Life*, chapter on "Parental Deprivation in the Past: A Note on Orphans and Step-parenthood in English history," 160–73; Maddern, "Between Households"; and Harrington, *The Unwanted Child.* On how separation affected children see Ben-Amos, *Adolescence and Youth*, 54–61.

48 Parsons, *The school class*, 80–85.

49 DRMH, vol. 4, paragraph 1514/60. I will examine other aspects of this law in Chapter 5.

50 Urbán Pásztor, who lived in the home of a widow in Paks, is an example of someone who rented private accommodation. APA vol. 69, fol. 111v–12r, 1522.

fellows to find out who made that noise [...]."[51] In some places, the school and dormitory were two separate buildings. The important thing is that the schoolmaster and students of vastly different ages all lived together, experiencing the advantages and disadvantages of life in a crowded residence.[52] Bertelan Fodor of Hodos, a poor nobleman, moved into a school where he came into conflict with a fellow student named András after having entered his room and taken his lute (or some similar instrument).[53] Their clash continued on the street and in the nearby parsonage to which Bertalan had fled.

Five students at a school in the Hungarian lowlands participated in a fight in the middle of the night. While it remains uncertain what caused tempers to flare, it is clear that the students lived in the same building. Awaking to the shouts of three fellow students, Péter Váradiai woke Antal Bakó in the neighboring room so that they might together separate those involved in the confrontation.[54] Schoolmaster György Ugrinagh seems to have shared living space at a school in a small Slavonian town with his students. One evening, one of Ugrinagh's students broke into his room and, aided by others, cast out his belongings. Meanwhile, some students who supported Ugrinagh ran to the house of the local judge, where the schoolmaster was having dinner, to tell him of the events.[55] These kinds of episodes, which are perhaps characteristic of student life regardless of time and place, explain why it has become widely accepted to consider the habits and lifestyles of students as part of a world of intense physical contact, violence and communal sentiments. While strong

---

51 APA vol 2bis, fol 405v–6r (1443, Zabrabien. dioc.). Schoolmaster Demeter Szentágotai returned home to the school with one of his students after dinner, thus indicating that he lived in the school building: "Unacum quodam alio scolare a domo cuiusdam providi viri prefate civitatis, cum quo cenarent aut commedebant et scolas ad quiescendum et dormiendum petebant." APA vol. 62, fol. 914rv (1518, Transylvanien. dioc.).

52 See for example: "Quidam rector scolarium, in cuius scola exponens moram trahebat et habitabat," APA, vol. 40, fol. 367v–68r (1491, Zagrabien. dioc.). With regard to students being boarders of their schoolmaster, see Ariès, *Centuries of Childhood*, 154, 191.

53 "Quod cum ipse olim quadam die quandam luttinam suam de camera cuiusdam Andree accoliti dicte diocesis, ad quam sine scientia et de camera ipsius exponentis dictus Andreas transportaverat, in presentia ipsius Andree inventam recepisset, ac in receptione huiusmodi quibusdam verbis paucis tamen rixosis cum dicto Andrea concertasset." APA vol. 37, fol. 248v–49r (1488, Strigonien. archdioc.). Hodos was a village in Pozsony County inhabited by poor noblemen. On the interpretation of *luta-lutina* to mean "lute," see Ramminger, *Neulateinische Wortliste*. Cf. students stole a writing table and an inkstand from each other at a Portuguese school. Esch, *Die Lebenswelt*, 71, 439.

54 APA vol. 57, fol. 225rv (1512, Waradien. dioc.).

55 APA vol. 68, fol. 233rv (1521, Zagrabien. dioc.).

communal feelings may have occasionally helped to blur the social differences between noble and non-noble students, they must have provoked the resentment of older generations.[56]

The Presence of Literate and "Civilized" Men in Rural Communities

Students did not frequently settle in alien parts: itinerant clerical students often returned home. To find lower pastoral clergy searching for a means of making a living in their native villages or regions appears to have been just as common as studying away from home.[57] "Disaffiliation" seems to have been a transitional phase in the lives of youths.[58] Traditional family and kinship ties helped them to find employment in their birthplaces as literate men or stipendiary clergymen.[59] It seems perfectly plausible that, much as in the case of burghers living in prosperous cities and establishing chantries with small benefices for their sons who had become priests, the inhabitants of villages also paid their native sons to perform votive masses. Just as the custom of "study-away" played a crucial role in the socialization of individuals, the return of these educated, "widely traveled" young clerics represented an important event in village communities. Balázs, who was to become the Helmec parish priest, in all likelihood took his books with him when he returned to the village, assuming that he had managed to get his books back from a fellow student who had stolen them, which had prompted Balázs to hit him on the head with a stone.[60]

In addition to books, the students took home knowledge. Perhaps the most obvious of their skills was their ability to read and write legal texts in Latin, which distinguished them from average village and town inhabitants. A case proving this point comes from Túr, a prosperous market town in the eastern part of the Great Hungarian Plain. The inhabitants of Túr asked their

56 Cf. Muchembled, *Die Jugend*, 40. Geremek describes how the diversity of social origins of the student body at universities created tensions and conflict between students, *The Margins of Society*, 148–49.

57 Instances in which parish clergymen returned to their birthplaces to assume employment become clear from their petitions, since close relatives are mentioned in the accounts of local conflicts, for example, APA vol. 9, fol. 242rv, etc. Those who did not manage to acquire a benefice remained self-supported itinerant priests.

58 The term was coined by Robert Castel, *From Manual Workers to Wage Laborers*.

59 We find for example *litterati* employed in villages in Pest County, one of whom worked as a bailiff and kept accounts. Tringli, *Pest megye*, 143.

60 APA vol. 66, fol. 1203rv (1521, Agrien. dioc.).

university trained schoolmaster Gergely, son of István, to read a letter that had been sent to them by the landlord, which had been written in "another language" (i.e., Latin) and which they "were unable to read or understand." The letter stated that either three of the peasants would act as bailsmen (*fideiussores*) for the person they had captured for some unspecified transgression or he would be hanged "according to the law and customs of the market town." As the captive was soon hanged, the schoolmaster who had translated the landlord's letter assumed some responsibility for his death and needed papal absolution before ordination.[61] The next case also shows that *litterati* had to be commonplace in order to ensure the smooth operation of local justice. The landlord of Ormány (Orman, Romania), a small village situated in northern Transylvania, found himself in similar trouble. He had detained a man named István Varga ("Shoemaker"), but was unable to decipher the official list of condemned criminals (*latrones*) produced by the congregation of the county nobility, so did not know how to proceed with his prisoner; he had to summon the local schoolmaster, Antal Szabó ("Tailor") to read the document. As the detained man was among the proscribed criminals and was executed, the schoolmaster needed the pope's pardon for his ordination.[62]

The fact that local people could not decipher complicated legal documents written in Latin did not necessarily mean that they were illiterate, as exemplified by the following case from the mining town of Körmöcbánya (Kremnica, Slovakia). One of the burghers approached Lőrinc, a student of the local school, and entrusted him with the task of writing down the following accusation: someone in town had stolen a horse and deflowered one of the maidens. Lőrinc was in need of money, so accepted the offer. The burgher then hung the note up in the cemetery chapel, obviously intending to spread malicious rumors about one of his fellow townsmen whom he clearly considered to be his enemy. Unsurprisingly, it was the kinsmen of the slandered girl, and not the alleged seducer, who began to seek out the slanderer after having found the note and quickly taken it down. It is worth noting that the rumormonger was, himself, unable to write. Furthermore, written slander implies the expectation that the targeted audience could read, reinforced by the circumstance that the girl's parents removed the note quickly before too

---

61 APA vol. 16, fol. 141rv (1468, Waradien. dioc.). The schoolmaster had earned a bachelor of liberal arts degree, probably acquired at the University of Kraków, where many residents of Túr studied during the fifteenth century. Kubinyi, *Városfejlődés*, 21–22.

62 APA vol. 70, fol. 321v–22r (1523, Transylvanien. dioc.).

many people saw it.[63] Relatives of the girl searched for the author of the note in the school, suggesting that it was evident to them that the ability to write was limited to students; indeed, they found seventeen-year-old Lőrinc.[64]

The situation in this northern Hungarian mining town demonstrates that the traditional dual model of a literate élite above an illiterate mass does not explain the much more complicated reality.[65] Many of the mostly German-speaking people of Körmöcbánya could read reasonably well, but were less able to write. This was not exceptional; nevertheless, it is not easy to explain how this came to be. It may well have been partially due to school curricula. As scholars have shown with regard to various regions, reading and writing instruction was often divided.[66] In England, for example, children began their first year of school with reading; thus, a child who only attended school for one year would not have learned to write.[67] By the middle of the sixteenth century, however, there were school regulations that indicate clearly that in Hungarian cities children began to learn to both read and write during their first year of school.[68] It is difficult to imagine that the situation had been much different one generation earlier. Perhaps in their everyday lives people had to read more often than they had to write.[69] Writing may have been regarded as a kind of specialized skill, for which one needed pen and paper, not easy obtained, and so was thought to be a skill better left to "experts."[70]

From the perspective of the present inquiry, the presence of educated men in rural communities must be stressed. They were not distinguished

---

63 From the widespread use of anonymous posted bills for political slander in fifteenth century England, Moran similarly concludes that lay literacy was increasing. Moran, *The Growth of English Schooling*, 174.

64 APA vol. 29, fol. 174v–75r (1479, Strigonien. archdioc.). The neighborhood conflict escalated when the slandered girl married and gave birth earlier than expected, which triggered further slander on the part of the earlier slanderer until her husband killed him.

65 For a more complete cultural history of different practices and uses of reading, see Chartier, *Lectures et lecteurs*; Chartier and Cavallo, eds., *The History of Reading*.

66 Wendehorts, "Wer konnte im Mittelalter lesen und schreiben?," 24–25. Young Pauline friars were expected during their first year in the cloister to learn to read and sing, though writing was not necessary. See Chapter 3 above.

67 Spufford, "First Steps in in Literacy."

68 For the regulations at the city school in Bártfa (Bardejov, Slovakia), see Mészáros, *XVI. századi városi iskoláink*, 152, 155.

69 With regard to reading and writing as separate skills, see Bouza, *Communication*.

70 Late sixteenth-century Reformed diocesan visitation records provide ample evidence of villagers entrusting the school rector with the task of writing their letters. Dienes, ed., *Református egyházlátogatási jegyzőkönyvek*, for example 56–58, 166.

from the rest of the community simply by their literacy, but also by their behavior. According to Norbert Elias, after the publication of Erasmus's 1530 essay on the regulation of children's behavior (*De civilitate morum puerilium*), the expression "civility" (*civilitas* in Latin, *civilité* in French) gained popularity as a term referring to good manners in lieu of the earlier, medieval term "courtesy" (*courtoisie* in French).[71] This insight is essential, since it follows that "good manners" became of public interest at the same that schooling, namely its method, content and purpose, began to attract special attention and trigger public debates.[72] In the first decades of the sixteenth century, discussions regarding the importance of education and good manners became widespread and fashionable, a trend best epitomized by the printed publication of a series of humanistic instructions on the education of children.[73] The notion of "civilized behavior" referred not to a particular skill or area of knowledge, but to the most basic gestures—appearance, posture, facial expressions, movement, dress, table manners, cleanliness and public behavior. It even included the expectation that one must reply when asked a question. István Kis, a Transylvanian student, recalled a time when his schoolmaster called on two of his fellow students, but the youths did not respond. The schoolmaster and the cantor approached the students to see why they were being defiant, but the students refused to speak. Provoked by their impudence, István spoke up: "You must reply to your teachers in all cases."[74] Even if István was not as well-mannered as he attempted to portray himself, his account clearly exemplifies a societal norm. In addition to texts, body language and behavior are also media of cultural memory.[75] The insistence that students adopt new habits taught in the cloister or parish schools can be seen as attempts to change certain existing patterns of behavior, since forms of conduct that had been entirely acceptable in the villages were no longer necessarily regarded as appropriate in the schools. This phenomenon

71 Elias, *The Civilizing Process*, 47–52. On the debates concerning the concept of the civilizing process, see Mennel, *Norbert Elias* and Schwerhoff, "Zivilisationsprozess."

72 For our argument here it will suffice to point out that a public discourse regarding good manners emerged in the early sixteenth century. For a critique of Elias concerning the issue of whether this codification of good manners represented a change of actual attitudes and feelings or rather just the transformation of respective norms, see Bryson, *From Courtesy to Civility*, 11–15.

73 See most importantly Margolin, *Erasme*, passim; Faber, "Humanitas."

74 APA vol. 57, fol. 232v–33r (1512, Transylvanien. dioc).

75 For more on habitual memory, see Connerton, *How Societies Remember*, 72–104.

can be seen as the "process of civilization." According to Elias, the rising interest in good manners at the beginning of the sixteenth century was due to a shift in the border that divided propriety from impropriety. Fortunately, we need not allude solely to the writings of Erasmus (whose essay on raising children had been translated and printed by Protestant printing presses in cities in Hungary by the 1590s) and their influence when examining this phenomenon in Hungary.[76]

In his writings from the 1510s (i.e., before the publication of Erasmus's aforementioned treatise), Gergely Gyöngyösi, the Pauline prior in Rome, displayed remarkable sensitivity to the question of behavior.[77] While Erasmus dedicated his writing to highborn youth, Gyöngyösi wrote for novices entering the order and their instructors. Obviously, he was continuing a medieval tradition. Educational instruction intended for clergymen, including regulations regarding behavior, had been around for centuries and Gyöngyösi may well have been as familiar with them as was Erasmus.[78] But Gyöngyösi's writing, like that of Erasmus, distinguishes itself from earlier treatises with a kind of freshness, which must be related to the fact that he did not simply imitate his predecessors, but was guided by his own personal experiences and observations of human behavior. Since common meals were the most important elements of sociability across all social strata, it is perhaps not surprising that the guidelines regarding conduct often focus on this activity.[79]

Regarding table settings and the manner of taking one's seat at the table, Erasmus writes, "the goblet and the thoroughly polished knife should be to the right, the bread to the left."[80] On the same question, Gyöngyösi suggests that one should "take a seat at the place indicated between the plate and the bread.

76 Erasmus's essay was published in 1591 in the town of Debrecen and in Latin in the town of Kolozsvár (Cluj-Napoca, Romania) under the title *Az erkölcsnek tisztességes volta* [The Honorable Character of Morals]. RMNY 1, 656 and 663.

77 For more on Gyöngyösi's career and ouvre, see Chapter 2.

78 Elias mentions several such handbooks (Elias, *The Civilizing Process*, 53) from the twelfth and thirteenth centuries: Johannes de Garlandia, *Morale scolarium*; Hugo de Saint-Victore, *De institutione novitiorum*; and Petrus Alphonsus, *Disciplina clericalis*.

79 Petrus Alphonsi devotes a mere two or three lines to the issue ("Cum ablueris manus ut comedas, nihil tangas nisi prandium, donec comedas; nec comedas panem priusquam veniat aliud ferculum super mensam, ne dicaris impatiens….") See Schmidt, ed. *Petri Alfonsi Disciplina Clericalis*, 74–75. Gyöngyösi's text is much more concrete and realistic. The process of transferring the act of taking meals from social life to the private sphere started in the royal courts in the sixteenth century. Benda, *Étkezési szokások*, 229.

80 Cited by Elias, *The Civilizing Process*, 49.

But do not crowd together, lest you vomit."[81] Both authors advise patience. Erasmus cautions, "Many people begin to reach for the platter once they have taken a seat. Wolves and gluttons behave in this manner. Do not be the first to reach for the platter that has been brought in!" Gyöngyösi offers similar advice: "If the plates have been placed on the table, do not eat until the prefect has given the sign."[82] Eating from a shared platter must have caused considerable inconvenience.[83] Two of Erasmus's injunctions are worth citing: "dipping your fingers into the sauce is better left to the peasants" and "do not rummage about the whole plate, but rather take the first piece that is within reach!" Similarly, Gyöngyösi cautions, "do not take many morsels and courses from the platter. Do not throw yourselves at the food, but rather, no matter how large the meal, eat in moderation, only as much as you need. Take care not to dirty the napkin or your hands with the soup."[84] With regard to eating noisily, Gyöngyösi exhorts the Pauline novices, "after the food has been served, do not slurp loudly and do not belch like drunks."[85] He also notes that one should hold the flagon with two hands, bones and leftovers should be placed quietly into the basket for the servants and upon completion of the meal napkins should be folded. Gyöngyösi also regarded it as rude for friars to let their gaze wander while eating or to stare at someone else's plate.[86]

Gyöngyösi was very well-read, though his comments are personal and distinctive. He drew lessons from extensive reading mixed with his experiences among his fellow friars and laypeople. As a precursor to Erasmus and as a religious superior endeavoring to confirm religious discipline, Gyöngyösi can hardly be expected to have struck the same direct and ironic tone as

81 Sarbak, Bellus and Weinrich, eds., *Gyöngyösi Gergely,* Directorium: Capitulum VIII: *secundo circa mensam*, 46–47. Handwashing before a meal, described at length by Erasmus, is absent from the monastic regulations regarding eating. However, it is mentioned in the manuals for both the Buda and the Viennese courts (both before and after a meal). See Pálffy, "*Koronázási lakomák,*" esp. 1045.

82 Cites Elias, *The Civilizing Process*, 50.; Sarbak, Bellus and Weinrich, eds., *Gyöngyösi Gergely*, Directorium, Capitulum VIII: *secundo circa mensam.*

83 In the royal courts of the Hunyadi and Jagiello dynasties (1456–1526) one finds similar customs pertaining to table manners, at least according to the accounts of the Italian humanists who lived for a time in Hungary and were sensitive to any deviation from Italian practices. People ate from a shared platter, without forks and they used napkins and served the food with sauce. Kubinyi, "A királyi udvar élete," esp. 330–31.

84 Cites Elias, *The Civilizing Process*, 50; Sarbak, Bellus and Weinrich, eds., *Gyöngyösi Gergely*, Directorium, Capitulum VIII: *secundo circa mensam.*

85 Ibid.

86 Ibid.

the humanist scholar who had shed the friar's garb. Yet while his style may not resemble that of Erasmus, the questions that preoccupied him show the affinity the two shared. Gyöngyösi wrote with circumspection and common sense not only on table manners, but also on everyday gestures, conversational strategies, dress and hygiene: "while sitting, [the students] should not have their knees apart, and they should not cross their legs [...]. When standing, they should not sway like a reed in the breeze [...]. They should bridle their tongues [...]. They should not lie prostrate, but rather should sleep on their sides [...]. Their faces should not be sad, but rather jovial, but their laughter should be restrained. They should not hold their heads up when they walk, but rather a bit forward [...]. They should not wiggle their noses, neither at a foul smell [...] nor at a pleasant one."[87] Gyöngyösi's admonitions were not limited to conduct in company (for instance, his insistence that one must always find a pretext for taking leave of others); he also provided guidelines on how students should behave after retreating to their quarters. He instructed them not to lift their feet too high when putting on their sandals. When washing their feet, they were not to uncover their legs higher than their knees. They were not to go barefoot or sleep naked (perfectly common among laypeople). He exhorted them to be restrained and orderly. They were to keep their bedding and clothes in a clean place, not under the bed (which must have been a secular habit), and after rising, they were to make their beds.[88]

Conclusion

Gyöngyösi's work plausibly testifies to the sensitivity of the Pauline superior to human behavior, rendering him a genuine Renaissance personality. His writings call attention to the important role of late medieval cloister and parish schools in the formation and diffusion of civilized behavior, the center of which was identified by Elias in the early modern royal court. The world of "civilized students" must therefore also be considered to have extended from the universities to parish and cloister schools. The surprisingly dense network of village schools in the Late Middle Ages is an important new finding since it reflects the educational demands of village and small town society. Furthermore, the high mobility of late medieval students within the country closely parallels the routes and geographical movements of Lutheran schoolmasters and preachers

87 Ibid., Capitulum VIII/3: *Circa statum et habitum.*

88 Ibid.

two generations later, at least in the northern regions of Hungary that escaped Ottoman Turkish occupation.[89]

The extended social group of literate clergymen of humble social origin lived in close coexistence with the laity in villages and small towns, which we will closely inspect in the following chapters (especially in chapters 6 and 7). Poor students, who returned to the outside world after having spent years within the walls of a cloister, or to their native villages after years of study in distant regions, taught the peasant world proper behavior. During their years in school, youths were compelled to accustom themselves to forms of behavior tied to stricter rules that required a higher degree of self-discipline, compliance and ability to manage one's time and follow a schedule. However, we can observe their process of socialization not only inside school buildings, but also within the context of leisure time spent collectively with their schoolmates, during which they constructed their masculine identity in violent and spontaneous street fights and tavern brawls. This snapshot of student leisure and festive practices will be further elaborated upon in chapter 7. As our cases also suggest, the routine appeal of self-defense to petitioners was tightly connected to codes of male honor.

While villagers may not have learned how to read and write from learned clergymen, they must have become familiar with their distinctive manners and patterns of conduct. How laypeople reacted to this otherness—imitation, rejection, mockery—would be another story. We can, however, conclude that runaway friars, the protagonists of this story, mediated at least two important things for village communities: the ability to read and write, and the norms of "civilized behavior." In doing so, they played important roles as mediators between élite and popular culture (assuming that we accept, at least tentatively, this dichotomous model of how cultures operate).

89 Csepregi, "A magyarországi iskolázás."

CHAPTER 5

Life Outside the Walls: Clergymen on the Road

What happened to the runaway young friars after they had left the closed and secure walls of the cloister? Did they manage to secure benefices or employment befitting literate men? Did they successfully integrate into the world outside the cloister or did they drift into the margins of society without connections and secure means of subsistence? I follow the destiny of these runaways analogically since, with a few exceptions, there is no data available regarding their non-cloistered lives.

Former Pauline friar Lukács Szakcsi, who became a parish priest in Pogány, just a short distance to the south of the market town where he was born and raised, represents one of these exceptions.[1] Priest Berec, son of Márton, identifies himself in his petition only as "presbyter in the diocese of Zagreb," although his story reveals that he left the Paulines in Garics (Garić, Croatia) to work at a hospital, where he was employed when he submitted his application to Rome.[2] The closest hospice for the sick and poor was located some thirty kilometers to the north of Garics in the market town of Császma (Časma, Croatia), south of Monoszló (Moslavina, Croatia).[3] Berec may have served as the chaplain at one of these places by administering mass, hearing confessions and caring for and burying the poor. Lukács and Berec thus obtained benefices that provided them with modest though secure and independent livelihoods as a village parish priest and a market town hospital chaplain, respectively. Both priests conspicuously decided to remain in the same small region within the counties in which they had been born. The petition of another runaway Pauline, Imre Litteratus of Bélc, provides hints regarding his life outside the cloister.[4] At the time, literate men with legal expertise generally used the title *litteratus*, which they acquired in their homeland parish or chapter schools as well as during their employment as clerks.[5]

1 Szakcsi's petition to Rome contains this piece of information. APA vol. 41, fol. 319rv (1492, Quinqueecclesien. dioc.).

2 "Habitu dimisso etiam de licentia sui superioris dictam domum exivit et ad seculum est reversus in quodam hospitali pauperum, quod de presenti obtinet" APA vol. 25, fol. 129r (1477).

3 Cf. Kubinyi, "Orvoslás, gyógyszerészek," 265–66.

4 ASV Arm. XXXII. Vol. 61, fol. 387v–88r (1522, Quinqueecclesien. dioc.).

5 Kubinyi, "Polgári értelmiség és hivatalnokréteg," vol. 2, 602.

 | DOI 10.1163/9789004361263_006

The fates of the three runaway Paulines mentioned above hold no significant surprises. It is generally presumed that there existed in the early sixteenth-century Kingdom of Hungary a large number of *literati* who served as lawyers and schoolmasters and filled an increasing number of positions as notaries, clerks and secretaries at the royal chancellery, aristocratic courts, municipal offices, church courts and *loca credibilia*.[6] The runaway Imre Deák (Litteratus) of Bélc probably pursued one of the above professions. The fact that the two other renegade friars managed to secure benefices as parish priest and hospital chaplain is also consistent with the longstanding scholarly hypothesis. Historians of the condition of the lesser clergy are unanimous that the number of small clerical benefices rose significantly at that time. Scholars uniformly state that, contrary to western European tendencies, this process did not exercise a negative impact on the living conditions of the lesser clergy in the Kingdom of Hungary; the multitude of lesser priests, including parish chaplains and chantry priests, continued to enjoy secure and comfortable lifestyles that must have seemed attractive to poor boys seeking ecclesiastical careers.[7] This rising number of clerical benefices was the result of an increase in lay demand for the sacraments and clergy-performed Church liturgies as well as the willingness and ability of parishioners to invest in pious bequests, legacies and endowments (votive masses and the maintenance of church buildings), all of which increased considerably in the second half of the fifteenth century.[8] Researchers agree that religious life in the kingdom differed from its western European counterparts only in quantitative terms: the size and density of Church institutions were understandably lower in smaller cities of a less populated country; however, similar devotional practices and forms ranging from the cult of the Eucharist to the religious practices of lay confraternities existed in both East Central and Western Europe.[9]

---

6 Bónis, "Men learned in the law" and Kubinyi, "Írástudás és értelmiségi foglalkozásúak." In medieval Hungary, chapters and larger monasteries, called *loca credibilia*, exercised the function of notaries: they issued and authenticated charters and participated in the administration of law.

7 Mályusz, *Egyházi társadalom*, 134–150; Cevins, *Az Egyház*, 30–33, 120–22.

8 On the late medieval Eucharistic and penitential devotional culture, which intensified the intercessory role of the clergy, the only legitimate administrators of the sacraments, see: Burgess, *The Parish*; Lutton, *Lollardy and Orthodox Religion*. With regard to parish religion in Hungary, see Pásztor, *A magyarság*, 73–75; Szende, "A soproni középkori végrendeletek," 269.

9 Cevins, *Az Egyház*, 169–73.

The Parish Church and Cloister in the Community

What did all of this mean for youth from small villages? How did young friars in friaries in towns and market towns perceive their social and religious environment during the early decades of the sixteenth century? For one, they realized that urban religious life was not focused on the mendicant cloisters in which they lived, but on the parish church,[10] even if cloisters were generally located in the center of town.

Parish priests were distinguished and well-to-do men earning incomes of up to one hundred forints per year. They required a large number of auxiliary personnel and chaplains to serve alongside them. Ordering masses for the dead became a widespread custom. Parishioners had weekly or monthly masses celebrated to further the spiritual salvation of their deceased kin and friends in exchange for both movable and immovable property. They entrusted these permanent or temporary chantry endowments—along with the administration of endowment property and the receipt of income derived from them—to appointed and familiar clerics, or to the parish priest. For example, in the town of Kassa (Košice, Slovakia), where Mátyás Zalzi lived in the Dominican friary not far from the parish church, ten chaplains earned their livelihoods in this way.[11] Eight priests in Beszterce lived on such incomes during the time native resident Mátyás Besztercei studied at the Dominican cloister located below the town walls.[12] In addition to the chaplains, the rector and students from the school located next to the church regularly helped the parish priest supply the laity with rituals such as singing festive masses and conducting funerary ceremonies. Preachers were employed in most towns to deliver sermons on festive occasions. Due to their training, mendicant friars had a fairly good chance of obtaining such positions.

Parish churches offered further opportunities to young priests seeking means of subsistence. Parishioners were not satisfied with chantry endowments only; those who could do so not only had masses celebrated, but founded chapel benefices as well. The chapel could be an independent building in the town or an internal construction within a parish church. Sometimes there was only enough money to erect an altar inside an existing chapel. Those who lacked the resources to have a new altar built simply paid for new ornamentation such as candles. As a result of this popular practice, there came to

10 The syntheses of Elemér Mályusz and Marie-Madeleine de Cevins serve as the basis for the following survey of lay religious practices and urban clergy.

11 APA vol. 70, fol. 313rv (1523).

12 Cevins, *Az Egyház*, 182 (ten chaplains in Kassa and eight in Beszterce).

be thirty-five chapels and altars at the cathedral of Eger.[13] András Machy of Eger and György Baktan may have observed this with a mixture of wonder and envy when they strolled from the Augustinian friary located below the walls of Eger toward the immense, opulent nearby cathedral church. They would have frequently encountered local secular clergymen, parish priests, chaplains and chantry priests from the town's four parish churches as well as dozens of canons who lived next to the cathedral. Adolescents who entered the friaries in the southern town of Pécs met with similar splendor, both at the local cathedral and at three parish churches. The most lavish was the one in the market square, where masses were regularly celebrated at ten different altars. Friars living in Pécs sooner or later came across one of the six chapel churches located in the town.[14] The income derived from lands dedicated to the construction and maintenance of these churches created further positions for priests, who in return celebrated mass and sang psalms for the salvation of the endowers and their families. The friars who lived a strictly regulated life in religious communities may have considered the relative independence of these chantry priests and chapelists, who often lived in individual urban houses on the income partly provided by parishioners for their services, to be attractive.

In sum, the number of pastoral priests engaged at parish churches and chapels could reach to forty or fifty even in non-cathedral towns.[15] Members of lay confraternities also employed chaplains and preachers to conduct religious services on feast days and commemorations for the dead. Hospitals for the poor and sick represented another possible source of employment for pastoral priests. In addition to the hospital chaplain officiating the sacraments for the growing number of poor, other priests also worked at these hospitals, since townsmen occasionally raised altars in hospital churches rather than overcrowded parish churches. As we saw, Berec managed to obtain a clerical position at such a hospital following his escape from the Paulines.

Friars could have discerned from within the walls of the cloister that, contrary to the pattern in other regions of continental Europe, parish churches, rather than mendicant cloisters, had become the focus of urban religious life.[16] Parish

---

13 Ibid., 183., 154.

14 Fedeles, Sarbak and Sümegi, *A pécsi egyházmegye*, 1,178–1, 180, 182 (map).

15 In the episcopal town of Pécs, only about 65 pastoral clergymen were active of between 270 and 300 ecclesiastics in the town, including canons, monks and friars. This represented 4 to 6 percent of the total urban population, which equaled the proportion of clergymen calculated for western European cities. Boockmann, *Die Stadt*, 192.

16 On the interactions of mendicants and lay society in the Holy Roman Empire, Italy and France, see the works of Kaspar Elm, Bernhard Neidiger, Roberto Rusconi, Daniel

churches were granted the most pious donations and the greatest number of new altars and chapels and served as the burial place for local residents.[17] They also received the greatest influx of capital, which naturally resulted in a growing civilian influence over their property. In comparison to parish churches, cloisters maintained a much looser connection to urban religious life. Although admission to mendicant confraternities—in exchange for pious donations—entailed prestige, parishioners erected fewer altars in cloister churches, and lay confraternities cherished closer ties to parish churches. The fact that burghers provided mendicant cloisters with fewer material resources is understandable, since—contrary to parish churches—municipal authorities exercised no influence over their administration. Young friars certainly perceived the balance of power that had developed between friaries and parish churches, specifically the relative prosperity of secular clergymen and the steadily increasing opportunities for learned priests beyond the walls of the cloister. If a friar became dissatisfied with his simple and strictly regulated communal lifestyle and desired to leave the cloister, walking the town streets with open eyes and developing good personal connections could result in securing a position as a schoolmaster or chaplain. Those who were lucky might even have been able to begin their lives in the outside world with an altar benefice. Well-educated non-local friars had a fairly good chance of acquiring small benefices because, for demographic reasons, members of the urban elite rarely chose a clerical career for their sons; the urban patriciate in Western Europe tended to monopolize urban church benefices.[18] This explains how clerical careers became important vehicles for social mobility among the lower social strata.

Masses of Unbeneficed Clergy

We have thus far gained an explanation of the destinies of three fugitive friars who employed their expertise as pastoral priests to obtain small benefices and livelihoods as literate professionals at various courts and administrative

Bornstein and Larissa Taylor. With regard to the vitality of parochial piety in Britain, see the works of Beat Kümin, Burgess Clive and Christopher Marsh.

17 This tendency was also manifested in Transylvanian Saxon towns, where mendicant orders, particularly the Dominicans and Franciscans, exercised great attraction over the local population. This was partially due to the fact that the towns had only one German parish each (Beszterce, Brassó, Nagyszeben), not enough to satisfy the spiritual needs of several thousand parishioners. Florea, *The Third Path*, 104.

18 Kubinyi, "Budai és pesti polgárok," 233–34.

offices. However, a problem emerges with regard to the rest of the runaways, who portrayed themselves simply as *presbyters* (ordained priests) or, in some cases, *clericus* (unordained clerics). In this way, renegade friars were classified as part of the largest group of petitioners to Rome—some 1,300 ambiguously identified *presbyter* (priests), *clericus* (clerics) and *scolaris* (students). The presence of this large number of priests, clerics and students among petitioners is both conspicuous and exasperating, since it is practically impossible to determine precisely who they were and how they derived a means of subsistence. The number of clergymen who included their ecclesiastical benefices in their petitions is unfortunately very low.[19]

It has become evident to many researchers that a large number of priests and clerics with no tangible livelihoods appear in late medieval sources. English and German historians characterize them as an "ecclesiastical proletariat" that failed to win competitions for benefices. This vast group of clergymen most often became stuck as stipendiary priests for their entire lives and had to earn their livings "singing for their suppers" day by day. A typical man of the cloth at the beginning of the sixteenth century was not a beneficed parish priest, but an auxiliary, hired cleric.[20]

The Unbeneficed as Outsiders

Members of this poor late medieval ecclesiastical stratum became the protagonists in the first social historical narratives of the Protestant Reformation. Seen from the perspective of careers, religious reforms of the early sixteenth century could be described as a social rebellion led by the impoverished and dissatisfied priesthood.[21] In Hungary, Elemér Mályusz, lacking such serial sources as ordination or benefice registers[22] and thus relying on sporadic data and normative texts, was the most important medievalist of the interwar period. He concluded that the majority of clergymen continued to acquire small benefices and secure permanent incomes, at the very least as chantry priests, in

19 The nearly 600 petitioners who listed such benefices included 5 prebendaries, 15 bishops, 17 provosts, 20 chapelists, 22 archdeacons (including 2 parish priest archdeacons and 10 canon archdeacons), 36 chantry priests, 88 canons, 106 friars and monks (including 12 abbots) and 286 parish priests.

20 Cooper, *The Last Generation*, 94–128 (with further literature on England). For more recent research on the German regions see: Meyer, "Der deutsche Pfründenmarkt"; idem, "*Arme Kleriker auf Pfründensuche*," 198–202.

21 Lortz, *Die Reformation*, vol, 1, 86.

22 For ordination registers, see Cooper, *The Last Generation*; and Virginia Davis, "Irish Clergy." For diocesan benefice registers with regard to Western Europe, see Cevins, *Az Egyház*, 21.

the decades prior to the Protestant Reformation.[23] However, there was a law containing thought-provoking stipulations. Following the 1514 peasant war in Hungary, one of the largest in Europe during that period, the nobility enacted several punitive measures at the Diet. Influenced by the war, the nobility prohibited peasants, as well as others, from carrying weapons, among other things. Paragraph 60 of the legislation began with the statement that "priests without benefices and students living in the schools should not hereafter dare to carry weapons and guns."[24] The nobles who convened at the 1514 National Diet specified that Church superiors should imprison violators. Only later did the legislators include *hajduks* and peasants in their prohibition. This law suggests that the nobility perceived these four groups—unbeneficed priests, student boarders, *hajduks* and peasants—as the main participants in the 1514 rebellion. The prescribed punishment clearly shows that the law considered students to be clerics subjected to Church disciplinary procedures. Thus, unbeneficed priests and students formed a single category: the former was composed of the latter who, as far as the nobles could tell, had not managed to acquire a benefice and had joined the peasant rebellion.

Decrees issued after the peasant war reflected the fears not only of the lords, but of the prelates as well. Church superiors who gathered at diocesan councils in the fourteenth and fifteenth centuries took repeated steps to counteract fraudulently ordaining clerics. In order to curb false ordinations, a measure was enacted that required archdeacons to provide ordaining bishops with information regarding the lives, morals and statuses of candidates. However, this regulation—which was renewed without amendment for centuries—does not highlight concurrent religious practices and conditions. Prelates who convened at the Diocesan Synod of Veszprém in 1515—one year after the peasant uprising—wrote an addendum to the regulation, in which it is revealed that those who had falsely ordained were primarily uneducated, vagabond priests (*sacerdotes ignorantes et vagabundi*). The synod urged archdeacons to verify the manner in which wandering priests administered the sacraments and to authenticate the episcopal letters substantiating their ordination.[25]

Thus, lords and prelates simultaneously cast suspicious eyes upon clerics roving the countryside in search of employment who, as auxiliary priests, helped parish incumbents tend to the spiritual needs of the faithful. It seems that the powerful rather feared itinerant clerics due to their mobility, education

---

23 Mályusz, *Egyházi Társadalom*, 139.

24 "Presbyteri non beneficiati et scholares scholas inhabitantes," DRMH, vol. 4, anno 1514/ paragraph 60.

25 Solymosi, ed., *A veszprémi egyház*, 86–87.

and lack of property. The lives of these clerics differed significantly from those of the majority of society. Beneficed lower clergy obtained their positions as rural parish priests with the help of patrons. In order for them to retain their benefices, they had to maintain good relations with landowners and the congregation. Lords engaged tax-paying heads of families that settled on tenant-peasant holdings, so the two parties typically knew one another;[26] however, wandering clerics did not enter into direct relations with the powerful. If they managed to find work in a parish, their employment was based on an agreement with the parish priest only. The fears of the lords and prelates were perhaps the products of both the 1514 peasant war and the fact that the vagabond clerics were strangers. This lack of familiarity may have been threatening in a culture based on personal relationships. The "stranger" differed only slightly from the "rogue."[27]

Using concepts of historical sociology, the appearance of a large group of unbeneficed priests and students, which the powerful regarded with fear, suggests that the patterns of social integration were undergoing transformation during the early sixteenth century. To use Robert Castel's expression, exceptionally mobile vagabond clerics, who had become disconnected from the traditional system of feudal obligations and reciprocal relations, had entered upon a path of social "disaffiliation."[28] These clerics were the "wage-laborers" of the Church who sought to make livings in the "religious market" by conducting religious services. The powerful typically reacted to their appearance with fear and criminalization (e.g., prohibiting carrying weapons); however, the most important question is whether their state of social disconnection became permanent. Did they become perpetually marginalized, living on the roadways, or did the "negative freedom of vagrants" represent a passing youthful episode and they subsequently managed to posit themselves in the traditional network of social relations that ensured individual recognition?[29]

The increased capacity of wandering priests for independent action was the result of their mobility, which meant that they had nothing to lose and

26 Péter, "Jobbágycsaládok."

27 For more on this issue see Chapter 7.

28 Robert Castel approaches the social transformation that attended the transition from feudalism to capitalism through an examination of the new modes of social integration (wage-earning work), their failures (unemployment) and their social problematization (the topos of the vagabond). Castel, *From Manual Workers to Wage Laborers.* I will also use the concept of marginality, which was first applied to the late medieval urban poor by Bronisław Geremek, *The Margins of Society.*

29 Castel, "The Roads to Disaffiliation."

were impossible to control. As a consequence, no written records remain regarding them. The names of all tenant peasants and heads of households who cultivated plots of land were carefully listed in records (*urbaria*) indicating feudal obligations, and diocesan superiors produced detailed records regarding the beneficed lower clergy in their diocese; however, prelates were not interested in clerics who worked temporarily in the service of parish priests--at least, I have not found any sixteenth-century visitation records that mention them.

The Unbeneficed as Criminals

Vagrant clergymen emerge at random in charters that served to safeguard privileges. Their heavy presence among petitioners to the papal curia—amounting to nearly half of all petitioners—does not accurately reflect their proportion within society at large, and stems from the nature of the source material. The most characteristic feature of petitioners was that they had violated a Church regulation or transgressed social norms and conventions. We find among them the troublemakers who struck fear into the lords during the autumn of 1514: clerical and student participants of the peasant uprising. Of the fifteen petitioners who asked the pope to absolve them for transgressions committed in the war, nine were priests, clerics or students. Priest Kelemen Canimich had taken part in the rebellion as secretary to a captain of the crusade in southern Hungary, forging letters that called the faithful to war in the name of the archbishop and king.[30] Imre Wolconz was still a student a 1514, although his petition stated that his literacy had been of use to the rebels.[31] In 1518, András Sokovics, a cleric from Obedszentkereszt, reported that he had joined the peasant rebellion with some fellow students in Halas, a southern market town where they had been studying.[32] Other rebels identified themselves as simple *presbiter*, as did the approximately 160 people who had become involved in murder, war and plunder.[33] In comparison to laymen and beneficed ecclesiastics, wandering clerics requested absolution with exceptional frequency

30 APA vol. 59, fol. 72rv (1515, Bachien. dioc.). For more detail and from another perspective see chapter 8.

31 APA vol. 66, fol. 24v–25r. (1520, Zagrabien. dioc.).

32 APA vol. 63, fol. 206v–7r (1518, Zagrabien. dioc.).

33 Around half of those who identified themselves simply as *presbyter* (340 people) needed papal absolution after having been excommunicated for committing grave sins.

for acts of collective and interpersonal violence connected to their peculiar lifestyle.[34]

Compared to parish priests, the number of offenses committed by vagabond clerics in conducting religious services was remarkably high: a large number requested absolution for having celebrated mass at places under interdiction or in churches that had not yet been consecrated.[35] Their narratives suggest a rural setting for their actions and that they had been unaware of the interdiction. Their identity as vagrant priests is reflected in their repeated requests for the pope to authorize them to celebrate mass in any diocese, which made it possible for them to bypass the authority of local parish incumbents and fulfill the orders of individual parishioners.[36] In the event that they became embroiled in amorous relations with married women, they risked coming into conflict not with the parish priest, but with the parishioners themselves. Vagrant priests, contrary to beneficed lower clergy, could indulge in such romantic liaisons with relative ease, since they had nothing to lose if they managed to flee to a distant location before the aggrieved husbands could get their hands on them.[37]

The vagabond lifestyle of these clerics also made them more prone to engage in certain types of financial delinquency. While either a chaplain or student at the St. Bartholomew parish church in the town of Pécs, priest Máté Perusics embezzled a significant sum from funds raised through the sale of indulgences for church renovations.[38] Stipendiary priests also operated a

34 The close connections between the world of poor priests and students and criminality and vagabondage was first analyzed in the late medieval urban milieu by Geremek, *The Margins of Society*, 135–66.

35 Irregular celebration of mass by petitioners: 65 *presbyteres* and 16 parish priests. Celebrating mass in places under interdict: 22 *presbyteres* and one parish priest.

36 For example APA vol. 3, fol. 138v (1450, Strigonien. archdioc.).

37 For example, Paulus Kralus de Culned: "Ipse olim quandam mulierem coniugatam actu fornicario pluries carnaliter [cognovit] et postmodum vero accidit, quod cum dicta mulier in quadam domo extitisset et exponens ipse cum ea concubuisset, maritus legitimus dicte mulieris insimul invenit in dicta domo et qualiter ipsos exponentem et mulierem incepit clamaret et dictum presbyterem exponentem cupiebat interficere, sed placuit deo quod de dicto domo et manibus mariti dicte mulieris illesus exivit et ad alienas partes se transtulit." APA vol. 2bis, fol. 225r (1441, Strigonien. archdioc.).

38 "Alias ipse sue salutis immemor viginti sex denarios hungaricales in ecclesia sancti Bartolomei Quinqueecclesiensi pro reparatione et manutentione cuiusdam ecclesie aut alias contemplationi certarum indulgentiarum eidem ecclesie a sede apostolica concessarum pie elargitos furtive accepit illosque in suos usus necessarios convertit." APA vol. 63, fol. 405v–6r (1518).

black market trade in church paraphernalia. Priest András, son of György, walked off with some of the liturgical objects belonging to the cathedral of Zagreb and sold some of them.[39] Priest Márton Nagy from the village of Vragovc admitted that he had stolen books and chalices from a smaller church.[40] Some vagrant priests apparently hoped that they could postpone—or perhaps completely avoid—repaying loans if they suddenly made off to a different location.[41]

Parish Incumbents and the Unbeneficed

Narratives representing violations of norms clearly reveal the enormous gulf that separated parish priests from the stipendiary clergy. The initial lines indicate whether petitioners identifying as presbyters had, either at the time of petitioning or previously, been parish priests.[42] The story of Priest Balázs, son of Miklós, began with the following phrase: "When he was standing around outside his house with his relatives and friends ..." The fact that Balázs had his own house suggests that he was a parish priest, since stipendiary priests usually referred only to their "own rooms" (*camera propria*). Priest Balázs continued as follows: "Then János, son of Lénárd, came by with a drawn sword and threatened the brother of priest Balázs with death. In response, the relatives and friends of the parish priest gave him a good beating. They subsequently concluded an agreement before arbiters that, along with a penalty of forty forints, in the future they would not offend and assault one another." A day later, priest Balázs celebrated a festive mass with his relatives. Afterwards, local villagers held a big feast from which the priest excused himself. Not long afterwards, the villagers sent Balázs a message asking him to return, because János and his companions had attacked his brother. Balázs rushed immediately to the scene of the confrontation, where his relatives killed János after finding out that he

39 "Olim in ecclesia Sancti Stephani Zagrabiensis nonnulla bona ad quosdam clericos ipsius ecclesie spectantia et pertinentia clam substraxit ipsaque bona alienavit" APA vol. 22, fol. 152v (1474).

40 APA vol. 3, fol. 129v (1450, Zagrabien. dioc.).

41 The widow of Péter Bodó, resident of Pécs, sued priest Ferenc Izdenci at the vicar's court over a loan of four ducats that the latter had failed to repay to her late husband. The procedure ended with the vicar excommunicating the priest, who petitioned Rome to have the censure lifted without having to repay the debt. ASV Arm XXXII. vol. 61, fol. 467rv (1522).

42 A total of 25 of the 657 simple *presbyters* turned out to have been parish priests.

had murdered his brother.[43] This episode clearly shows that "priest Balázs" was the village parish priest and the head of a large "familia" that depended on his protection. The account also reveals that the "parish priest clan" conducted religious services together. The figure of the parish priest tends to appear in these narratives as a true lord who, like Balázs, possessed a large house with servants, a household full of relatives and land with tenant peasants, and rode around on horseback with a sword sheathed at his side. [44] Balázs, son of Bálint, identified himself only as a "priest." Following the murder of a judge investigating those who had robbed an innkeeper, villagers turned to him for help. Balázs immediately called his congregation together and dispatched a few men to apprehend the villains. Thus priest Balázs must have been the local parish priest who, along with the judge, was responsible for maintaining peace and security in the village.[45]

The large majority of the several hundred "priests" mentioned in the petitions, however, appear as unbeneficed, stipendiary priests. Many of them were employed in the service of parish priests with a one-year contract as chaplains. The possessive construction used in the petitions reflects the relationship that existed between the chaplain and the parish priest: "chaplain Lukács Scopzich, the chaplain of the parish priest named Pál of the Holy Trinity Church in Toplica"; "Ambrus Kemléki, parish priest of the St. Peter church in Gradec and Antal Gradeci, the chaplain of the said Ambrus."[46] Parish priest János Bognár of Körmöcbánya requested permission for his four unnamed chaplains to absolve parishioners of grave sins reserved for the pope.[47] The story of Györgу Prodavizi reveals that he, too, had served as a chaplain: "He was taking his supper with

43 "Ipse cum suis fratribus et nonnullis suis amicis esset ante domum suam propriam, supervenit quidam Johannes Leonardi laicus dicte diocesis nescitur quo spiritu ductus cum gladio evaginato volens consanguineum germanum oratoris, quiquidem exponens cum fratribus et amicis suis huiusmodi sine aliqua effusione sanguinis predictum Johannem Leonardi aliquantulum verberarunt et eum in futurum similia non facere rogarunt, et post aliquod dies interventu quorundam virorum fuit inter eos concordia, ut ad penam xxxx florenorum nemo ipsorum aliqua iniuriosa verba contra aliquem proferret seu manus violentas apponeret." APA vol. 44, fol. 291rv–92r (1495, Chanadien. dioc.).

44 For more regarding the everyday lives of the parish priests, see chapter 7. Ambrus Kemléki, incumbent of Gradec (modern-day Croatia) sent his retainers (*familiares*) to help one of the tenant peasants of the bishop of Zagreb to escape. APA vol. 37, fol. 221rv (1487).

45 APA vol. 8, fol. 217v (1460, Quinqueecclesien. dioc.).

46 APA vol. 37, fol. 221rv and 225v (1487, Zagrabien. dioc.).

47 "Johannes Bognar presbyter plebanus rector parrochialis ecclesie Beate Marie Virginis de Cremnicia et quatuor eius in dicta ecclesia vicarii capellani nuncupati." APA vol. 25, fol. 202v (1477, Strigonien. archdioc.).

other chaplains and meanwhile he and one of his colleagues began to quarrel, argue and fight. When he brought a complaint against his opponent in front of the parish priest, it aroused such anger against him that one night when he came out of his room, he attacked him with a drawn sword and cut off one of his fingers."[48] When János Vragovci was summoned by his parish priest, he replied that he could not come because he was in the process of celebrating mass. The furious parish priest again sent for János with the message that if he did not report to him immediately, he could no longer remain in his service. In this way he unwillingly became involved in a major scrap. The parish priest's "troops"—armed priests dressed in disguise (*sub habitu quasi dissumulato*) to appear as laymen—clashed in the cemetery with the laypeople who had mocked and inflicted wounds upon some of their fellow clerics.[49] The parish priest who employed Priest Illés summoned him to help "take care of some affairs" in a neighboring village and sent Priest Bálint Lybar to a nearby hillside vineyard to fetch some wine.[50] The parish priest under whom Márton Fábri served assigned him the thankless task of disciplining some of his disobedient domestic servants.[51] The above narratives suggest that chaplains not only helped parish priests to conduct religious services, they also acted as a kind of clerical retainer (*familiares*) who belonged to the incumbent's *familia* and assisted their "lord" in all spheres of everyday life, including occasional violent confrontations. Their status was similar to that of clerics who entered into the service of landlords as retainers or private chaplains, some of whom appear among the petitioners who identified themselves as "presbyter."[52]

The petitions provide clear evidence of the existence of a substantial layer of unbeneficed, stipendiary priests; however, I would not dare to speculate on whether this group of poor priests expanded in Hungary at the end of the Middle Ages or whether they had difficulty earning livelihoods during this

48 APA vol. 10, fol. 160r (1462, Zagrabien. dioc.). The market town of Prodaviz situated in Kőrös County.

49 APA vol. 15, fol. 202v–3r (1467, Zagrabien. dioc.).

50 "Ipse olim a suo plebano, ut cum eo ad quandam villam pro negotiis suis expediendis iret, vocatus fuisset" APA vol. 45, fol. 374r (1496, Zagrabien. dioc.); and ibid. vol. 117, fol. 700v–2r (1547, Iaurien. dioc.).

51 "Cum alias quidam Stephanus rector parrochialis ecclesie Sanctorum Cosme et Damiani dicte diocesis, cui orator ipse inserviebat, eidem oratori, ut quosdam alios ipsius Stephani famulos delinquentes castigaret, mandasset."APA vol. 55, fol. 230v–31r (1510, Wesprimien. dioc.).

52 "Olim fuisse capellanus unius nobilis" (APA vol. 15, fol. 102r, 1467, Iaurien. dioc.); "Alias eo servitiis domini temporalis castri de Erdwd dicte diocesis tunc insistente" (ASV Arm. XXXII. vol. 61, fol. 247v–8r, 1522, Transylvanien. dioc.).

period.[53] For one thing, we gain only a transitory image of these priests. The chaplains whose cases appeared at the Apostolic Penitentiary may have been young men at the beginning of their careers who later acquired benefices. The Transylvanian Saxon priest Máté Hosszúfalvi stated openly in 1450 that he "had no Church benefice," though he may have obtained one a few years later.[54] The narrative of Priest Pál Szepetki reveals that the events in question took place "when during his youth he served a parish priest in the church and around the house as a cleric."[55] However, we are unaware of his fate. At most, some light is shed upon their pasts. It becomes evident that Priest János Perlaki had previously been a chapel rector.[56] He left this position, presumably in the hope of finding better opportunities elsewhere. Priest Gergely Gueak had previously been a parish priest in the village of Radvány; the reason he decided to leave cannot be determined. The hypothesis that the death of a student he had beaten as punishment for some transgression had caused indignation in the village seems to be overly modern.[57] Priest Mátyás Zhewer declared that the local landowner had removed him from his parish benefice.[58] Priest Tamás had also previously had a benefice. This represents the one credible element

53 The Hungarian medievalist Elemér Mályusz remarked that, contrary to the tendency in the West, the number of chaplains in Hungary grew more sharply than that of chantry priests. Petitions to the Penitentiary do not clearly reflect this. Chantry priests, particularly from urban settings, submitted a total of around forty petitions to the papal curia beginning in the 1440s.

54 "Nullum ecclesiasticum habens beneficium [petit], ut possit dicere officium secundum Romane Curie stilum et non ad aliud possit compelli." APA vol. 3, fol. 137v (1450, Transylvanien. dioc.) The Saxon village of Lankendorff (Hosszúfalu in Hungarian), located in Fehér County to the east of Brassó.

55 "Cum ipse olim tempore iuventutis sue cuidam plebano tanquam clericus in ecclesia et alias in domo sua famularetur." APA vol. 2bis, fol. 143rv (1440, Wesprimien. dioc.). The village of Szepetk located in Zala County.

56 "Ipse olim capellanus capelle Beate Marie Montis Grecensis nuncupate prope Petoniam situate Aquilegiensis diocesis existeret." APA vol. 2, fol. 226r (1441, Zagrabien. dioc.).

57 "Alias ipse ecclesie loci de Radelban plebanus tunc existens quendam Erasmum de Benis scolarem suum, qui furtum et quedam alia enorma crimina comiserat correctionis gratia, ne de cetero talia committere auderet, quadam parva assella seu tabula, qua magistri scolares suos castigare solent, [...] citra sanguinis effusionem percussit." APA vol. 53, fol. 321r (1507, Waradien. dioc.). I have identified *Radelban* as the village of Radvány (Nagyradvány, Kisrandvány) in Bihar County. Priest István Hatai was also previously a parish priest "Alias ipse tunc parochialis ecclesie de Koch rector." Ibid., vol. 57, fol. 224v, 1512, Iaurien. dioc. The village of Kocs is situated in Vas County.

58 "Cum ipse olim ut capellanus cuiusdam parrochialis ecclesie serviret et quidam dominus temporalis ipsum exponentem de huiusmodi servitio deponeret et quendam alium

in the priest's otherwise extremely dubious story. Although there is nothing unique about the claim that the landowner had dismissed the previous incumbent, Priest János, from the parsonage of the village of Bocsárd, the assertion that the landowner had managed to persuade Priest Tamás to take possession of Priest János's vacated benefice by threating to confiscate his family property, sounds very unlikely. It is also peculiar that Tamás did not appear before the vicar of Eger during the proceedings that Priest János brought against him. What did Tamás fear if his actions had been justifiable? In the end, Tamás's brothers settled the dispute by murdering János. According to Tamás, the only reason he had agreed to this method of resolving the issue was that he had been so drunk that he had not known what he was saying.[59]

The above cases interestingly suggest that the holders of smaller benefices, including small parsonages and altar benefices, fluctuated considerably. Priests decided to move on to different locations not only because they were forced to do so, as in the examples above, but also because they believed they could gain larger benefices and greater opportunity elsewhere. Such priests spent much time on the road. As the examples show, disputes and small benefices were very common. However, I would not venture to state, on the basis of the conflicts that emerged here and there over benefices and the occasional case of simonist priests (those who purchased their benefices), that they were the result of competition for benefices.[60] Simonist priests, competition for better benefices, had existed for several centuries. The stereotypes of the "ignorant parish priest" and the "benefice hunting schoolmaster," the contention between whom was discussed earlier in this book, could have become ingrained in the popular consciousness through several centuries of experience.

---

presbyterem in eadem ecclesia pro capellano locaret, dictusque exponens cum suis bonis et rebus abinde recedere vellet…." APA vol. 18, fol. 83v–84r, (1470, Zagrabien. dioc.). Although the Latin term usually used for "parish priest" is *rector parrochialis ecclesie*, within the context of this text the term *capellanus parrochialis ecclesie* can only indicate this position (*capellanus* and *rector* are occasionally used interchangeably: cf. *capellanus/ rector capellanie*).

59 APA vol. 73, fol. 602rv–3r (1525, Agrien. dioc.). I identified *Bochenad* as the village of Bocsárd in Abaúj County.

60 Cases of simony were not generally referred to the Apostolic Penitentiary, but to the Dataria: I found only thirteen such cases at the Penitentiary over a period of 150 years. In five instances, the fathers of "presbyters" purchased parsonages for them from the landowner (APA vol. 5, fol. 211v); the purchase of the Orod archdeaconry from another archdeacon (vol. 2bis, fol. 318v); purchase of a parsonage in Zagreb County from the previous parish priest (vol. 5, fol. 349v); during the visitation to the diocese of Zagreb, the auxiliary priest visitors accepted small gifts "as was customary" (vol. 5, fol. 414r; vol. 16, fol. 91v).

Ordained in Rome

With regard to the issue of rivalry for benefices, a closer scrutiny of petitions concerning priestly ordinations may be useful. Dispensations for such impediments (for example minority of age, bodily defects or illegitimate birth) as well as absolutions for having violated the strict regulations of ordination form a significant group, and such cases compose 650 of the 3,000 petitions from the Kingdom of Hungary.[61] Clerics most often violated the rule concerning the place of their ordination: they were ordained elsewhere, typically in Italy and very often in the papal curia.[62] What might have prompted this multitude of clerics to undertake this complicated enterprise? According to one explanation, the strict canonical regulation and ecclesiastical control of ordination was the cause of many offenses, and clerics participating in pilgrimages to Rome frequently exploited the opportunity to receive curial consecration to the ministry.[63] A few priests stated that on their way home from such pilgrimages they had had a bishop in northern Italy ordain them.[64] However, this does not explain the motives of the large majority. Was it fashionable to be ordained in Rome, similarly to how clergymen competed for the opportunity to celebrate mass in the Eternal City?[65]

---

61 This proportion (21.7 percent) remains far below the overall average, which was as high as 56 percent during the pontificate of Pius II (1458–64). See the recent analysis of several thousand petitions concerning ordinations from throughout Europe that were handled by the Penitentiary and the Apostolic Chamber: Salonen and Hanska, *Entering a Clerical Career*.

62 Some 330 cases, or about half of the total number of applications for priestly ordination at the Penitentiary.

63 Lukcsics, *XV. századi pápák*, 19–21. Recently Salonen and Hanska as well as Rehberg have argued that the late medieval papacy stringently controled ordinations and thus laxities were the result of individual shortcomings and the limited possibility of curial officials to check the statements of clerical candidates coming from far away regions. Our findings below reinforce this conclusion. Salonen and Hanska, *Entering a Clerical Career*, passim; with regard to Easter pilgrim petitioners, see 130 and 154. Rehberg, "L'affluenza di ordinandi a Roma," 188, 223. For information regarding the canonical rules of ordination, see CIC vol. 2, 118–24, 975–76 (*De temporibus ordinationum et qualitate ordinandorum*).

64 APA vol. 2bis, fol. 417v (1443, a cleric from the diocese of Pécs); vol. 2bis, fol. 417r (1443, two clerics from Zagreb diocese); vol. 13, fol. 124r (1464, a cleric from the diocese of Veszprém).

65 Luther wrote, in connection to his trip to Rome, that there was great competition to celebrate mass because it was believed that one soul could be rescued from purgatory for each mass celebrated in the city. Virágh, *Dr. Luther*, 22.

Acting according to regulations entailed an enormous amount of administration. First, authorization (*littera dimissoria*) was needed from the diocesan bishop or the pope. Obtaining such permission was not easy. It appears that Albert Szabó ("Tailor") concluded that it would be impossible to obtain approval from Dénes Szécsi, and therefore decided to resort to fraud. When a sealed letter from the archbishop summoning the clergy from the diocese to attend a synod was nailed on the church door, Szabó secretly removed the letter and used the prelate's seal to forge a permit authorizing any bishop to ordain him.[66]

Papal decrees had for centuries prohibited non-Italian clergy from receiving ordination in Italy,[67] but this changed nothing with regard to the practice. Priests ordained in the curia later claimed that they had been unaware of the prohibition. They portrayed themselves as victims of greedy curial lawyers and corrupt bishops. Priest Barnabás Sormási reported that his lawyer had written his petition in his presence and acted as if he was taking it to the Curia. However, the lawyer forged the signature and took Barnabás to the house of the bishop, where he made the following request: "Your excellency, please ordain this person to the holy orders, since his petition has been approved!" However, the bishop was suspicious and compelled Barnabás to swear to the authenticity of the papal permission before ordaining him.[68] Others also asserted that curial bishops had ordained them based on forged papal authorizations in expedited procedures in exchange for financial compensation.[69]

---

66 "Cum eius ordinarius presbyteros eiusdem diocesis per suas litteras, ut ad sinodum venirent, monuisset, et illas in valvis ecclesie sub sigillo affigisset, postquam certum temporis spatium idem exponens huiusmodi litteras amovit et de sigillo earundem sibi quandam dimissorialem fecit." APA vol. 10, vol. 179v (1462).

67 Petitioners claimed that they were unaware of the relevant resolution of Pope Clement IV (1265–68).

68 "Nuper ad omnes ordines sacros promoveri desiderans ad quendam presbiterem in Romana Curia solicitatorem accessit, quiquidem presbiter eidem exponenti abusionem proponens supplicatione dicti oratoris prius confecte ad signaturam portare finxit. Demum ad domum cuiusdam episcopi cum dicto oratore reversus eidem episcopo dixit: Domine episcope, ordinare et promovere ad sacros ordines dignemini oratorem predictum, quia supplicatio est signata. Episcopus vero hec minime credens sacramentum ab eodem presbitero ad sanctam dei evangelia et in verbo sacerdotis recepit, quo recepto oratorem ipsum ad diaconatus ordinem promovit, ignoranter tamen." APA vol. 23, fol. 214r (1475, Zagrabien. dioc.). I have identified Solmes as the village of Sormás in the southern part of Zala County.

69 "Vigore cuiusdam false fabricate supplicationis, quam videbatur per Sanctitatem Vestram signatum fuisse [...] quam exponens ipse falsum esse ignorabat, extra tempora a iure statuta et absque vitio symonie per quendam episcopum catholicum etc. in romana curia."

Obviously both parties benefited from this thriving industry. Curial officials satisfied an existing demand. In order to meet the urgent needs of their many clients, these officials perhaps did, in fact, occasionally provide them with forged documents. In order to accelerate the process of ordination, bishops conferred holy orders in a single day and demanded money for this service. The clients participated fully in this business. What did the clerics gain from these transactions, in light of the fact that their petitions to the Apostolic Penitentiary reveal that they entailed further complications and expenses?

On the basis of the examined ordination petitions, I have gained the impression that from among the three basic preconditions of ordination—sufficient knowledge, good morals and adequate financial standing—most petitioning clerics had difficulties in proving the existence of the third requirement (called *titulus*). In other words, they did not have a benefice that would provide a living worthy of a priest, which the Church expected candidates to have upon taking the examination prior to ordination.[70] Some of these petitions state that clerics had been ordained "without sufficient title" (*sine titulo sufficienti*).[71] This could simply indicate that the bishop conducting the ordination had not always demanded the latter. But what might the repeated declaration that they lacked the required *titulus* when they were preparing to receive the holy orders and thus have themselves ordained to a false title have meant?[72] As has already been shown with regard to Erasmus, Bucer and the runaway friars, it was not easy for a young cleric to obtain a benefice if his family lacked property and connections. Petitions of more talkative clerics reveal the meaning of the term *fictus titulus*: Ferenc Wablay sought a papal letter proclaiming his innocence as the passive participant in a tavern brawl that ended in murder. In his petition,

---

APA vol. 23, fol. 213r (priest Kelemen, 1475, Iaurien. dioc.). A curial bishop had his chaplain ordain two clerics from Veszprém before a portable altar in his own house to nonexistent benefices (*ad fictum titulum*) in one day without the required papal authorization (1498, ibid., vol. 47, fol. 212v). On the institutional framework of ordination in Rome, see Rehberg, "L'affluenza di ordinandi a Roma." In addition to the Apostolic Chamber and the Vicar of Roman, ordinations in the curia were carried out by individual bishops authorized to do so, who often came from poorer dioceses and were in need of financial resources. They were usually authorized to ordain to the four minor orders only. Ibid, 204–5.

70 This phenomenon has been examined in connection with the petition of Péter Ferriani in chapter 2, "Runaway Friars."

71 "Ipse olim tanquam simplex et iuris ignarus Rome [...] sine licentia etc. et sine titulo se fecit ad omnes promoveri." APA vol. 2bis, vol. 128v (1440).

72 "Ipse olim ad sacros ordines promoveri desideraret et sufficientem titulum non haberet, ad quendam fictum titulum se fecit alias tamen rite ad omnes ordines promoveri." APA vol. 2bis, fol. 189rv (1440).

Wablay identified himself as the perpetual chaplain of the St. John altar at the St. Bartholomew parish church in the village of Bese. As a result of this lie, the papal letter issued in connection with this murder defined Wablay as the priest of the stipulated altar benefice. Wablay subsequently used this letter to certify his fictitious benefice in order to become ordained as a priest.[73]

Obtaining written proof of a non-existent benefice apparently required much planning and tactical maneuvering. It was much easier to achieve success with such counterfeit benefices in Italy, where, on the one hand, people were unfamiliar with conditions in faraway Hungary and, on the other hand, the ordination of foreign priests had become a flourishing business.[74] It therefore seems reasonable to suppose that the thousands of clerics who sought an ordination in Italy did so because they wished "to handle" their lack of benefice in this way, not because they wanted to be trendy or to exploit the opportunity connected to their participation in Roman pilgrimages. There seem to have been many clerics unable to demonstrate that they had benefices and who therefore were willing to do anything to correct this deficiency, such as forging documents, traveling to Rome and turning to the pope in order to have themselves ordained as priests. I have therefore returned to my previous proposition that young men of lowly origins attempted to achieve social advancement via a clerical career, many through education acquired within the mendicant orders. Typically, such people made use of the Apostolic Penitentiary in the fifteenth and sixteenth centuries in order to attain this objective. This is understandable, because it was much cheaper to obtain papal permission through the Penitentiary than through the Apostolic Dataria. Interestingly, nobody turned to the latter curial office with regard to the issue of fraudulent benefices. Those who applied to the Apostolic Dataria to obtain the more expensive papal letter were presumably more affluent clerics who had ready access to benefices, though had trouble satisfying the canonical stipulation that they be ordained celebrant priests within a year of acquiring a benefice.[75] Petitioner Albert

73 APA vol. 57, fol. 373rv (1512, Quinqueecclesien. dioc.). Salonen and Hanska (page 162, for example) also cite examples of clergymen being ordained without benefices or on falsified titles, but they do not dwell on its social consequences.

74 A dozen clerics from Hungary requested absolution for the following irregular ordinations: being ordained without having a benefice or a falsified one, or for being ordained in Italy without the permission from their own diocesan bishop.

75 Lukcsics, *XV. századi pápák*, 22. On the variety of the financial resources of clerical candidates and their distribution (clerics in possession of benefices ordained by the Apostolic Chamber in return for a higher fee, while poorer candidates were ordained by authorized bishops and the vicar of Rome), see Rehberg, "L'affluenza di ordinandi a Roma," 223.

Swerth of Győr cannot be classified among the latter. In 1468, Swerth submitted a request to the Penitentiary to have a bishop from the neighboring diocese ordain him on the grounds that the local bishop of Győr, Demeter Csupor of Monoszló, invested only those with priestly authority who had served him for a period of one year at their own expense in the cathedral liturgies. Swerth claimed that he lacked the financial resources to participate in the religious services of the chapter and to sing with the students at the chapter school for one year without pay.[76] The fact that Swerth asked to be transferred to a neighboring diocese suggests that the conditions that the bishop of Győr had established for the ordination of priests were uncommon. This case nevertheless shows that the Church required candidates for the priesthood to first satisfy several material requirements.

As young men who had joined the mendicant orders fled in violation of their religious vows, Albert Swerth remained undeterred. He presumably believed that if he was able to become invested as a priest, his efforts would pay off. The cleverer and more capable sooner or later managed to acquire a benefice. Priest Imre, for example, had himself ordained to a forged *titulus*, before asking for absolution for this offense in 1455, as the parish priest in the village of Dorog.[77] It appears that the majority of those who falsified their *tituli* served as unbeneficed priests at the time they submitted their petitions. The nobility at the National Diet shortly after the peasant rebellion in 1514 recorded the existence of this stratum of young, educated, stipendiary priests who had shown willingness to take up arms against them. They did not participate in the uprising out of bitterness or because they felt that their situations were hopeless, but because they were the sons of tenant peasants. Learning was a tactic aimed at negotiating their social status with their overlords. Armed rebellion was another collective tactic that served the same purpose.[78]

---

76 "Episcopus semel in anno presbyteros ordinat et quos ordinat, sunt coacti per annum in choro ipsius ecclesie Jauriensis sumptibus eorum, et quia dictus exponens est pauper et sumptibus suis per annum stare non posset, quare petit licentiam ut a vicinori episcopo [...] dictos ordines recipere possit." APA vol. 16, fol. 93r (1468, Iaurien. dioc.). On the *clericus chori*, see Mezey, *Deákság és Európa*, 175–81.

77 APA vol. 5, fol. 33r (1455, Wesprimien. dioc.).

78 For this interpretation of peasant rebellions, see Erdélyi, Introduction to *Armed Memory*, 23–24.

Conclusion

The Church had provided ambitious individuals with a channel of social mobility for several centuries. One of the most knowledgeable Hungarian medievalists observed that by the end of the Middle Ages, the division between nobles and magnates as well as between nobles and tenant peasants had become sharper.[79] With the increasing stratification of society and the closing of established channels of mobility, the traditional function of the Church became even more important in the early sixteenth century. Of course, it looks as though the Church attached increasingly strict conditions on entrance to the priesthood, not with regard to knowledge, but in financial terms. Poverty represented an increasing impediment for the large majority of those wanting to enter the clerical estate, as indicated by the appearance in the 1510s of those who attempted to attain priesthood via a detour through the mendicant orders. It is hard to determine whether the Church had begun to close its gates or if the pool of those with higher aspirations had begun to broaden lower down the social scale; young men of more meagre origins strove to gain entry into the privileged estate of the clergy, which they achieved through discovering the least expensive opportunities. The prospect of becoming priests, ex-friars or otherwise and earning a small Church benefice did not seem impossible for smart peasant boys. The most competent among them were able to become canons and bishops.[80] Even if, as others argue, only the brightest boys attained wealth and fame and the majority continued to live their lives under their birth status, an increasing number tried to change their lot, to which end even the poorest deemed and used learning as a viable route.[81]

---

79 Kubinyi, *Változások*, 8–13.

80 See more in chapter 4 on canons and bishops with peasant origins.

81 In late medieval England, as Philippa Maddern argues, social immobility remained the norm. Maddern, "Social Mobility." Even if this statement is true, it does not exclude a change at the level of individual and collective social behavior and ambitions.

CHAPTER 6

The Heyday of Popular Culture: The Shared Time and Space of Laity and Clergy

Defending Male Honor

Priest György, son of Máté Kalasta, was visiting one of his friends. After a time, György sent one of his relatives—perhaps his nephew—to purchase more wine at a nearby tavern, which was in fact a private house, where the owner opened a barrel and measured out wine for neighbors invited in by the sign over the door.[1] Such private houses became village centers of communal sociability; thus, it is not surprising that the errant boy encountered some chaplains and priests, colleagues of his kinsman, sitting at the table. The clergymen sent the boy back with the message that they were waiting for György to join them. György decided to accept the invitation, and prepared to take leave of his friend. However, before departing, his host warned him that the hour was late and he should therefore take some sort of weapon. Priest György went to the house at which his fellow clerics had congregated and knocked on the door. After the owner of the house let him in, one of the men, András Ács ("Carpenter"), picked a fight with him, asking drunkenly "Why did you knock so loudly?" The two men exchanged words before coming to blows. György had to ask for absolution in Rome for the death of Ács as a result of this fight a few days after the incident.[2]

The detailed description of the quarrel and subsequent brawl in the petition followed a recurrent script. Petitioners tended to claim that they had been provoked without cause and had responded in a calm and conciliatory manner, which had simply heightened the anger of the aggressor, who attacked without warning. Priest György, like several other petitioners, asserted that he had launched a counterattack only after it had become apparent that his life was in danger. Before that, as was typically claimed, the petitioner had left the scene of the confrontation, though later returning in the belief that tempers had calmed only to face a renewed and even more ferocious attack against which he had to defend himself. Priest György further excused himself by stating that

1 Rural taverns often operated in private houses elsewhere in Europe. See Krug-Richter, "Das Privathaus als Wirthshaus"; Kümin, *Drinking Matters*, 17–23.

2 APA vol. 2bis, fol. 136rv (1440, Agrien. dioc.).

 | DOI 10.1163/9789004361263_007

he had been armed only with a very small knife and had struck his opponent only once, inflicting a barely visible wound with a log he had randomly found in the room. Despite the modesty of petitioners unwillingly embroiled in self-defense, their opponents, described as "rogues," nevertheless died soon after the incidents.

This standard recounting of a tavern brawl seems improbable, almost ludicrous, to the modern reader. However, interpreted within their own context, the narratives reflect the craftiness of their authors, the petitioners themselves and their lawyers. In order to obtain papal clemency, these stories had to establish the legality of the petitioner's actions rather than offer a truthful account of relevant events. Remission stories were thus built upon fragments of fact that became stylized stories framed according to their own narrative logic and legal strategy. The narrative of priest György represents a very typical pardon letter recounting a standard sequence of events: drinking laced with insults that led to blows and a fatal injury. The supplicant was guilty of homicide committed in self-defense against an irrational adversary. György's storyline is exculpatory, acknowledging the crime, but at the same time justifying it. Explaining away violence was the essence of any good pardon tale. The mitigating factors in this case were also common denominators of the pleas for clemency: the petitioner adamantly sought peace, but his enemy was excessively aggressive, thus the supplicant had been "forced" to save his life by committing violence. Self-defense was the most common justification for the unintended killing of an adversary.

The stability of the script of the unfolding conflicts resulted, moreover, from the fact that in a society built upon interpersonal relations and orality, conflicts revolved around one central issue—personal honor.[3] Pardon requests often depicted events in which male honor was placed in jeopardy and had to be defended. The origin of conflicts narrated in requests of remission was a perceived insult or offensive gesture, such as András Ács's provocative question addressed to priest György. Another story reports that somebody from among a group of men drinking at a tavern threw a piece of roast goose onto the neighboring table. The petitioner described this act using the word *ignominiose* to indicate that the offender had "dishonored their name and good reputation," characterizing the entire incident as an insult (*iniuria*).[4] Actions interpreted as slander could not be left unaddressed: failure to act brought shame not only upon the target

3 On the late medieval culture of honor in which male self-worth was based on the opinion of others (i.e., *fama publica*), see, for example, Fenster and Smail, Introduction to *Fama*.

4 APA vol. 2bis, fol. 143rv (1440, Wesprimien. dioc.).

of ostensible insult, but upon all associated friends and family, such as those sitting at the table upon which the roast goose had landed. There was a fleeting chance of avoiding confrontation through an appeasing gesture or rapid departure; however, in the event that the parties made no attempt to forestall conflict or rejected conciliation, the ritual of challenge and response automatically began, pushing the situation inexorably in the direction of violent conflict.

György Kalasta initially reacted to András Ács's insulting remark with a conciliatory gesture: "Oh, my good man, sit down and keep calm." However, after a minute or two, when it became apparent that Ács had not listened to his advice, Kalasta lashed him gently with a whip that he had brought with him. Only then did tempers flare: Ács, as he struggled up from the floor, became so filled with anger and malice (*colore iracundie accensus et cum malo animo ductus*) that he lunged toward György Kalasta with a sword, injuring two fingers on his hand. This same sequence of events is repeated in the report of another tavern brawl. Four clerical students were sitting in a tavern, when one of them began to sing. An ill-humored noble sitting at an adjacent table was in no mood for song, so he went to the table where the students were amusing themselves and insulted them with offensive words (*nonnulla leadiosa*). After one student

FIGURE 7 *Calvary. Probably Central Panel of Tryptich, detail (fighters).*

responded to "insult with insult," weapons replaced words. Outside the tavern the noble and his armed men attacked the students, who defended themselves by shooting arrows at their assailants. Student Tamás Székely claimed in his petition that the arrows inflicted only a minor wound on one of the attackers, who died from his injury two weeks later as a result of his poor behavior and inadequate medical treatment.[5]

Pardon requests narrate interactions between laymen and clergymen shaped and informed by codes of male honor, and provide insight into how honor guided human action in scripted ways and served as a rhetorical tool applied strategically in emergencies.

Shared Spaces of Leisure

The story of György Kalasta reveals the presence of several clergymen in private homes and taverns in the course of evening social life in a small locality. The papal requests offer us an exceptionally colorful glimpse into the daily lives of the surprisingly large number of clergymen in the countryside. Reading these accounts, one gains the impression, as the present chapter will demonstrate, that the late medieval clergy and laity engaged in a lot of common activities in their everyday lives and on feast days.

In addition to the parish priest, chaplains, a schoolmaster and a dozen or so clerical students inhabited rural parsonages. János Bercop, the incumbent of St. Michael's church in the village of Edelény in northern Hungary, was forced to dismiss his chaplain because he regularly behaved aggressively after returning home from the tavern in the middle of the night.[6] Smaller groups of priests and clerics are also depicted in public houses, inns and taverns, centers of leisure, trade and gossip. Late one night, Márton Nagy and a fellow chaplain entered a public house, where they met two other priests.[7] The clerics János and Lőrinc Chekme, and at least three or four companions, had dinner together at the house of Mihály Certor at a village in the south.[8] István Kis and some fellow students encountered parish priest Ambrus on the road as they were on their way home after eating dinner at the local public house. Ambrus, apparently accustomed to taking his dinner in the company of others,

5 APA vol. 70, fol. 315v–16r (1523, Quinqueecclesien. dioc.).

6 APA vol. 13, fol. 375v–76r (1464, Strigonien. archdioc., Szepes County).

7 APA vol. 2bis, fol. 114r (1440, Agrien. dioc.).

8 APA vol. 53, fol. 316v–17r (1507, Bachien. dioc.).

asked the students to return to the tavern in order to spend the rest of the evening with him there.[9]

Priests and laymen sat comfortably together within the semi-public space of the tavern, eating, drinking and engaging in informal conversation. Parish priest Miklós Karomi sold his own wine at the parsonage in a small town in southern Hungary. Selling wine at a parsonage could not have been unusual, since late medieval diocesan synods prohibited lower clergy from conducting commerce in wine on the grounds that such activity was secular and therefore unsuitable for priests.[10] Priests and laymen did not share company with one another by accident. Local priests and clerics were nearly obligatory guests at dinners held in private houses, an everyday social practice.[11] A schoolmaster became angry at one of his students because the local judge had invited him, but not the schoolmaster, for dinner. A parish priest likewise invited guests to have dinner at his house, among them the student Benedek Marcali and another cleric from the nearby market town of Paks as well as several laypeople.[12]

The fact that the clergy and the laity spent their leisure time together is not surprising. All historical paradigms that attempt to comprehend and describe early modern social and cultural transitions are based on the premise that at the beginning of the era, in the fifteenth and early sixteenth centuries, both the nobility and clergy participated in popular culture. The relations between noblemen and peasants as well as between clergymen and peasants were based on personal contact, including common leisure, festive rites and

---

9 "Alias ipse postquam una cum quibusdam suis sociis refectionem sumpserat corporalem in quodam hospitio, iter versus domum suam faciens quendam Ambrosium presbyterem dicte diocesis obviam habuisset, et demum dictus Ambrosius oratorem et socios, ut ad dictum hospitium iterum redirent, quia collationem solvere volebat, rogaret. Orator et socii huiusmodi verbis ipsius Ambrosii confisi versus dictum hospitium unacum dicto Ambrosio ambulaverunt…." APA vol. 57, fol. 232v–33r (1512, Transylvanien. dioc.).

10 Parish priest Karomi: "Olim quidam Raciani in domo ipsius oratoris, in qua vinum vendebatur ad bibendum, collocassent." APA vol. 23, fol. 166r (1475, Bachien. dioc.). Solymosi, ed., *A veszprémi egyház*, 82–83.

11 Until the sixteenth and seventeenth centuries, people customarily ate two meals a day whether they were villagers or members of royal or aristocratic courts: the forenoon lunch (*prandium*) and the early evening dinner (*cena*). Cf. Benda, *Étkezési szokások*, 199–200; Kisbán, "Az étkezések." Terms used in the petitions to describe other common repasts—*collatio, refectio corporalis* and *convivium*—refer to casual meals that supplemented regular lunches and dinners.

12 APA vol. 68, fol. 233rv (1521, Zagrabien. dioc.); Ibid. vol. 23, fol. 182rv (1475, Wesprimien. dioc.).

activities.[13] The unanimous master narratives of change notwithstanding, in-depth analyses of the late-medieval scene seem to be lacking.[14] Some works of Norbert Schindler serve to partially fill this gap; the author provides the reader with a vivid depiction of some of the shared activities of noblemen and peasants.[15] With regard to clergymen, there is a prevailing consensus that the shared culture of the lower clergy and laity began to disintegrate in the latter part of the sixteenth century and that the process of separation climaxed in the eighteenth century. While this chronology is generally accepted, there is disagreement concerning the reasons for this phenomenon: was it the result of change in clerical education or in the social background of the new clergy that provided for the professionalization and the elite-consciousness of the clergies of the confessional era and turned them from local boys into outsiders?[16]

Carnival Every Day

The image that emerges from papal pardons about local priests and parishioners spending leisure time together in the East Central European countryside is particularly interesting because the recurring episodes suggest that feasting, drinking, revelry and jesting, frequently ending in violence, were everyday occurrences. These accounts include all the familiar elements of carnival festivities; thus, we might characterize the events collectively as having evoked an atmosphere of everyday carnival with an emphasis on the qualifier "everyday." Nearly an entire library's worth of theory and literature has been produced regarding the merrymaking that took place during the festive season before Lent. Although opinions diverge regarding the social function of this period of pre-Lenten feasting, the central themes of carnival celebrations are identified unequivocally regardless of time and place as related to food, sexuality

13 Here I think primarily of Elias's theory regarding the process of civilization, Gerhard Oestreich's theory of social control, the idea of the reform of popular culture promoted by Peter Burke and the confessionalization thesis pioneered by Wolfgang Reinhard and Heinz Schilling. See Burke, *Popular Culture*. Chia Hsia, *Social Discipline*, 8.

14 For an important case study, see Kurze, "Der niedere Klerus."

15 Schindler, "Nocturnal Disturbances."

16 On the relationship between the Protestant ministry and its parishioners, see: Gordon, "Preaching and the Reform of the Clergy"; and Goodale, "Die Pfarrer als Außenseiter." On the impact of post-Tridentine clerical education, see Quéniart, *Les hommes*, 63, 85; Forster, *The Counter-Reformation in the Villages*, 58–93; Kaufmann, "*The Clergy*." On the intellectual social origin of the early modern clergy, see Barnes, "The Social Transformation."

and violence. The mood and gestures of carnival can best be characterized by jesting, games, pranks, laughter, freedom and a world turned upside down.[17] I found the frequency and spontaneity with which the elements of the carnival spirit appeared in the course of everyday life in rural Hungary to be surprising.

Both adults and children engaged in jest and play, including forms of merry-making that can be clearly distinguished. Cleric Damián Szedeci claimed that "he and his friends played together every day," in an attempt to obtain papal pardon for the death of his childhood friend, who had died at the age of ten after being struck in the head during a game of what might today be called dodgeball, though played using rocks instead of a ball.[18] While the street served as the locus of children's play, the tavern was incontestably the main venue of revelry for men. Once, as priest Lőrinc Waygai sat eating and drinking peacefully, one of his companions playfully pulled him down from his chair onto the floor. Waygai admonished his companion, "Leave me alone! I am not in the mood for this game!" However, the latter did not heed this request, maintaining his grip around the priest's neck and pinning him down to signify his triumph.[19] Another time, at a tavern located in the Saxon Lands of Transylvania, a friend of Melchior Szászvárosi began to spatter water on him after he had eaten a good meal. In the course of the subsequent chase, Melchior's companion suffered the misfortune of falling into a pit.[20] Entertaining guests frequently entailed games in addition to meals. Péter, the parish priest of the village of Valkó, invited friends to lunch, after which a spontaneous tournament took place in his courtyard. As they prepared to hold an equestrian *mêlée*, one of the guests playfully fell on one of his servants, attempting to knock him out of the saddle. In response, the servant engaged in a similarly playful attack.[21]

Male prowess, which evidence suggests included an element of priestly identity, had to be proven through regular tests. Target practice, for example, served

17 Some of the most salient interpretations: Ladurie, *Le Carnaval;* Davis, "The Reasons of Misrule"; Schindler, "'Karneval"; Muir, "Carnival."

18 APA vol. 2, fol. 118v (1439, Chanadien. dioc.). The village of Szedec in Temes County.

19 "Ipse olim per aliquos ad collationem invitatus esset, quidam laicus ex quadam precepta malitia finxit ludem cum ipso exponente, de banco, super quo sedebat, ad terram traxit, qui exponens eidem laico dixit, dimittas me in pace, quia ludus ille michi non placet…." APA vol. 2, fol. 121v–22r (1439, Transylvanien. dioc.).

20 APA vol. 64, fol. 68v–69r (1519, Transylvanien. dioc.).

21 APA vol. 1, fol. 79v (1411, Quinqueecclesien. dioc.) The petitioning parish priest lost parts of two of his fingers during the incident. The chivalric tournament was one of the most common forms of entertainment in the courts of medieval Europe, the ritual parody of which was a popular folk game. See Kubinyi, *A királyi udvar élete*, 329; and Endrei and Zolnay, *Társasjáték és szórakozás*, 146, 150.

as competition, recreation and military training. Bow ownership was likely not universal among inhabitants of the southern borderlands, where clerics cited exposure to attack from the Turks as the reason for being armed.[22] Those who attempted to justify their violation of the prohibition against members of the clergy carrying weapons claimed that they had carried only a single arrow, if possible one made of wood rather than the more deadly metal.[23] Students consistently referred to their weapons as "tool[s] of game."[24] It seems that the favorite form of entertainment was target practice with bow and arrows. The schoolmaster in Lippa (Lipova, Romania) wanted to hold archery practice in the cemetery of the St. Stephen parish church, requesting that one of his students, Lukács, test a borrowed bow, using a cap placed a significant distance away as the target. Priest Máté and two students practiced their archery skills during their leisure time in Perlak, a market town in Zala County, using the window of Máté's house as a target. We are well informed of such customary leisure practices in relation to the above episodes because both came to an unfortunate end when arrows ricocheted from the targets and inflicted mortal wounds upon students who were observing the practice.[25] In another incident, Priest György Palicsnai and his companions were holding a competition on the outskirts of a village in Slavonia to see who could shoot an arrow the farthest. This contest also ended in catastrophe when a wayward arrow became lodged in the throat of a peasant who had just happened to be passing down a nearby road in an oxcart.[26]

Not only nobles carried swords as weapons and toys. Priest György Buti was returning home from the market in the company of village parishioners. "Coming to a field, they drew their swords and began to duel for amusement in the course of their playful competition," but one of the participants accidently

22 "Propter metum turcorum horthodoxorum fidei inimicorum tunc illas partes invadentium prout et omnes alii tam clerici quam laici continue armatus pro sui defensione et sagitas penes se etiam portando extiterunt." APA vol. 2bis, fol. 311v (Priest György Palicsnai; 1442, Zagrabien. dioc.).

23 "Ipse in oppido Kurland, Collocensis diocesis, in scolis moram traheret et arcum quendam cum unica sagita haberet, quem exercitii causa, ut sit in partibus illis, portaverat." (APA vol. 8, fol. 210v–11r, 1460, Colonien. dioc.).

24 "Se defendendo arcu seu arcibus, quibus muniti recreationis causa erant, in dictos satellitos seu soldates sagitas traxerant, vulnerando…." APA vol. 112, fol. 211rv–12r (1545, Zagrabien. dioc.).

25 APA vol. 66, fol. 45rv (1520, Chanadien. dioc.) Lippa was a town in the possession of a secular landlord in Arad county; Ibid., vol. 68, fol. 235v–36r (Mihály Ivánci, *scolaris*, 1521, Zagrabien. dioc.).

26 APA vol. 2bis, fol. 311v (1442, Zagrabien. dioc.).

received a serious head injury.[27] Buti interestingly made no attempt to excuse the fact that he had been armed with a sword in the manner of a layman and that he had participated in a spontaneous test of swordsmanship.

Shared Practices

The case of Priest György is interesting because it suggests that collective trips to the market were an established social practice that served both as a means of making a living as well as a form of entertainment. Roadside inns were full of guests during weekly markets and annual fairs. Benedek Szakályi and a fellow cleric named András were on their way from their village to a market at a nearby town when they met a friend named Lőrinc, who invited them to refresh themselves at a public house. After continuing toward the market town, András realized that he had forgotten his walking stick at the tavern, but encountered trouble when he returned for it.[28]

Conflict and disorder tended to develop when and where many people were assembled. Those who were lucky encountered friends at such places, though it was easy to encounter enemies as well.[29] The nobles who convened

27 "Ipse de foro cuiusdam ville cum nonnullis aliis laicis hominibus tamen honestis ad domum redierat in campis iidem laici iocose et solatiose inter se cum eodem exponente cum gladiis nudis dimicare interceperunt et sic dimicantibus sive potius ludentibus unus dictorum laicorum per alterum in capite modicum tetigit et vulneravit, non tamen voluntarie sed inadvertenter." APA vol. 46, fol. 337v–38r (1498, Wesprimien. dioc.).

28 APA vol. 46, fol. 270v–71r (1498, Quinqueecclesien. dioc.). The village of Szakály situated in Tolna County. More cases with regard to going to the market: "Cum ipse olim in quodam foro certo bona emisset et illa ad domum sua defferret, quidem laicus in eius societate se posuit" (ibid., vol. 17, fol. 210v–11r, 1469, Bachien. dioc.); "Alias non sui culpa veniens ex nundinis ville Kezeth Albensis diocesis quibusdam latronibus in via obviavit…." (ibid., vol. 28, fol. 154r, 1479, Waradien. dioc., cleric Péter Varga); and "Cum alias per opidum de Simeg […] ubi nondine tunc temporis vigebant inter ambulandum a nonnullis laicis aggressus…." (ASV Arm. XXXII, vol. 61, fol. 719r, 1522, Wesprimien. dioc., Péter Szűcs ["Furrier"], parish priest in the village of Görbő).

29 Ambrus, the parish priest in the village of Béd, went to visit his relatives in the village of *Pataij*, where he met his friend Péter Földvári, who invited him to his home. ("Ipsum exponentem, qui sibi amicitia coniunctus est, a casu reperisset, eundem ad faciendum collationem in domo, in qua ipse plebanus hospitabatur, duxit.") Afterwards, Ambrus took a room at an inn, where he met a peasant who turned out to be an old adversary and therefore beat him "for no reason." ("Quidem rusticus me maxime verberavit et dubito per eum amplius verberari, rogo te, ut fratrem meum voces et provideatis, ut saluus hinc exire possim.") APA vol. 47, fol. 299rv (1499, Quinqueecclesien. dioc.).

at the 1486 National Diet evidently realized that passions tended to flare out of control more easily when people came together; therefore, they passed a law intended to prevent brawls at taverns and markets. The nobles decided that the best way to prevent violent confrontations would be to prohibit carrying weapons at these locations. The legislation stipulated that when people left their quarters with the intent of drinking spirits and engaging in commerce, they should leave their weapons at their lodgings.[30] However, nobody could have seriously expected people to travel to markets and fairs without weapons to defend themselves from brigands who targeted people on their way to such events; therefore, weapons were usually left in front of buildings, since not even those on their way to religious processions could risk traveling without them.[31]

Public processions connected to Church feasts were a particularly common sight on the streets of towns and villages during the late medieval period. People marched, sang and carried religious symbols.[32] In cities, processions usually took place in central squares and streets, though in villages they often wended their way out onto country roads. Highwaymen regarded participants of crowded processions as well as large groups of pilgrims traveling to distant shrines to be easy prey; however, bandits occasionally encountered clerical students among the faithful who not only possessed strong singing voices, but great physical strength and fighting spirit as well.[33] Therefore, not only rogues who had robbed pilgrims asked for absolution from the Apostolic Penitentiary, but also priests and laymen who had committed murder defending themselves and fellow pilgrims. Lay and clerical pilgrims alike claimed, in their remission requests, that they had accidentally killed highwaymen while trying to ward

---

30 DRMH, vol. 3, anno 1486/paragraph 66.

31 "Armis muniti ad huiusmodi hospitium similiter redierunt, dicta arma prope et extra domum huiusmodi dimittentes dictum hospitium animo bibendi, ut dicebant, vinum petentes, intrarunt." APA vol. 70, fol. 295rv (1523, Wesprimien. dioc.).

32 On Corpus Christi processions in Hungary, see Pásztor, *A magyarság vallásos élete* 26–27. On popular practices connected to official processions, see Dömötör, *Naptári ünnepek*, 202–6. For an interpretation of the procession as a political ritual, see Trexler, *Public Life*, 191–94.

33 Student Imre offered an account of the armed attack launched against a procession headed toward a nearby parish church (APA vol. 9, fol. 230v–31r, 1461, Zagrabien. dioc.). Another incident was recalled by the schoolmaster János Rudabányai, who was on his way home from a procession with his students when they came into conflict with a peasant who was driving his wagon down the road (ibid., vol. 72, fol. 318v–19r, 1524, Agrien. dioc.).

them off with swords and rocks.[34] The pilgrim's staff often came in handy as a bludgeon.[35]

Groups of priests and laymen traveled distances of several kilometers not only to attend markets, processions and shrines, but sometimes to obtain wine as well. Such wine tours served not only to revitalize thirsty travelers, but also to acquire available wine reserves of a given village and as a form of communal entertainment. Reverend János Szalatnoki traveled from the Slavonian village of Vidóc with a large group of parishioners to a neighboring settlement to procure some wine. On their way home, one of the inebriated parishioners began to strike the parish priest with a stick just for fun, which the latter playfully attempted to parry with his knife. According to Szalatnoki, this little game ended in double misfortune: first, the parishioner suffered an accidental wound to his knee; secondly, his knee became contaminated after a dog bit it, causing an infection that resulted in his death.[36]

Public executions and rituals of public torture and punishment such as placing offenders in the stocks and the pillory provided people with regular occasions to interrupt work and participate.[37] Authorities intended these carefully orchestrated theatrical scenes to serve as means of deterrence and discipline,

---

34 Szilveszter Balog forced pilgrims on their way to Rome to hand over three ducats. (APA vol. 18, fol. 149r, 1470, Waradien. dioc.). A layman killed his attacker in self-defense during a pilgrimage (ibid., vol. 3, fol. 167r, 1450, Transylvanien. dioc). Six priests asked for absolution for having killed some rogues who attacked them in German regions on their way to Rome Ibid., vol. 2bis, fol. 319v (1442, Zagrabien., Quinqueecclesien., and Wesprimien. dioc.).

35 "Quodam clavo, quem baculo secum more peregrini gerebat, accepto eundem Michaelem unico ictu percussit et vulneravit." (APA vol. 81, fol. 608v–9v, 1533, Priest Ambrus, chaplain in the diocese of Zagreb).

36 "olim quidam laici dicti exponentis parrochiani, quia in dicta parrochia tunc vinum non reperiebatur, ut biberent, velint causa recreationis et solatii ad quandam villam Zopia nuncupatum ire, prefatum exponentem, ut cum eis iret, rogarunt et postulaverunt, et cum in eandem villam venirent, quidam Stephanus laicus dicti exponenti notus et amicus quasi ebrius et vino plenus ad eundem exponentem iocose et solatiose accessit et cum quodam remo, quem secum habebat, dictum exponentem iocosis ictibus invadens, exponens vero volens se etiam iocose defendere quendam cultellum longum, quem tunc penes se gestabat, ictibus dicti laici eius amici et benivolentis iocose obviare conatus est." APA vol. 2bis, fol. 189v–90r (1441).

37 During his days as a student, Priest Benedek went with his schoolmaster to watch the rogues who had robbed the latter be broken on the wheel. APA vol. 3, fol. 122v (1450, Quinqueecclesien. dioc.). Máté Váci happened upon a scene of public torture as he strolled across the main square of the town of Debrecen: "Postquam alias in oppido Debrecen dicte diocesis quidam laicus propter sua demerita in platea ipsius oppidi

though they did not mind if they provided the spectators with an opportunity to release their passions as well. Hurling stones and insults at the culprits implied that they identified with the punishment and the authorities.[38] Public execution, however, not only served to establish norms, but also made it possible for spectators to become active participants. Cleric Antal Kis of Szécsény and other spectators who had gathered to observe the execution of two thieves assumed an important role in the communal ritual of manorial court justice. One of the thieves attempted to escape as he was being transported toward the gallows. Antal, along with the landowner he served, János Ebecki and other spectators, some on horseback, pursued the condemned man who, after this brief interlude, met with his prescribed fate at the end of a hangman's rope.[39]

Schedules and activities connected to work and leisure were not distinguished or separated from one another in an urban milieu, as recorded by historians; however, according to Peter Burke's dual model explaining the reform of popular culture, this increasingly violated the tastes and interests of the educated elite.[40] In the seventeenth century, members of the elite made a vigorous effort to restrain immoderacy by trying to bring order to the prevailing chaos to increase their own sense of security. In order to achieve this, landowners and urban magistrates attempted to divide the schedules of their subjects into distinct segments, separating time spent working from hours of amusement, and reducing the latter. In order to ensure that nighttime hours would be spent relaxing and sleeping, authorities limited the opening hours of public houses and established evening curfews. Notwithstanding the disparities in the chronology of such changes and the motives that impelled them, one can state with certainty that the powerful endeavored to parsimoniously structure the lives of their subjects, imposing greater discipline in terms of working hours and restricting the amount of time spent at profligate leisure activities.[41] Our scattered data regarding the everyday lives of rural priests, students and villagers assumes a unique meaning and significance in light of the historiographical discourse regarding the process of discipline.[42] This data illuminates

publice tormentis sive questionibus subiceretur et orator inibi casualiter pertransiret." APA vol. 66, fol. 46rv (1520, Agrien. dioc.).

38 For such an interpretation of the social function of public executions, see Dülmen, *Theatre of Horror*, 127–39.

39 APA vol. 14, fol. 116rv (1466, Strigonien. archdioc.). Szécsény is in Nógrád County, where the Ebecki family owned considerable estates.

40 Burke, *Popular Culture*, 289–334.

41 Thompson, "Time, Work-Discipline."

42 This does not mean that we do not encounter occasional prohibitions in the fifteenth and early sixteenth centuries. For the banning of dice and card games in the city of

the relatively "undisturbed" final period of a thriving popular culture of laughter and carnival in so far as we accept the proposition that "popular culture" existed in "untouched form" during certain periods.[43] This notion, accepted to this day, cannot be separated from the approach that contrasts modern societies with traditional communities and, in the course of the twentieth century, idealized the interpersonal relations that prevailed in the societies of the old world.[44]

Leisure and Crime in the Dark

It appears that in the age before disturbing the peace became a punishable offense, it was not the quiet of the night that was undisturbed, but public nocturnal sociability. Priests and laymen could be sitting together in taverns at dawn and be set upon by "their enemies." Priests, students and villagers returned home from public houses and social gatherings in private houses "at one o'clock in the morning" and "four o'clock in the morning."[45] "Peace disturbers" changed little over the centuries, consisting primarily of patrons of public houses and taverns and students seeking fun and entertainment at night.[46] Students frequently roved from one tavern to another in the course of an evening with ample opportunity to play pranks. Priest Dénes, who would later

---

Sopron during the Late Middle Ages, see Házi, *Sopron*, 322–23. However, such measures remained isolated episodes during this period and had not yet become part of a continual and coordinated campaign.

43 For classic descriptions of an original folk or popular culture, see the seminal works of the Italian microhistorian Carlo Ginzburg (*The Cheese and the Worms*) and the Russian literary critic Mikhail Bakhtin (*Rabelais and his World*) from the 1960–70s.

44 For over a hundred years, the prevalent notion within the social sciences of impersonal, contract-based "capitalist societies" standing in opposition to collective, confidence-based "feudal communities" has defined our image of society to a significant degree. Ferdinand Tönnies has made a distinction between society and community based on this concept. See Tönnies, *Gemeinschaft*.

45 For example, "Ipse certa hora prima noctis voluisset versus domum habitationis transire, quidam laici, quos tunc dictus exponens penitus ignorabat, ipsum gladiis invaserunt." APA vol. 22, fol. 183v, the cleric Balázs Majtényi (1474, Transylvanien. dioc.).

46 Cleric Lukács Raszinjai and his friends were suddenly attacked while returning home from an evening of revelry, resulting in one death and one injury. APA vol. 8, fol. 223v–24r, 1460 (Zagrabien. dioc.). Raszinja is a market town in Slavonia, Kőrös County. Students from Zagreb were on their way home from dinner when they encountered some drunken soldiers, an encounter that claimed a life. Ibid., vol. 112, fol. 211rv–12r, 1545.

become a rural parish incumbent and rose to occupy a place in the middle clergy as a canon, had to account for the theft of fruit he had committed during his student years.[47] The ransacking of private houses as an act of vengeance unsurprisingly occurred most frequently under the cover of darkness, and nighttime hours also provided a prime opportunity to avenge insults by surprising the enemy in his bed.[48] Priest Dénes attacked cleric Mátyás Mindszenti with a big knife as the latter slept at four o'clock in the morning "due to the anger that he had long harbored against him." Mátyás demanded, to no avail, that Dénes allow him to resume his slumber. The drunken priest attacked him with even greater fury and swore that he would kill him before the night was over. Coming to his senses, Mátyás grabbed a knife in order to save his own life and stabbed his foe in the calf. Dénes sought to mitigate his crime in his pardon request by citing the routine argument that Mátyás' death had not been the result of the wound he had inflicted, but of the priest's relentless and unreasonable character, traits manifested in his refusal to heed orders from his physician not to drink alcohol, frolic about and spend time at the baths.[49]

Nighttime recreation and crime were closely connected: carousers either turned against each other after a time or fell victim to thieves and bandits as they moved about in the dark. Such nocturnal attacks have allowed us occasional glimpses into the most common forms of popular entertainment. If possible, people traveled in groups and carried arms and a source of light in order to defend themselves. György Steflin, for example, carried a burning torch in order to illuminate the road as he and some of his fellow students returned home from dinner at the house of a burgher of Zagreb. Gyögy emphasized this fact in his pardon story in order to prove that he had held a torch in his hand rather than a weapon and therefore could not have been culpable for the death of a drunken soldier who had assaulted them.[50]

47 "Quadam nocte cum quibusdam suis sociis in quendam ortum pro colligendis et furendis fructibus dicti orti armatus intrasset." APA vol. 2bis, fol. 67r, 1439 (Strigonien. archdioc.). The former thief later apprehended a thief: as parish priest in Galambok, Priest Dénes instigated the execution of a church burglar. Ibid., vol. 2bis, fol. 66rv and Lukcsics, *XV. századi pápák oklevelei*, 2, no. 311 (1433).

48 Attack "tempore nocturno" on the house of Priest György Stenzi (ibid., vol. 2bis, fol 105rv–6r, 1439, Agrien. dioc.).

49 APA vol. 1, fol. 82v (1411, Bachien. dioc.). One night two laymen attacked the house of Gergely Enyedi, canon in Esztergom, to avenge an insult that one of them had suffered at the hands of his servant as they drank wine together (ibid., vol. 3, fol. 59v–60r, 1449).

50 APA vol. 112, fol. 211rv–12r (1545). Torches were used to illuminate the king's route as he returned to Buda on horseback from his hunting grounds in Nyék. Fraknói, "II. Lajos," 125, 146, 148, 159, etc.

Some cultural historical studies argue that medieval and early modern people were terrified of the night;[51] however, such collective anxiety seems unlikely in light of the animated nightlife and constant nocturnal comings and goings described in the petitions to Rome, and may rather be the projection of fears of modern people accustomed to street lighting. People in past centuries carried torches not because they were frightened of the dark, but because they needed to identify approaching strangers. One night, Demeter Jakószerdahelyi heard the sound of rocks striking the walls of the school. When he went out with his companions to investigate, they found nobody. However, after the noise resumed, they fetched their bows and went back outside. The armed group "noticed two people whom they could not identify in the dark." Demeter shot one of them in the heart with an arrow; however, it turned out that the victim had not been up to any mischief.[52] Strangers were often thought to be enemies when encountered in the dark of night. As was the case with the students from Slavonia, people tended to act in unrestrained self-defense when attacking unrecognized acquaintances or strangers in the dark. Péter Nagy of Tamanya was serving as the schoolmaster in a village in southern Hungary when, according to his petition, he heard noises outside his house as he was preparing to go to sleep. Thinking that a thief might be lurking in the dark, he seized his sword, stepped outside and shouted, "Who's there?" After receiving no reply and seeing nobody, Péter proceeded toward a corner to relieve himself. However, on the way he stumbled upon someone, who replied defiantly to his request to identify himself: "You'll soon see and feel it too!" The two men began a scuffle that ended in the death of the prowler.[53] People were accustomed to knowing almost everybody in their immediate environment, thus strangers represented an inherent threat to which they often responded with violence justified as self-defense.

51 Delumeau, *Angst im Abendland*, 125–39; and Muchembled, *Popular Culture*, 25, 85–86.

52 APA vol. 2bis, fol. 405v–6r (1443, Zagrabien. dioc.).

53 "Cum ipse olim magister scolarium in loco quodam fuisset, et quadam nocte se ad lectum dormiendum posuisset [...] quosdam audivit rumores credens furem ibidem esse gladium suum in manibus suis arripuit et domum exivit clamando quis ibi est, nullum vidit vel audivit, volens facere opus nature se declinavit versus unum angulum, ubi quendam laicum stare et austheltare invenit, cui dixit, quis es, qui respondit, statim videbis et sentries ...." APA vol. 16, fol. 139r (1468, Bachien. dioc.) The village of Tamanya in Bács County is located in present day Serbia in the territory of Bačka Palanka.

Festivities and Violence

In addition to their regular nighttime recreations, feast days were also regarded as prime occasions for engaging in "undisturbed" amusement. We of course encounter sporadic instances in which Church or urban authorities prohibited certain popular festivities; however, only in the seventeenth century did they begin to organize campaigns to suppress mass festivities, which they considered to be pagan and extravagant hotbeds of sin and all genres of vice, including drunkenness, fornication and violence.[54] Clergy in the fifteenth and early sixteenth centuries had not yet begun to object to popular games and entertainment connected to religious feasts and, in fact, participated enthusiastically in them. Priest Antal Horvát ("Croatian"), for example, described in detail how he took part in the Europe-wide customary bonfire lighting near Modrus (Modruš, Croatia) as part of the feast on St. John's Eve, or Midsummer.[55] Antal wrote that villagers had gathered at the sound of thunder, which he, himself, had helped to produce by attempting to load some kind of small weapon (*scopetum*), resulting in an accident. It is impossible to determine whether this weapon was actually some sort of pyrotechnical device, like the fireworks used to celebrate the same feast in Florence, or a loaded weapon used to fire celebratory shots.[56] According to historical ethnographers and anthropologists, the popular celebration of the feast of St. John in Hungary usually entailed lighting a bonfire over which people jumped and around which they engaged in various activities ranging from spinning yarn to amorous games.[57]

Priest Antal's description of the celebration is even more interesting: "The eve of the birth of St. John the Baptist, the night when it is customary to light a fire for common and public joy and entertainment in honor of the saint." [58] The Croatian priest thus appears to have found nothing wrong with the fact

54 On the methods of social disciplining in Hungary, particularly those of the Reformed Church in Transylvania, see Kiss, "Református egyházfegyelmi iratok." The process of prohibiting and imposing discipline on popular games and entertainment is well reflected in the church visitations of Reformed Dean István Csulyak of Miskolcz to locations in northeastern Hungary between 1625 and 1645. In this regard, see recently Péter, *Házasság*, 96–97.

55 APA vol. 81, fol. 1025rv (1533, Modrusien. dioc.).

56 On the fireworks shot off in Florence in honor of St. John the Baptist, see Trexler, "The Feast of St. John." For a description of the custom practiced throughout Europe of setting celebratory bonfires, see Chartier, "Phantasie und Disziplin," 160–61.

57 Dömötör, *Naptári ünnepek*, 140–47.

58 APA vol. 81, fol. 1025rv.

that villagers spent St. John's Eve joyfully amusing themselves in preparation for the following day's feast, whereas the Church theoretically required that they fast. Priest Antal was undoubtedly not the only ecclesiastic who joined the popular festivities; thus, the prescribed vigil of fasting was transformed into a joyful festival.

What would have stopped people from engaging in revelry on such occasions? The fusion of the sacred and profane and the intimate relationship with saints, which over time became regarded as improper and pagan, had not yet begun to bother the learned and the powerful.[59] In the middle of the fifteenth century, Vince Szilasi, bishop of Vác, organized a wrestling competition at his palace on the occasion of an official religious feast in order to entertain the noblemen he had invited to his table.[60] Upon finishing the funeral ceremonies, a simple village priest, Ambrus and his co-celebrating chaplains had no misgivings about attending a big village feast that lasted into the night at which he and the local faithful "celebrated in great abundance according to the custom of the region."[61] Such feasts appear to have been common, since several clerics remembered in their requests that, after celebrating mass or assisting in the celebration as auxiliary priests, they had spent the evening cheerfully eating and drinking as guests of parishioners.[62] The parish priest and his parishioners in a southern village beseeched the Virgin Mary during mass to protect them from the plague that was ravaging the countryside, and then had a big party. Priest Balázs and his relatives joined the festivities, though they went home early after politely asking fellow revelers for permission to do so.[63] Similarly, the Croatian priest István Zettini sat at the communal table to eat dinner with villagers following mass, though in this instance the latter refused to accept the cleric's request to be excused from subsequent gaming on the grounds that he

59 Burke, *Popular Culture*, 209–12, 215–16.

60 APA vol. 5, fol. 65v–66r (1455).

61 APA vol. 81, fol. 608v–9v (1533, Zagrabien. dioc.).

62 The cleric Balázs Izdenci was invited by the parish priest to assist with the patronal feast mass "Cum olim dedicatio ecclesie in quadam villa fuisset, et dictus accolitus propter hoc per quendam presbyterem plebanum dicte ecclesie ad serviendum in eadem ecclesia vocatus esset et finito officio divino dictus exponens per quosdam presbyteros et laicos ad collationem invitaretur faciendum." APA vol. 16, fol. 133r (1468, Zagrabien. dioc.).

63 "Postmodum vero durante pestilentia, cum predictus exponens cum fratribus suis missas ad honorem Beate Marie Virginis celebrare fecisset, et in fine dictarum missarum magnam convivium fecissent et ibi quamplures probi viri essent, sero facto prefatus exponens de omnium astantium licentia recessit et ad domum suam accessit." APA vol. 44, fol. 291rv–92r, (1495, Chanadien. dioc.)

had to celebrate early morning mass. The slumbering priest therefore had to be roused from his bed the following dawn.[64]

We cannot determine what kind of game—cards or dice, dancing or martial competitions—Priest István wished to forgo and the reason he was not really in the mood to revel with the villagers: was he really tired or did he consider the company to be beneath him? Due to the purpose and targeted audience of their stories, one should read the above accounts of Balázs and István with some skepticism. The above-mentioned bishop of Vác, who was of noble origin,[65] had not gone out among the villagers, though he had held a very profane entertainment in his courtyard, which had ended in the death of his participating retainer; the youth had made the mistake of overestimating his strength and had challenged four opponents to wrestle him simultaneously. The bishop therefore felt compelled to reassure the Roman clergy that "this respectable game is authorized and practiced throughout Hungary."[66] However, the clerical student Ferenc Cernichi did not attempt to make excuses for the fact that he had joined "frolicking or dancing and other games" that had taken place on the main square of the Croatian port town of Bakar. Ferenc's narrative reveals that he had participated in a men's martial dance. During the dance, one of Ferenc's friends dropped his sword, which the cleric picked up, though as a prankish gesture refused to return it. However, during the subsequent playful wrangle over the sword, a young boy who had wandered into the group of dancing men was accidentally stabbed in the neck, and Péter needed to obtain papal pardon for the boy's death.[67]

---

64 "Quod cum alias per certos villanos ad celebrandum eis missam ad certam villam conductus fuisset et cenam ab villanis recepisset, et deinde dormiendum in lecto se posuisset, quidem ex villanis post repletionem vini exponentem per capillos ex lecto ideo, quod cum eis ad ludere recusavit, extraxerunt, qui villanos causa dei, ut eum quietum permitterent attento, quod de mane eis missam esset dicturus rogavit, ipsi vero cum bene potati essent, exponentem per crines capere, trudere et percutere non cessarunt." APA vol. 30, fol. 188v–89r, 1481, Modrusien. dioc.)

65 Vince Szilasi, bishop of Vác between 1450 and 1475, was a learned humanist prelate, who earlier in his career served as public notary in the royal chancery and was employed as a diplomat in the service of János Hunyadi, governor of Hungary (1446–53).

66 "Olim in quadam sollepnitate pro sollatio et recreatione quorundam nobilium amicorum suorum et familiarium honestum ludum videlicet duos et duos invicem conluctari seu ad brachia ludere […], quisquis ludus in regno Vngarie esse communis honestus et usitatus." APA vol. 5, fol. 65v–66r (1455). On wrestling as a courtly and popular form of entertainment, see Endrei and Zolnay, *Társasjáték és szórakozás*, 128–29.

67 "Alias ipse recreationis causa in quadam dicti loci platea seu loco, ubi saltationes seu tripudia et alia jocosa fiebant et exercebantur, esset, et a quodam Martino Grizi eius amico seu cognato quidam pugio, quem a tergo deferebat, saltando seu volvendo evaginatus

Sacred and profane rituals, priests and laymen, adults and children—all of them existed comfortably alongside one another not only during the large-scale communal festivals that attended church feasts, but as part of family celebrations as well. Márton, the parish priest in Mecske, a tiny village inhabited by peasants in Baranya County, joined a wedding feast in a nearby village as an official guest. The parish priest remembered that as he paraded down the road on his way to the wedding as part of a large group of people, a young man had stopped him and asked if he could borrow his horse; he intended to ride it in the jumping contest which unmarried youth usually organized and for which purpose "they built hedgerows on the outskirts of the village according to the custom of the region." Priest Márton must have owned a particularly good horse, because everybody requested to use his mount in the jumping competition.[68] His story is interesting in several regards, reconfirming that people moved through the countryside in groups, highlighting the prestige connected to owning a good horse and revealing that the wedding ritual, which served the symbolic entry into adulthood, provided a good opportunity for unmarried youth to enter competitions based on dexterity and courage which prepared them for the manly roles they would play.[69]

---

humi cecidisset et orator illum non animo aliquem offendendi sublevasset et accepisset et postmodum plura verba iocosa cum dicto Martino pugionem petente habuisset et tandem dictus Martinus, ut dictum pugionem suum a dicto oratore illum dare iocose renuente auferret ambabus manibus eundem arripuisset et agiliter ab oratoris manibus extraxisset, accidit, quod quidem puer nomine Mathias retro dictum Martinum adfuit, quem idem Martinus pugionem prefatum, ut prefertur, extrahendo preter suam et oratoris mentem et intentionem, cum illum non viderent, ipso pugione in gutture seu collo uno ictu percussit et vulneravit." (APA vol. 117, fol. 456v–57rv, 1547, Modrusien. dioc.). On the more well-known war and sword dances of the early modern period, see Ortutay, ed., *Magyar Néprajzi Lexikon*, vol. 2, 91 and vol. 3, 74–75.

68 "Ipse alias ad quasdam nuptias invitatus fuisset et cuidam equo veloci insideret, dumque ad nuptias catervatim procederent quidam iuvenes, ut illius regionis consuetudo est, in ingressu ville quandam septem erexerant, quam concito gradu unusquisque iuvenis conscendere tum transilire moliebatur, dumque quidam iuvenis equum dicti exponentis vidisse velocem ad ipsam sepem transiliendi ab eodem exponente sibi ad sepem ipsam transiliendam expetiit, qui illico gratia amicitie eidem concessit, et dum predictus iuvenis spectaret in transiliendo, alter iuvenis superveniens etiam equi velocitatem cognoscens prescripto iuveni inquit, Carissime michi socie, cedere debes, volo siquidem, ut ego ipsum equum plebani conscendens sepem ipsam transilire debeam." The second rider, however, broke his neck after an unsuccessful jump. APA vol. 42, fol. 374rv, 1493, Quinqueecclesien. dioc.

69 On the equestrian competitions held in connection to the Pentecost festivities in May: Dömötör, *Naptári ünnepek*, 125–27.

Moving from the public spaces in which the conspicuous activities of young men predominated into private homes celebrating family feasts, we encounter women and elderly people. István Mészáros, who served as the rector of a school located in a gently sloping region of southern Transdanubia, was traveling the countryside collecting alms with his students when he found himself a guest at a wedding in the village of Újfalu. The students, one of whose relatives was presumably the host, were seated at the table of the peacefully celebrating group of guests, when a quarrel between "a disreputable woman" and an elderly person suddenly disrupted the cheerful banquet. At the unanimous request of the guests, Mészáros undertook the task of reconciling the disputants;[70] however, the role of peacemaker placed the schoolmaster in the middle of an armed skirmish that resulted in a fatality. The same thing happened in the Transylvanian village of Kaczafalva, where family members and their friends were "playfully" celebrating an engagement. Two women who had been invited to the event became involved in an altercation that spoiled the mood of the guests and the parents who had betrothed their daughter. The intervention of men to separate the women as they pulled one another's hair quickly produced a mass brawl.[71]

We have gained information about festive games and other customary forms of leisure and entertainment that ended in physical violence, and the resulting legal consequences; should we regard such violence as exceptional or common? Members of the elite, who approached popular festivities with increasing reservation, considered feasts to be prime occasions for fighting, violence and brutality. Similar perceptions must have prompted the Hungarian nobility to ban the carrying of weapons in taverns. At the same time, modern theories surrounding games and leisure maintain that popular feasts and games infused with a carnivalesque atmosphere performed important social functions. Temporary suspension of order, values and hierarchy, as the argument goes, might have served to challenge and reconfirm established social norms. The rites of disorder and violence ensued in a regulated and controlled manner and resulted in genuine turmoil only in exceptional instances.[72] This concept

70 APA vol. 62, fol. 49v–50r, 1517, Quinqueecclesien. dioc. There are several villages called Újfalu ("New Village") in both Baranya and Tolna Counties.

71 Reference in the account of the joy of the parents: "Ne in tanta letitia parentum aliquod sinistri eveniret." On time spent together in a playful manner: "Ad domum paternam predictam, in qua dicta sponsalia, ut prefertur, gratiose, jocose inter amicos fiebant." APA vol. 66, fol. 62v–63r, 1520.

72 For a functionalist approach to popular entertainment, see: Burke, *Popular Culture*, 199–204; and Davis, "Reasons of Misrule." On the control of violence, see Müller-Wirthmann, "Raufhändel. Gewalt und Ehre im Dorf."

of order amid chaos presumes the existence of social customs intended to prevent the escalation of conflict and violence previously described in this chapter. Apparently uninteresting, repetitive details in the narratives refer to the "built-in brakes" that inhibited violence. The customary intervention of conciliators served in this capacity and provided petitioners with an established crime-mitigating role they were able to use in their narratives in the hope of gaining papal pardon. The aforementioned schoolmaster who found himself at a wedding feast in the village of Újfalu claimed that his fellow guests had impelled him to "separate the adversaries and make peace." Student Benedek Marcali, acting upon orders from his parish priest, attempted to make peace between dinner guests gathered at the parsonage.[73] Many others intervened to prevent the fracas and the subsequent "bloodshed." The rector of the hospital in the market town of Csepreg, for example, interceded in a fight between young men in order to extricate his brother from the altercation.[74] The brother of the bride likewise tried to pacify brawling guests at the aforementioned betrothal in Kaczafalva: "For the sake of tranquility and lest some calamity occur in the midst of such great joy of the parents, he cordially attempted to calm Fülöp [the husband of one of the enraged women], though when he saw that kind words were getting nowhere with him, he threw him out of the house."[75] This story continued according to the established script, ending in a bloody free-for-all in front of the house.

Armed clashes did not take place inside public houses, taverns or private homes, but outside, due to the fact that when disagreements veered uncontrollably in the direction of physical confrontation, the challenging party routinely

---

73 "Ipse olim in domo cuiusdam plebani in convivio collocatus esset et quidam laici cum quodam Georgio de Paks clerico [...], quem percutere conabantur, rixam haberent, prefatus exponens iussu dicti plebani accedens, ut pacem inter eos imponeret...." APA vol. 23, fol. 182rv (1475, Wesprimien. dioc.).

74 "Alias certe iniurie et rixe inter quosdam iuvenes laicos dicti opidi exorte sive commote fuissent, quorum societati quidam Johannes Vadas eiusdem exponentis germanus adierat, dictus autem exponens dubitans propter huiusmodi rixas inter eosdem laicos motas ad maximum prolabari periculum in ipsorum laicorum detrimentum, ne ipsi invecem offenderentur, causa eos separandi et pacem inter eos ponendi, et non alias, se in medium ipsorum posuit...." APA vol. 45, fol. 317rv (1486, Iaurien. dioc.). Sebestyén was the rector of the St. Dorothea hospital in the Vas County market town Csepreg.

75 "Orator causa pacis et ne in tanta letitia parentum aliquod sinistri eveniret ipsum Philippum gratiose pacificare voluit, et cum videret nihil in eum proficere bonis verbis eundem extra domum conduxit." APA vol. 66, fol. 62v–63r.

went outside and waited for his adversary.[76] This is precisely what the aforementioned nobleman did when he become involved in an argument with four students.[77] Those who lacked the patience to wait for their foes simply dragged them outside.[78] However, those who followed the convention of waiting outdoors gained the opportunity of quickly recruiting allies, thus transforming personal conflicts into mass brawls. The custom of "going outside" or "calling outside" has also been observed in Bavaria, where they concluded that this practice was intended to comply with laws regarding the maintenance of household peace.[79] Leaving indoor venues in order to fight enabled combatants to avoid compounding the offense of physical assault with that of damage to private property. This custom also served as a means of preventing the eruption of violence, providing the challenged party with the possibility of simply remaining inside rather than going outside to skirmish with his adversary. If the person who pursued such a course of action was lucky, his foe did not break down the locked door to get back inside.[80]

Shared Concepts of Magic

The scenes of everyday village life and festivals depicted above suggest that clergymen and laymen lived together in close symbiosis. Using the dichotomy model that Peter Burke developed based on the theory of anthropologist Robert Redfield, we can state that clergy participated in popular culture. We have seen priests and clerics joining villagers on collective trips for wine and eating and drinking together in taverns as well as engaging side-by-side in

---

76 For example, "Deinde de dicta domo exiens prope ipsius portam, unde comune ipsi transitum habere debebant, cum quibusdam aliis suis sacellitibus armatis eos expectabat"—where the fatal confrontation finally did take place. APA vol. 53, fol. 316v–17r (1507, Bachien. dioc.).

77 "Nobilis ipse cum eius famulis hospitium exiens in ipsos scolares irruere cepit, propter quod unus ex dictis oratoris sociis vim vi repellendo et se necessarie defendendo cum aliter evadere non valeret, quendam arcum sagitta munita in alterum ex aggressoribus laxavit et unum vulnus non tamen letale sibi intulit"—revealing that the students also went outside to confront their challengers. APA vol. 70, fol. 315v–16r.

78 "Hoc videns dictus stipendiarius erripiens eum per brachium extra domum extraxit et venientes ad arma…." APA vol. 23, fol. 166r.

79 Dülmen, *Das Haus*, 12, 245.

80 During the fight that took place at the engagement banquet in Kaczafalva, the hosts did not go outside to join the fray, but locked themselves inside the house while friends and family of the bridegroom attempted to break down the door. APA vol. 66, fol. 62v–63r.

fisticuffs. Members of the clergy took part in games, playful sword fights and mock tournaments just as they participated in village festivities, weddings and martial dances. We have observed the temporal and spatial framework of their shared social practices, and now have the chance to gain exceptional insight into the thoughts of lesser priests regarding popular traditions connected to witches. Did the lower clergy share popular notions regarding witches and, if so, did they take part in related magical practices? Ethnography and historical anthropology regards the figure of the witch as one of the most conspicuous examples of interaction between learned and popular traditions. As a result of several decades of ethnographic research, it has become possible to separate the learned from the popular elements of the image of the witch, which enables us to orient ourselves with relative ease within the complex system of witchcraft over the coming pages.[81]

According to scholarly typology, a case that took place in Esztár, a tiny village in Bihar County, introduces us to popular witch beliefs at the beginning of the sixteenth century. The incident, involving the parish priest and an old woman known for her poisons, was related by Priest Pál in his petition to the pope:

> After they stole my brother's horse and they searched for it to no avail, they turned to an old poisoner (*vetula venefica*). The woman, after doing something in front of them underneath a shroud for a time at both his own house and his brother's, asked Pál to take her in a carriage to a place that she had specified where she would show them the horse. When they reached there, she set a fire and she melted wax generally used in sorcery in the fire. They both then felt that this was not permitted, but was some diabolical and prohibited craft, and as such heresy, so they passed the woman stripped naked through the fire with her face turned backward. After her skin became well scorched, they finally let her go. The woman whom had been burned somewhat in warning then quickly fled and has not been seen in the region ever since.[82]

The words of the village parish priest show that he shared the popular view that the sacred operated in the same way as the demonic. In other words, the practice of magic was perceived as either good or evil, helping or harming

81 On the typology of *maleficium* narratives and of witches in Central Europe, see Klaniczay, "Hungary: The Accusations and the Universe of Popular Magic," and Pócs, *Between the Living and the Dead.*

82 APA vol. 64. fol. 107v. (1519, Waradien. dioc.). In 1552 Esztár had a little more than a dozen peasant tenant plots under the authority of the Esztári noble family.

individuals and the community. By contrast, theologians devised the so-called diabolical witch belief that regarded all forms of sorcery as pacts with the devil.[83] The parish priest of Esztár, similarly to the villagers, saw the old woman as a seer, sorcerer and poisoner whose duties included, in addition to exposing thefts, treasure-hunting, fortune-telling and seeing the dead.[84]

A similar incident took place at another location in the Great Hungarian Plain, in the market town of Csanád. Here Márton, the parish priest, felt that he had got himself into trouble, because a woman, whom he considered to be his enemy, had come under communal suspicion of witchcraft. Similar to the case of the old woman of Esztár, the local peasants regarded Ilona Kardos as a poisoner, a viewpoint that the parish priest shared. Priest Márton was therefore very frightened of the suspected witch, who threatened both his reputation and his life. He therefore prohibited Ilona Kardos from going to his house, placing in his courtyard a wooden log with which the woman would be beaten if she dared to violate this command.[85]

Like the above village priests from the Great Hungarian Plain, a cleric student, Márton, from the diocese of Zagreb, also believed in the dual capacity of witches. Márton had become ill and concluded that a woman named Katalin, who openly admitted to being an herb specialist, had brought trouble upon him. Márton and his fellow villagers believed that she was the only person who could cure him by withdrawing the *maleficium*. In order to force her to do so, Márton accused the woman of sorcery before the local secular magistrates and had her placed under arrest. The image of Katalin outlined by the village priest is a familiar figure in the system of popular witchcraft. The woman was likely a traditional healer who had become engaged in some sort of "disturbance" in neighborly reciprocal relations, perhaps refusing to offer aid to Márton, and had thereby, in the eyes of the community, become a witch capable of harmful *maleficium*.[86] Although I could only find three cases of witchcraft, it

83 Klaniczay, "Hungary."

84 Pócs, *Between the Living and the Dead*, 121–22.

85 „Alias quondam Helena Cardos de Canadino, que suspecta de intosicatione erat et eundem oratorem odio prosequabatur non modico, postquam prefatus orator eam propter suspitionem huiusmodi quam pro conservatione vite et fame sue eidem Helene, ne ad eiusdem oratoris domum accederet, expresse prohibuerat, et ut ipsam Helenam saltem timore ab accessu huiusmodi abstineret, quendam baculum ligneum in curia seu claustro eiusdem domus ad terrorem dicte Helene posuerat." APA vol. 63. fol. 98v–99v (1518, Wesprimien. dioc.).

86 "Ipse alias a quadam Catherina muliere, ut declarative dicebat, facturaria fuisset, et propterea gravi egritudine detineretur, ex qua sanitatem recuperare non sperabat, intellecto per eum quod dicta Caterina eum facturaverat, eandem Catherinam per curiam

is nevertheless interesting that the priests involved all espoused beliefs about magic that formed part of the popular belief in witches and witchcraft.

Conclusion

In the course of my argument that the clergy took part in popular culture in the late fifteenth and early sixteenth centuries, we received a glimpse into the everyday lives and festive customs of villagers. Fields, streets, cemeteries, marketplaces, taverns and private homes served as venues for the described episodes. The priests who participated in popular culture were also part of the learned cultural tradition, which emerged not at the previously cited public locations, but from schools and universities. Whereas the public spaces of oral culture were open to all, educational institutions were accessible to only a small minority. In chapter 3 we saw that the level of learning of rural priests varied considerably, ranging from university degrees to practical skills needed to perform the liturgical duties of a priest. One can state conclusively, based on the dense network of village schools and the intense geographical mobility of clerical students, that many of the clergy had obtained formal education in a series of schools over a period of several years. Since we have learned in the present chapter that rural clergy lived in close coexistence with the laity, it follows that this schooled society of rural clerics and clergymen was able to effectively play the role of mediator between the learned and popular cultural traditions.[87] The shared free time and daily leisure practices of parishioners and their priests, described as an "everyday carnival," and their festive rituals, contained both joy and anger, laughter and violence. In the next chapter we will turn our attention to the conflicts inherent in their close coexistence. What might have triggered these lay-clerical conflicts and how did the parties negotiate and represent these disputes?

temporalem capi fecit et incarcerari ad effectum solum, quod illa compelleretur ad eliberandum eum ab eius egritudine." APA vol. 44. fol. 281rv (1495, Zagrabien. dioc.). The term *facturatio* does not arise during witch trials in Hungary, but appears exclusively in Italian, Venetian and Dalmatian sources. The term means healing or bewitching using herbs. The use of this term in Zagreb can be attributed to the Dalmatian influence, though it may also be a contrivance of the curial lawyer who drafted the final version of the petition.

87 Burke regards noblewomen and pedlars (or journeymen printers) as typical mediators between the two traditions. See Burke, *Popular Culture*, 28, 63.

CHAPTER 7

Contested Coexistence: Lay-Clerical Disputes and Their Settlement

Hermán, son of Márton, a layman from Slavonia, opened his petition to the pope in 1456 with the salutation "Most Holy Father!" His request, as usual, was composed in the third person, which reminds us of the mediating role of professional lawyers. Hermán was one of the several hundred priest killers from Hungary: "The beloved son of Your Holiness humbly relates that by diabolic inspirations he killed a priest and thus suffered excommunication. Therefore, he requests the Holy Father to absolve him from this sentence and the sin of killing a priest."[1] The rest of the story, to the historian's dismay, was reported orally before the curial judges who tested the credibility of petitioners.[2] During the period prior to the Protestant Reformation, between around 1450 and 1520, a total of 250 ordinary laypeople—peasants, petty nobles and burghers—requested papal absolution at the Apostolic Penitentiary for having killed a priest, while another 135 asked to be pardoned for having committed violence against clerics. Other papal offices, such as the Apostolic Datary and the Apostolic Chancery, also dealt with affairs involving violence, although their more prestigious services cost considerably more.[3]

Petitions also exist from violent clergymen who did not personally attend the papal court, but provided written explanations of their crimes. Such petitions provide the researcher with some consolation and more material for conflict analysis.[4] Ordinary clerics and priests, in fabricating stories they hoped

1 APA, vol. 5, fol. 174r (Zagrabien. dioc.).

2 It seems that laypeople requesting absolution for the killing of clerics had to appear personally at the curia, where their cases were further investigated. See the note which is inserted in an informal list of taxes (1455–58) to be paid for the letters of the Penitentiary: "Nota quod ista ultima absolutio [pro homicidio clericale] raro conceditur pro absentibus." Müller, "Die Gebühren," 240.

3 That which cost ten ducats at the Apostolic Chancery cost just four or five ducats at the Apostolic Penitentiary in spite of the "inflation" that occurred in the late fifteenth century. Laymen paid two ducats to obtain simple absolution for the murder of a cleric. The simplest pardon, which came in the form of a letter without a seal, cost five or six groschen (see also Introduction). Cf. Müller, "The Price of Papal Pardon," 457–81. In this chapter I will deal, with a few exceptions, with cases handled at the Penitentiary.

4 The majority of petitions requesting absolution for homicide involved lay-clerical conflicts: out of the 373 clerical narratives, the victims were clerics in just 39 cases.

 | DOI 10.1163/9789004361263_008

would bring about the forgiveness of their sins, translated the actual plots of local conflicts into the language and scenarios expected by the Roman center.[5] Such clerics and priests submitted 373 murder-related petitions, the majority of which contain accounts of their conflicts with laypeople.

These stories of lay-clerical conflicts are from the same period during which runaway friars without ecclesiastical benefices were irregularly ordained; however, this was not the only reason I found the large number of petitions regarding the murder of priests, in which the petitioner claimed innocence, to be interesting. These appeals for pardon reflect everyday conflicts between the lower clergy and the laity at a time when—partially as a result of the greater degree of social mobility that the mendicant friaries had provided—relations between priests and parishioners might have been undergoing change. We can presume that such change was taking place when we examine lay-clerical relations from the perspective of the impending Protestant Reformation, and adjust ourselves to the expectations of teleological historiography. It is possible, however, that clerical roles were merely being reinterpreted, for violence can represent not only conflict, but also interdependence.

By the minute reading of representations of lay-clerical conflicts, this chapter aims to furnish the reader with a better understanding of the relationship between ordinary parishioners and their priests in the decades preceding the Protestant Reformation. What kind of conflicting interests lurked behind the laconic and seemingly routine narrations of priest killings? It is generally argued that under the impact of the Protestant Reformation, lay-clerical relations underwent substantial transformation. In the Late Middle Ages, parishioners expected pastoral clergy to mediate between this world and the next by delivering the sacraments.[6] As a result of the new theology professed by the Protestant Churches of the confessional period, the Protestant clergy had lost their function as *sacerdos*: they did not mediate divine grace by performing rituals, but educated the laity from the pulpit. In theory, the Lutheran tenet of the priesthood of all believers eliminated the difference between the laity and clergy. The laity therefore turned to the clergy with a new set of expectations based on more secularized values: they considered local priests to be models, exemplary husbands and fathers as well as honest members of the community fulfilling their professional duties.[7]

Taking issue with the above argument on a general level, I reject the notion that social practice was primarily guided by abstract ideas that common

5 For more on this phenomenon, see Smail, *Consumption of Justice*, passim.

6 Swanson, "Before the Protestant Clergy."

7 Dixon and Schorn-Schütte, "The Protestant Clergy," with further literature listed.

people blindly followed. This is a broad brushstroke of a much more complex picture, but I suggest that it is fruitful to examine how the relationship between the laity and clergy played out in concrete situations rather than in terms of abstract principles. I will therefore explore contexts in which common people emerge as active agents. Scholars focusing on the social and cultural factors of early modern transformations rather than on religious tenets have reached opposing conclusions. They argue that early modern transitions implied the social and cultural disintegration of clergy and laity.[8] Therefore, it seems plausible that during the time of confessional rivalry it was not the laity's expectations that underwent major changes, but the practices of legitimation regarding rival clergies as well as the public representation of lay-clerical conflicts.

Before I demonstrate the ambivalent nature of relations between clergy and laity in the Late Middle Ages, I will first briefly describe the expectations of parishioners with regard to the sacred role of priests, then I will present the secular roles of the late medieval clergy.[9] This chapter will demonstrate that the disputes negotiated before the Apostolic Penitentiary between laypeople and local clergymen were typically rooted in their conflicting interests as neighbors rather than in their different social status.[10] Although pardon tales were officially designed to regulate vertical social relations, I will draw upon the historical record and try to show how laypeople—with their terse petitions—appropriated the complex scenario of pardoning in the process of resolving their local conflict negotiations. I will demonstrate how the papal tribunal was used by ordinary people and priests as a stage for negotiating local conflicts, where the innocence of the petitioning party was justified not by his or her actions, but by the emotions from which these actions stemmed.

---

8 For more detail regarding this thesis see Chapter 6 note 13.

9 The complexity of the position of parish priests between Church and laity was described in a contemporary satirical pamphlet, which stated that the parish priest had to put up with nine demons, including the ignorant peasant, the patron who regarded the parish benefice as his own property, the female cook who ruled over him, the sexton who betrayed him and the bishop who demanded taxes. Quoted by Bünz, "Thüringens Pfarrgeistlichkeit," 61–62.

10 The differences between priests and their parishioners were the sacred functions of the clergy and their judicial and feudal power. These could also generate conflicts in the event that priests and parishioners did not live up to one another's expectations. A few such cases appeared before the Roman office related to unpaid ecclesiastical taxes and their forcible collection as well as theft of church devotional objects and subsequent punishments.

Enmities and the Language of Emotions

Reading these narratives, I was initially shocked by the high level of self-consciousness and reflexivity among the actors. Sentences such as "in order to restore his reputation, he made expenses and initiated legal proceedings" suggest that petitioners were highly aware of what they were doing.[11] Priest Hypolite Rutz from the diocese of Mainz wrote that "his enemy delivered insulting words disparaging the entire clergy, which made him somewhat angry and he fought with words in order to defend his honor, but finally he could not restrain his temper and grabbed with a bowl with his right hand."[12] This gesture induced a fatal fight. His words illustrate the conscious choice of weaponry on the battlefield of honor. They also reflect the norm of self-restraint and the communicative nature of emotional behavior: a display of anger served to publicize enmity, while the "cooling" of emotions, expected and respected today, was counter-effective.[13] In other words, it seems that contemporaries were not as incapable of self-restraint as proponents of the civilizing process have advocated, but that emotions and their staging had different functions and values in late medieval society.[14]

These stories show that denunciations were not, as a rule, interpreted by contemporaries as being "more civilized" or "more rational" than acts of physical violence. Expressions such as *violenter spoliare* ("to plunder by force") and *violenter in causam trahere* ("to initiate a suit by force") reflect that violence and litigation were placed on an equal footing. Taking someone to court was not necessarily perceived as a more acceptable or friendlier tool of conflict negotiation, but as a process of social competition performed not by swords, but by a financially and psychically more burdensome "armory of legal expertise."[15] Such a perception is reflected in their language: they denoted their

11 "Ut famam suam recuperaret, expensam fecit et litem habuit": petition of Gál, son of Bálint Redolich, 1482. APA vol. 31, fol. 179r (Zagrabien. dioc.).

12 "Verba iniuriosa honori exponentis detractoria totum clerum vituperando explorasset, exponens aliquantulum commotus pro honoris defensione verbis impugnavit et se continere non valens quendam cantarum ibidem manu dextra apprehendit" (1491). RPG Online.

13 Riis and Woodhead, *A Sociology*, 186–87.

14 On the history of emotions (i.e., the meaning of emotions staged in public), see Rosenwein, Introduction to *Emotional Communities*. For a useful survey of the literature on violence, emotions and their interplay, see Susan Broomhall, ed., Introduction to *Violence and Emotions*.

15 Kagan, *Lawsuits*, 161.

actions in both domains with a vocabulary of enmity directed by emotion, hatred and love.[16]

In an effort to prove their innocence within the framework of canon law, lay-clerical conflicts tended to be represented as innocent folly, but hidden tensions are evident in "emotion talk."[17] György, a market town parish priest, related how he had once mocked and beaten one of his servants as they were on their way home one night. Instead of giving a reason for the insult, he cited drunkenness as an excuse for his foolish behavior. György describes the road brawl in which he killed the servant in self-defense, and casually mentions that a year earlier the servant had beaten his adopted father.[18] This last piece of information suggests that what was portrayed as an isolated spur-of-the-moment episode gone wrong was, in fact, a revenge killing. There is therefore good reason to suppose that physical clashes that claimed the lives of priests were episodes within protracted family feuds and neighborhood conflicts. This is less surprising in light of the fact that rural pastoral clergymen, as will be discussed below, were deeply rooted in local networks of families and friends. We learn only incidentally from the story of Miklós, son of Mátyás, that the priest Márton, who he killed, was, in fact, his brother.[19]

Generally speaking, supplicants tended to simplify complicated and messy family feuds in order to make them appear as isolated conflicts, typically self-contained tavern brawls and street fights. This was a strategy, applied also by petitioners for royal pardon, motivated by legal expectations: violence was remissible if committed in self-defense or in a fit of passion.[20] Tempers could be legitimately provoked by drunkenness or "hot anger." Such a pattern of emotion and action is inherent in the story of Gergely Pap ("Priest"), a priest from the village Orbányosfalva: "A layman called Demeter nurtured such a tremendous anger against him and his servant that he regularly threatened to kill them. One day Demeter came to his house and impudently killed his servant while he was absent."[21] Informed of the homicide, Gergely set off for

---

16 On the discussion of emotions in juristic literature, the product of the effort to regulate enmities, see Bartlett, "*Mortal Enmities.*"

17 On the role of emotions and their representation in neighborhood conflict and litigation, see Smail, *Consumption of Justice*. "Emotion talk" is his term (e.g., 134).

18 MREV vol. 3, 310–11 (1489).

19 "Olim quendam Martinum presbyterem fratrem carnalem diabolo instigante interfecit." APA vol. 14, fol. 205r (1466, Transylvanien. dioc.).

20 Carroll, Introduction to *Cultures of Violence*, esp. 21; Arnade and Prevenier, *Honor*, 27–35, 52–67.

21 "Gregorius ... Pap presbyter ville Vrbanusfalua Wesprimiensis diocesis exponit, quod cum alias quondam Demetrius laicus Jauriensis diocesis in ipsum oratorem et quendam eius

home accompanied by friends, in such an upset state of mind that, when he ran into Demeter, he was "overcome by anger" (*furore repletus*) and started to chase the priest with a sword and an axe. Gergely's life was saved with the help of his friends, who beat Demeter *hungarico more* ("in the manner of the Hungarians") so severely that he died six weeks later. In this story, as in several others, the enmity lurking beneath the surface of events becomes apparent as the narrator describes his foe as having acted out of pre-determined malevolence (*ex preconcepta/precogitata malitia et animo malivolo* or *malo proposito*). Hatred (*odium*) was the other key word used to denote long-standing tensions between individuals or families.[22] From hatred followed acts of premeditated violence, which were officially outlawed. Gergely legitimized his counter-reactions as having been motivated by anger—partly from a sudden outburst of rage and partly from a just response to the injuries he had suffered. The quality and legitimacy of emotions justified actions. Portraying revenge killings as self-contained incidents was a legal strategy on the part of both lay and clerical petitioners, one which enhanced the plausibility of committing spontaneous, unintentional violence rather than an unpardonable, intentional murder.

Clergymen as the Mediators of the Sacred

Traditional scholarly narratives examining the antecedents and causes of the Reformation identified with the humanist criticisms of the Church. Seen from this perspective, motives for violent actions against priests appeared self-evident. A history of the Reformation in Hungary published in 1921 referred to the "widespread abuses" of the late medieval Church and the "moral decline of the clergy" that "engendered and sustained discontent." The author concludes: "In general, immorality of every kind had become prevalent among them [...]. This slowly subjected the entire body to the contempt of the people, while monks in particular were the objects of public scorn and hatred."[23] This

famulum maximum odium concepisset et in dies eis mortem minaretur et die quadam, quod prefatus idem Demetrius ad dicti oratoris domum accesserit ... et certas insolentias faciebat, quod unum ex ipsius oratoris famulum interfecerat, eidem oratori in domo cuiusdam amici tunc existenti relatum fuisset." APA vol. 70, fols 95v–96r (1522). Orbányosfalva is a village in Zala County, in Transdanubia.

22 See, for example, APA, vol. 2, fol. 130v; vol. 2, fols 20v–1r; vol. 2bis, fols 105rv–6r; vol. 117, fols 700v–702r.

23 Zoványi, *A reformáczió Magyarországon*, 6, 10, 12.

normative argument maintains that the medieval Church was in a state of crisis and that the immoral acts of the clergy had turned the faithful against it.

More recent interpretations of the Reformation agree, regardless of their specific subject and region of concentration, that late medieval Europeans tended to turn toward the Church rather than away from it.[24] Laypeople were familiar with Christian doctrine, practices and institutions and made use of them. The chantries and confraternities endowed by lay society required the services of an increasingly large number of parochial clergymen. These lay endowments produced minimal livelihoods for auxiliary priests, attractive for ambitious peasant boys. This expanding layer of lesser clergy, with little or no benefice, formed a considerable proportion of the petitioners to the Penitentiary in the century before the Reformation.[25]

Parishioners were, of course, not familiar with the precise text of the centuries-old synodal decree that provided clerics with increasing protection against physical assault.[26] They likely did not read theological treatises regarding the notion of the two distinct societal bodies, clerical and temporal, nor did they get the chance to observe the rite of ordination that symbolically furnished priests with their special status through anointing their hands and presenting the host and the chalice.[27] I nevertheless believe that laypeople regarded the special function and status of priests to be self-evident. Those who petitioned the Apostolic Penitentiary perceived this special status in financial terms as well: the life of a clergyman was worth twice as much as that of a layman.[28] Only priests endowed with special *facultas* via ordination were authorized to perform religious rites that parishioners either ordered from them or in which they participated. They paid for the celebration of masses aimed at abbreviating the amount of time their deceased family members would have to spend in Purgatory. Ordinary parishioners regularly attended mass on days other than Sunday as well as during morning and evening canonical hours. In addition,

---

24 The model study of this is Duffy, *Stripping off the Altars*. For a succinct overview of the old and new approaches, see: Dixon, *Contesting the Reformation*, 34–43. In terms of Hungarian historiography, the seminal monograph on this subject is still Pásztor, *A magyarság vallásos élete*. From the recent, anthropologically informed approaches of lay religious practice, see Majorossy, "Church in Town."

25 For more detail on the poor parish clergy, see Chapter 5.

26 The Second Lateran Council in 1139 stipulated that only the pope could lift excommunication imposed due to violence committed against the clergy. COD, 220, canon 15.

27 On the ritual of ordination, see LTK vol. 8, 2107; Radó, ed. *Libri liturgici manuscripti*, 450–51 (Pontificale ad usum Metropoliae Strigoniensis).

28 Müller, "Die Gebühren," 240.

they typically went to holy confession and took communion once a year at Easter, established by determining that those who neglected Easter communion thought it necessary to justify their omission. Parishioners might have found themselves in an uncomfortable situation if they had been called as witnesses. The justification for their failure to participate in Easter communion was compatible with Church doctrine: they had not taken the sacrament because they had not become reconciled with their enemies. Some parishioners even referred to the clear conscience needed in order to receive the host.[29] A serf from a small town in western Hungary attempted to deflect suspicion that he had sworn a false oath with the following categorical statement reflecting the official concept of the two realms: "Having taken an oath, he fears God more than man and is rather willing to relinquish his body than his soul." In other words, his spiritual salvation mattered more to him than his temporal life.[30]

All of this suggests that simple parishioners were not only familiar with Church doctrine, but were able to utilize ecclesiastical concepts and teachings in concrete situations, thus indicating their internalization. Moreover, they needed the clergy to mediate the sacred, most importantly receiving the body of Christ from the hands of a priest. Exceptional statements of simple parishioners reveal that they expected priests to not only mediate the sacred, but also to directly influence the workings of the sacraments, thereby helping as well as harming them. They believed that priests were imbued with both sacred and demonic powers.[31] Parishioners must have considered the physical assault or murder of priests as a very grave sin. Why, then, did the clergy and laity so frequently commit acts of violence against one another within the seemingly harmonious system?

Clergymen as Members of Local Communities

If lay-clerical conflicts were the results of emotionally laden neighborhood disputes, it follows that the parties lived in close coexistence, as demonstrated in the previous chapter. The rural parish clergy were normally local boys, the sons of

29 For information regarding the religious practices and notions of the residents of an average market town in western Hungary, Körmend, see Erdélyi, *A Cloister on Trial*, 139–53.

30 In the witness deposition of Körmend, resident István Tóth from Báta, we read: "Et dicit testis, quod licet esset iobagio domini Petri Erdedÿ, tamen non eum tantum timeret, quod subticeret veritatem, quoniam postquam iurasset, plus Deum, quam hominem timeret, mallet enim perdere corpus, quam animam." Erdélyi, ed., *The Register*, 119.

31 Erdélyi, *A Cloister On Trial*, 165–70. See the previous chapter for concepts regarding the demonic (helping-harming) character of witches.

peasants, integrated socially—by kinship, affinity and friendship—into local communities. They continued to farm and head households. They usually lived with a woman, often a female relative, who was in charge of housekeeping. The parish priest might have tutored some of his nephews in preparation for the priesthood, kept a chaplain who helped to perform religious liturgies, and retained some servants. Priests often entered their own stories as authoritative and responsible patriarchs imposing punishments "in accordance with the committed crime" on "impertinent" "irreverent" and "misbehaving" matrons and nephews.[32]

Parish priest Benedek was "doing some bookkeeping at his house with some laymen for whom he had an elderly female relative prepare dinner." The woman was drinking wine with the guests, which loosened her tongue, and she began to insult him. Benedek wrote that he seized the woman by the hair, not with an angry spirit, but with corrective intent in order to help her sober up, thus causing the drunken house servant to fall to the ground. After struggling to her feet, she headed back to the kitchen, grumbling to herself along the way, so the parish priest went after her and slapped her in the face repeatedly. The fight became rough and the servant suffocated the following night due to drunkenness, according to the priest."[33]

Ecclesiastical and secular authorities considered moderate "rebukes" utilized with the intent to edify to be the lesser of two evils, recommending them in case of need.[34] Priests who acted as heads of households claimed

32 For details regarding physical punishment of disobedient female servants, see ibid., vol. 3, fol. 122r; vol. 14. fol. 138v; vol. 24, fols 144v–45r, etc. With regard to nephews, for example: "Quendam puerum eius nepotem annorum etatis duodecim vel circa, quem unacum fratre ipsius pueris secum in domo tenebat … [quem] animo corrigendi et sine gravi excessu vel enormi eundem puerum cum manu sua in latus eius dexterum percussit seu trusit." Ibid., vol. 2, fols 123r–v (1439, Wesprimien. dioc.).

33 "Ipse olim quosdam laicos ad calculandum quasdam rationes in domo sua convocasse et collatione eis per certam mulierem antiquam eius consanguineam preparare fecisset, ipsaque mulier quia cum dictis laicis ex diversis vinis bibit, ipsis laicis […] tanquam vino capta contra dictum exponentem alloqui cepit, quam dictus exponens non animo irato, sed correctionis causa cognoscens eam vino completam esse sobridens ipsam in crinibus accepit, que propter ebrietatem in terram cecidit surgensque versus coquinam prorexit et dictam exponentem murmurans molestabat accedensque ad eam dictus exponens unam alapam sibi dedit."; "nocte sequenti propter huiusmodi ebrietates suffocatione vita finita fuit." Ibid., vol. 14, fol. 138v (1466, Zagrabien. dioc.).

34 Regarding the contemporary recommendation and acceptance of moderate beatings of children and pupils (as well as wives) for remedial purposes, see Ozment, *When Fathers Ruled*, 148–49. With regard to relations between master and servant, see Kovács, ed., *Temesvári Pelbárt*, 31.

that beatings were administered "for corrective purposes, to deter household members from doing such things again," and that corporal punishment was employed "without exceeding the bounds of moderation." They only had to account for the beatings that accompanied everyday household conflicts if, as in the case of parish priest Benedek, they somehow ended in a death, usually the result—according to the petitions—of some sort of existing sickness or "deep-rooted depravity." Péter, the parish priest in the village of Zámor, "corrected" his pupil with a whip and hit him on the head with a switch because he had forgotten the Apostles' Creed. János, the parish priest in the village of Kutas, elbowed his nephew in the side after the twelve-year-old boy, whom he was raising, "took no notice" of his request to go out and find a lost cow, and "laughed at him, running back and forth in the house like a lunatic."[35]

In addition to safeguarding the order and morals of the household, parish priests also acted responsibly for the well-being and safety of household members within the local network of relationships. The *paterfamilias* role of village incumbents is well reflected in the case of Pál Albi, the parish priest of the Transylvanian Saxon village of Schlattendorf (Zlagna, Romania). Albi betrothed one of his female servants, endowed with a respectable dowry, to a male servant. After a while, however, the husband took to beating his wife and one day tried to kill her. According to the priest's version of events, the desperate wife was forced to take refuge at his house, although the husband continued to bedevil her. Priest Pál could not bear this harassment with "a peaceful soul," so one night he snuck into the husband's house and stabbed him.[36] The story demonstrates not only the parish priest's sense of responsibility for members of his household, but also that anti-violent behavior was an effective form of argument corresponding to official expectations of obtaining papal grace.

35 "Ex eo, quod simbolum ipsum oblivioni tradiderat, tribus vicibus cum quodam flagello de corio correxit eumque cum palmatorio ligneo in manibus percussit." APA vol. 16, fol. 126r (1467, Wesprimien. dioc.). The village of Zámor in Fejér County. "Quendam puerum eius nepotem annorum etatis duodecim vel circa, quem unacum fratre ipsius pueris secum in domo tenebat, [...], cui ipse exponens, dum quendam bovem suum in eadem domo non reperit, dixit illi, ubi est bos noster, qui respondit, nescio ubi est, et licet idem exponens dicto puero mandaverat, ut eundem bovem quereant, cum verba ipsius exponentis minime curavit, imo eum derisit et per domum hincinde tanquam insanus cucurrit, tunc prenominatus exponens animo corrigendi et sine gravi excessu vel enormi eundem puerum cum manu sua in latus eius dexterum percussit seu trusit." Ibid., vol. 2, fol. 123rv (1439, Wesprimien. dioc.). The village of Kutas in Zala County.

36 APA, Armadio XXXII, vol. 61, fols 427v–28v (1522, Milkowien.-Strigonien. dioc.).

Assaults against the parsonage were directed not so much against the priest, but against his family: house raids were the most common acts of "rightfully" avenging an earlier offense by force.[37] Family feuds that involved local priests tended to be highlighted by hatred. Like their parishioners, village incumbents were not unwilling to deal severely both with negligent servants who wasted wealth and harmful neighbors. Priest Ambrus Cserepes ("Tiler") was shocked when he arrived home at the parsonage to find foreign cattle trampling his hedges even though he had earlier admonished the herdsman not to permit the animals to graze in the parsonage garden. In his frustration, so he maintained, he lost his temper (*ira motus*) and beat the herdsman so severely that he died soon afterwards from head wounds. Ambrus had brought himself to ruin through murder committed in "hot anger": he had to leave his benefice and office and could only function as a priest at a location where his past was unknown.[38] The defense of property was not free of danger. Péter, the son of Pál from Croatia, was probably aware of this when he rode out daily to his lands to save his crops from being trampled and eaten by cattle. On one of these occasions his neighbor's servants, who let their cattle graze on his land, made an armed attack after he attempted to expel them. They first wounded his horse and then sought to take his life, which impelled him to draw his knife in self-defense and kill one of the aggressors.[39]

In addition to these acts of vindicatory violence, rural clergymen also became involved in tavern brawls even though their superiors had repeatedly prohibited them from frequenting public houses. One evening, cleric Pál from the village of Szepetk, together with the parish priest who he was serving at the time, entered a tavern "where they spoke and drank together with laymen in an honorable manner." Paulus described how the laymen who arrived later gathered at a nearby table; once drunk, one of them threw a roast goose over to their table and attacked the parish priest and his company with a sword.[40]

Members of the local clergy not only passed their leisure hours in taverns, they were also regular guests at family feasts and participated in village festivities and popular games tied to cyclical festivals (sacred and profane rituals intermingled). However, these activities occasionally went wrong and ended in violent brawls, sometimes due to enmity and revenge. Priest Ambrus, after performing funeral ceremonies, joined his chaplains at a village feast

37 House raids (*invasio domorum*) were handled as acts of public violence (*actus potentialis*). Tringli, "Fehde und Gewalttätigkeit," 283.

38 APA, vol. 70, fols 104v–5r (1522, Strigonien. archdioc.).

39 APA, vol. 78, fols 541rv–42r (1532, Zagrabien. dioc.).

40 Ibid., vol. 2bis, fols 143r–v (1440, Wesprimien. dioc.).

and "celebrated with abundant eating and drinking according to local customs."[41] We know of this fairly common scene only because of its violent outcome: when the clergymen departed late at night, one of their companions stayed behind. He tried to catch up with the rest of the company, shouting for the parish priest to wait for him. When he finally reached his fellow clerics, he attacked them with his sword, resulting in the death of the vehement and drunken colleague.

Another instance of parishioners and clergy sharing in popular festivity after a religious ritual is presented to us as an episode in a feud. Priest János, son of Miklós, was the incumbent in a village in southern Hungary. He commanded a large household that included some of his siblings who he tutored; they, in return, helped him perform religious services. The main character in the story is one of the priest's siblings, who was on hostile terms with a local man named János, son of Lénárt. After the latter János threatened to kill the priest's sibling by brandishing a sword, his brothers thrashed the aggressor. The rival parties subsequently made peace through the mediation of arbiters (*interventu quorundam virorum fuit inter eos concordia*), promising, under pain of punishment amounting to forty forints, not to cause any damage to one another either through words or deeds. However, this did not stop the layman, portrayed according to the usual script as a restless and wicked person, from engaging in further violent harassment. The village had been stricken by pestilence, and requested the incumbent to celebrate a mass with the assistance of his siblings in order to solicit and pray for the Virgin Mary's aid. When the public ritual finished, clergy and laity joined in a great convivial evening. It was late by the time Priest Balázs politely asked permission to leave, and departed for home.[42] However, he arrived too late and was unable to prevent János and his accomplices from murdering his sibling in his own house. Priest Balázs did, however, take immediate revenge for the killing.

Beyond attesting to the common leisure of clergy and laity, as highlighted in the previous chapter, this story demonstrates that local priests, embedded in the local network of reciprocal relationships, applied the same tools of conflict negotiation as their parishioners: they used violent self-help, negotiated enmities with communal mediation (arbiters) or went to court. Laymen used

41 Ibid., vol. 81, fols 608v–9v (1533, Zagrabien. dioc.).

42 "Postmodum vero durante pestilentia, cum predictus exponens cum fratribus suis missas ad honorem Beate Marie Virginis celebrare fecisset, et in fine dictarum missarum magnam convivium fecissent et ibi quamplures probi viri essent, sero facto prefatus exponens de omnium astantium licentia recessit et ad domum suam accessit." Ibid., vol. 44, fols 291r–92r (1495, Chanadien. dioc.).

verbal strategies, portraying their clerical enemies as bad priests rather than as malicious neighbors. The personal adversary thus appeared to be a priest who failed to satisfy local expectations or fulfill his clerical duties. This kind of representation made it possible for personal conflicts to appear as communal affairs, and was debated as such before public authorities. The peculiarities of neighborhood disputes, laden with individual interests and emotions, were translated into the universal issue of priestly honor that was comprehensible for the targeted audience.[43]

Honor and Hatred: The Script of Lay-Clerical Conflicts

Priestly honor, like female reputation, revolved primarily around sexual virtue.[44] The power of symbolic language becomes starkly clear when examining a case that took place in the Zagreb County village of Toplica, where two participants tried to present acceptable stories about the same event. Priest Pál Worscki, the incumbent at the Holy Trinity Parish Church, fabricated a homicide story in which the alleged conflict took place between his chaplain, Lukács Scopzich and two of his parishioners, Mihály Borbély ("Barber") and Péter Varga ("Shoemaker"). The laymen accused the chaplain of adultery; in other words, of seducing a married woman. The parish priest tried to mediate between the parties, but his intervention only drew the ire of Mihály Borbély. According to Priest Pál, the conflict reached its climax when Borbély unexpectedly shot and killed his neighbor, Péter Varga, with an arrow.[45] The outcome is incomprehensible: why did two laymen turn against each other when it seemed that they were united in conflict against the adulterous chaplain? We learn from chaplain Lukács's story, submitted to the Penitentiary on the same date as Priest Pál's request, December 13, 1487, that he had only been a secondary figure in the conflict between the two laymen: the two neighbors had been engaged in a dispute during which both men had named the other's wife as the chaplain's lover.[46] Most likely the conflict had developed over some sort

43 Honor functioned as a central concept constituting a person's individual identity and social relations. For this interpretation of the concept of honor, see Dinges, "Die Ehre"; and Burghartz, "Disziplinierung oder Konfliktregelung?"

44 Gowing, *Domestic Dangers* 4, 111–38.

45 APA, vol. 37, fols 224v–225r (1487).

46 "Lucas Scopzich presbyter Zagrabiensis diocesis capellanus Pauli plebani ecclesie Sancte Trinitatis in Toplica dicte diocesis, quod cum ipse olim a quibusdam laicis super

of material damage, as was most often the case, but this had gone unnoticed in the public debate concerning the fidelity and reputation of their wives. This had important consequences for their own status. One of the central components of a man's honor was his ability to ensure the fidelity of his wife, as well as the virginity of his daughters.[47] This paternalistic quality of male honor was the issue at stake in this particular dispute. We do not know how it resolved or the fate of Mihály Borbély, since he did not ask the pope's pardon for committing murder. The two priests who had become entangled in the affair of their parishioners, however, needed the pope to declare their innocence. The parish priest, whose attempted mediation had failed, felt responsible for the death of one of his parishioners.[48] His narrative, which misrepresented the conflict between the two laymen as a lay-clerical dispute, must have seemed credible to the Roman office, where stories about laymen killing priests were handled routinely.

The varied but always very concrete causes of disputes were translated into a symbolic language over the course of the verbal clashes. The script is found in the petition of the cleric Imre Corcunctal from Majsa, a village in southern Hungary. The clergyman claimed that a layman named Balázs had "falsely denounced him" for fornication, first at the landlord's tribunal and later before the parish priest. Balázs was portrayed by Imre as "an evil man of ill repute" who had behaved aggressively towards him. However, the charges against Imre fell flat; both the landlord and the parish priest recognized his "innocence" and the "malevolent intrigues" of his enemy, who refused at court to reconcile with the defamed party and ask for his pardon. The efforts of the man to defeat his clerical enemy with the support of legal authorities appear to have come to nothing. Imre continued the story as follows:

> Finally, one night on his way home, Balázs assailed him with insults and threats, to which he responded "Balázs, I have had enough of your defamations; be considerate of Christ's passion and leave me in peace." Balázs, bursting into diabolic anger, replied: "Rascal and son of

---

crimine adulterii licet falso accusatus fuisset, et propterea lis inter quosdam Michaelem Barbitonsorem et Petrum Sutorem dicte plebanie parrochianos orta fuisset ita, quod alter alterum increpabat dicendo Lucas presbyter habuit rem cum uxore tua et non cum mea, et econverso alter dicebat de altero adeo, quod propter huiusmodi frivola et inepta verba prefatum Petrum ictu sagitte interfecit." APA, vol. 37, fol. 225v.

47 Roper, *Oedipus and the Devil*, 65, 107–9.

48 On the role of the pastoral clergy as promoters of peace within the parish, see Castan, *"The Arbitration of Disputes,"* 239.

> a whore, I have recently failed to destroy you, but today I'll drag you out of your house, smash you, drink over your tunic and pass my sword through you."[49]

This battle of words, performed in the language of honor, devolved into a fistfight that made the priest the victor and the actual reasons for their hostilities concealed. In other instances, like that of the priest Mátyás, son of János, it was not the alleged sexual misconduct of his mother (who had been referred to as a "whore"), but his own alleged adultery that had been the target of insult. The parish priest related in great detail how one night at his house he had been assaulted *ex precogitata malitia et animo malivolo*—in other words, by his enemies. His chaplain had been the first to notice intruders, warned by barking dogs. When he inquired who was outside, he received the unambiguous reply: "Once I get my hands on you, I will kill you!" The aggressor broke down the house door and shouted outside the pastor's room, "Pastor, give us your concubine!" Priest Mátyás awoke in alarm. According to the usual script, the pacifying words of the parish priest only added to the aggressor's rage. The priest opened the door and claimed he had done nothing to merit such treatment. "You'll see now what you deserve: you will have to die shamefully!" his enemy yelled, drawing his sword and wounding the priest. The defenseless priest and his coward chaplain escaped death by turning the aggressor's sword and knife against him.[50]

When attacks on clerical sexual behavior—in other words, on priestly honor—proved ineffective, the language of the battle shifted to worldly honor, with people addressing their clerical enemies as "rogues" and "rascals."[51] This double coding of insults seems to have been applied with the conscious weighing of circumstances and odds in both tavern and courtroom as well as in moments of self-defense. The cleric György Rojcsai criminalized his enemy thus:

49 "Aliquibus postremo diebus elapsis idem Blasius exponentem ipsum tunc serotivo tempore ad domum sue habitationis revertentem … iniuriis affecit et minis sibique dicenti, O Blasii iam satis me … diffamasti, rogo te ob passionem Christi ut sinas me in pace talia aut similia verba, respondit furore diabolico inflammatus, O latro et meretricis filius, pridie non potui te spoliare sed hodie extraham te de domo tua et te spoliabo et bibam supra tunicam tuam et meo ense te perforabo." APA, vol. 54, fols 300v–301r (1508, Quinqueecclesien. dioc.). Majsa is a village in Tolna County.

50 APA, vol. 2, fols 20v–21r (1439, Strigonien. archdioc.).

51 Tringli, "Jagelló-kori levelesítő jegyzék," 19.

> For the sake of leisure, he visited once a house where many had gathered already. After talking for a while, a man, who had already attacked a cleric that day and committed several homicides ... turned against him by quarrelling and with insulting words. He called him and his parents thieves and rogues and therefore unworthy of the company of virtuous men. He responded to the insult: "Neither I nor my parents have ever been thieves or rogues and I ask you in the name of God to leave me in peace, since I have nothing to do with you, neither good nor bad."[52]

Soon afterwards, swords and knives were drawn. As the above cases reflect, clergymen preferred to call their lay enemies murderers and present them as stubbornly hostile and aggressive towards priests.

Enmities were pursued in multiple frames of action: interpersonal and collective violence (house raids), court procedures and extra-judicial negotiations. The actual choice seems to have been regulated not by emotions, but by a constant calculation of risk. János Csonka ("Maimed"), the expelled parish priest of the village of Belesz (in modern-day Serbia), sought redress by denouncing his successor, Priest György Vágó, at the diocesan court. Vágó tried to forestall a long lawsuit by offering an out-of-court settlement with the help of arbiters. János, however, broke this mediated contract by demanding a huge amount of money from his successor, and took the case to the tribunal of the vice-archdeacon. During the ongoing judicial process, he did not refrain from battering his enemy when they randomly bumped into each other on the road. In fact, what he later depicted as a random road brawl seems to have been a preplanned revenge killing. His brother was with him, which ensured their physical advantage, and the original lawsuit seems to have served both to mask his real intentions and to make it possible for him to follow his enemy's movements.[53]

---

52 "Quandam domum ubi plurimi laici causa solatii convenissent et eadem causa idem exponens similiter intrasset, cum autem idem exponens ibidem per modicum spatium inter homines conversasset, quidem laicus qui eadem die alium clericum percusisset et per prius diversa homicidia in diversis locis perpetrasset ... ipsum exponentem verbis litigiosis et iniuriosis invasit et publice coram omnibus hominibus ipsum furem et latronem unacum suis parentibus appellavit, et ipsum exponentem asseruit non dignum cum ipsis et aliis bonis hominibus conversare; cui idem exponens Ego nunquam fur aut lator fui, nec parentes mei, sed peto causa dei dimitte me in pace, nam tecum nichil habeo agere sive bonum sive malum ..." APA, vol. 2, fol. 148v (1439, Zagrabien. dioc.). Rojcsa was a market town in Kőrös County (Rovišće, Croatia).

53 APA, vol. 55, fols 214v–5r (1510, Quinqeecclesien. dioc.).

FIGURE 8 *The boy is arrested as a thief and brought to appear before a judge. Part of Tryptich from Szentjakabfalva (Svätý Jakub, Slovakia): Scenes from the legend of the apostle St. James the Elder.*

As elsewhere in Europe, the social norm was peacemaking, the halting of the flow of hatred and the making of *concordia amicitie* ("pacts of friendship"). There were numerous ways to achieve this, but the use of so-called private settlements mediated by arbiters—which were, of course, also public, since they entailed the involvement of several members of the local community—seems to have been very common. My findings at this point do not agree with Thomas Kuehn's conclusion that, in his reading of Florentine civil court cases, the initiation of lawsuits in the late medieval and early modern period served to enforce private settlements.[54] Instead,

54 Kuehn, *Law, Family and Women*, 22.

a different, looser pattern emerges from the papal petitions. It seems to me that going to court, just as engaging in violence, almost always entailed varied effects and interpretations, depending on the circumstances and participants. Therefore, I consider the view that the calculated use of violence was intended to accelerate lengthy, delayed and obstructed court procedures.[55] In one situation a lawsuit could no doubt promote an agreement mediated by arbiters, but in another it might facilitate violence. Although the incident involving the two priests supports Kuehn's assertion that lawsuits tended to enforce private settlements, several stories testify to an opposite claim. One was related by the cleric Miklós, son of István, in the diocese of Pécs in southern Hungary. He was the victim of false accusations by a layman named Mayus and ostracized by the county assembly as a "malefactor" who could be killed by anyone.[56] Unsurprisingly, Miklós became very perplexed by his vulnerable position, and ordered his servants to tear out the tongue of his enemy, hoping this would deter him from engaging in further harassment. In his petition, Miklós claimed that only part of his tongue had been torn out and added that ultimately his enemy had reconciled with him before he had been killed *propter suam malam linguam* ("because of his wicked tongue") by enemies other than himself.[57] As Miklós obviously considered his denunciation to be unbearably humiliating, it pushed him toward violence that deepened the conflict. Since customary law punished unjustified slander by tearing out tongues, he may well have believed his actions to have been legitimate.[58]

The Communal Definition of Criminals

Let me finally return to my starting point regarding lay petitions involving priest killings. Although these petitions were very short, they still reveal the working of intense emotions. Some of the petitioners wanted to be absolved by curial confessors instead of their local bishops, since, as the usual argument went, "In fear of death he does not dare to return to the presence of the bishop

55 Rady, "Justice Delayed?," 9.

56 On the *congregatio generalis* and its jurisdiction, see Tringli, "Az 1481. évi szlavóniai közgyűlés."

57 APA, vol. 1, fol. 89v (1411, Quinqueecclesien. dioc.).

58 The tearing out of one's tongue under the pillory could be evaded by paying a tongue fine. Eckhart, *A földesúri büntetőbíráskodás*, 126–7; Csukovits, "Bűn és büntetés," 217.

and the place of the committed crime."[59] In other words, after the crime the perpetrators were so scared that they fled as far as Rome; but what were they afraid of? No doubt they dreaded the imminent revenge of their victim's kin. In principle, they may also have been afraid of the death penalty, the official punishment for homicide, but it was possible to evade this, unlike the wrath of enemies. The death penalty, as in other parts of early modern continental Europe, was rarely implemented, since hostilities normally ended through peacemaking procedures and the payment of fines (*homagium*).[60]

Priest killers were also subjected to spiritual punishment and were automatically sentenced to excommunication, which could be absolved solely by the pope. The rite of absolution included the public penance of sinners on the spot, intended to prevent crime.[61] The sinner requested a penance that, in the established formula, entailed "his own salvation and the deterrence of others."[62] However, besides averting divine anger, the penance also needed to avert the wrath of the offended party. Since violent crimes against the clergy fell under ecclesiastical jurisdiction, the family of the victim could turn to the diocesan vicar's tribunal. In the course of the unfolding legal procedure, the parties usually reached an agreement, which included the payment of fines.[63] In this context, those people seem to have run to Rome either because the usual script of peacemaking had not been available, since they were outsiders to local communities, or because negotiations had for some reason broken down and they reckoned it wise to disappear for a while. From this perspective,

---

59 For example: "Committantur in Sancto Petro attento quod exponentes ad ordinarium suum et locum commissi delicti propter metum personarum suarum accedere non sunt ausi." APA, vol. 42, fol. 210r.

60 For a comparison of continental inquisitorial procedure and the English adjudicatory courts, the first producing fewer executions, see Carroll, Introduction to *Cultures of Violence*. For Hungary, see Eckhart, *Földesúri büntetőbíráskodás*, 108–9; Rady, "Hungarian Procedural Law," 65.

61 On the contemporary practice of public humiliation, see Clarke, "Central Authority and Local Powers," 429. In the town of Pécs in southern Hungary, a married woman (aborting her child) was instructed by her confessor to join the public penitents performing penance collectively during the Holy Friday liturgy *secundum morem illius patrie* ("according to the customs of the region"). APA, vol. 5, fol. 187r (1456).

62 "Penitentiam talem, que sibi sit ad salutem et aliis ad terrorem." APA, vol. 64, fol. 698r (1520).

63 For example, in 1464, a sum of 190 florins was paid as *homagium* to the sister of a murdered priest, Sebestyén, by a noble servant of the Amadé of Várkony family, according to their agreement before the archiepiscopal court of Esztergom. MNL OL, DL 48650. See also MREV, vol. 3, 279–80.

petitioning to the Roman office served to suspend enmity and avert the vengeance of outraged enemies.[64]

Irrespective of legal norms, men and women embedded in local networks of relationship were seldom sentenced to death. Even if the court passed a capital sentence, it functioned more as a step towards reconciliation.[65] The situation was very different, however, for those who were outsiders. Robbers and highwaymen with no ties to local communities had a good chance of ending up on the gallows. Notaries and judges of the Penitentiary regularly read dramatic stories about such executions. Clerics robbed and wounded on the road used their petitions to explain how villagers or townspeople had forced them to take active parts in the hangings of their assailants who had been arrested and sentenced to death. In a world of social reciprocities, only the offended party could initiate a suit and, when he was an outsider, he was expected to participate in the punishment.[66] Clerics having to place a noose around the neck of the condemned were forced to take the role of hangman, an act difficult to justify as it entailed bodily pollution that impinged on clerical duties.[67]

Lőrinc of Nádasd knew the ins and outs of dramatic storytelling. He was galloping alone in deep snow across the woods, he wrote, using words that provoke the sympathy and anxiety of the reader, when highwaymen assaulted him, stole his clothes, horse and money, cut off one of his ears and tied him to a tree. He was just about to freeze to death when out of God's mercy he escaped. This was not, however, the last twist of his story: when he reached the nearest village, he witnessed the following:

> One of the robbers, sitting on his horse and wearing his clothes, was just presented to the village judge, who asked him: "Whose clothes and money are these?" The robber turned towards cleric Lőrinc and replied: "They

64 Carroll, *Blood and Violence*, 128.

65 In the Transylvanian town of Nagyenyed (Aiud, Romania), an adulterous woman whose lover had killed her husband in a fistfight was sentenced to death. As a result of a private agreement, the woman was not executed, but was sent on a penitential pilgrimage and forbidden to marry her lover. APA, vol. 48, fols. 475v–6r (1500).

66 On the practice of late medieval private accusations as opposed to the modern institution of public accusations, see Mezey, ed., *Magyar Jogtörténet*, 357–8. As one cleric related the stance of the villagers: "Since the villagers did not find anything that the robber, whom they had arrested, had taken away from them, they forced the petitioner to hang him." APA, vol. 2bis, fol. 146r.

67 On the abundance of medieval pollution taboos, see Elliott, *Fallen Bodies*.

> belong to that priest." The judge asked again: "And to whom belongs the horse?" "To the same priest," so the robber answered. "And who cut his ear off?", the judge interrogated further. "I did."

After the robber had confessed everything, Lőrinc was forced to hang him.[68] We are able to imagine the tension that vibrated in the crowd gathered to watch the execution. "After he [Lőrinc] escorted the robber to the scaffold, the robber said: 'I ask you by the love of God not to hang me, just ascend and tie the knot to the column and then leave. I have sinned against you, still I beg you to intervene for me with God.'" Lőrinc ascended the stairs, tied the knot and left him. "The robber begged the crowd to pray for him, then jumped off the stairs and died."[69] Although priests were officially expected to refrain from all forms of violence, including the execution of criminals, neither laymen nor possibly clerics, even if they apologized, were concerned about this.

Two clerics from the diocese of Eger attempted to prove their innocence in a more effective way, placing themselves in the role of captive. They were traveling to Várad (Oradea, Romania), the seat of the neighboring diocese, in order to be ordained as priests. After leaving the market town of Bihar (Biharia, Romania), they were robbed in the hills. They returned to the village and reported the robbery to the first two people they encountered. One of them happened to be the local judge, who quickly produced one of the thieves. The two clerics told the judge that they wanted nothing more than to have their stolen belongings returned; however, the judge responded, "You cannot get your things back so easily. You must first bring charges against the offenders in accordance with our laws." The bewildered clerics found themselves captives, locked in jail alongside the felon. They waited in chains for four days for the village tribunal to convene. The clerics had to swear before the court that the accused had been the one who had robbed them. Weeping, they dropped onto their knees and begged not to be forced to swear an oath, because they wanted to become priests; however, the jurors insisted that they do so so that nobody could later accuse them of injustice. "Since there was no other way for them to be released from the hands of the judge and the jurors," the clerics were compelled to accompany the condemned man to the execution site, where they were forced to turn the wheel on which he was broken three times, and pull the rope that was around his neck. As they completed the execution, they shouted

68 For the *jus gladii* of some late medieval villages, as well as village courts announcing capital punishment, see Szabó, *A középkori magyar falu*, 94.

69 APA, vol. 2bis, fol. 146r (1440, Iaurien. dioc.).

FIGURE 9 *Breaking Wheel. Panel Painting with Scenes from the legend of Felix, Regula and Exuperantius.*

"We do not want this man's death, we do not want him to be executed because of us!"[70] Stories like this suggest that the appraisal of participation in legal executions might have been changing in Rome and Hungary.[71]

70 The two identical petitions were from the two clerics: APA vol. 20, fol. 87v–88r (September 4, 1471) and vol. 22, fol. 103r (September 21, 1471).

71 There were eleven such cases registered at the Apostolic Penitentiary between 1440 and 1523.

Conclusion

We can conclude, on the one hand, that the contradictions inherent in lay expectations towards the clergy derived from the duality of their sacred and social roles. The complexity of their status is also reflected in the language of insults, which targeted either their priestly or their worldly honor. Playing a variety of sacred and profane roles from hangmen to the minister of the Eucharist, they had a difficult time fulfilling both ecclesiastical and lay expectations. Although they also had families, households and farms, their household structure differed from those of their parishioners. Behind apparent similarities lurked differences: between a housemaid and a wife, a niece and a son, moderate drinking and drunkenness, and between the taxes paid by serfs and their own tax exemption.

Everyday disputes between parishioners and priests most often arose as the result of conventional discord between neighbors and tavern patrons, and reflected the similarity between the laity and the clergy. Since priests were also part of the local network of reciprocal relations composed of friends and enemies, they employed the same means of settling conflicts as their secular associates. They resorted to violence or engaged in litigation, depending on the calculated efficacy of action. When priests were compelled to justify the actions they had taken in the course of conflict, they employed the same language as their secular adversaries, claiming that their acts of physical violence had been legitimate because they had been the product of sincere emotion, rightful hatred or genuine affection. According to the standard script, their conflicts with laymen ended in peace. Incidents that resulted in deaths, sometimes those of priests, were portrayed as exceptional, in which attempts to achieve reconciliation had for some reason failed. Often the narrow boundary between cultural practice and violent assertion of interests came within a hair's breadth of breaking.

With regard to the late medieval practices of the negotiation of conflicts, on a more general level, we may wish to reflect on the words of the U.S. legal scholar Robert Cover. In a famous study, Cover claimed that the modern practice of law, with its formal adjudications, to be "a field of pain and death." His point was that it is a form of institutionalized violence, since it not only justifies violence that has occurred, but also occasions the imposition of violence on others.[72] Given the reinterpretations of late medieval and early modern cultures of honor that are now taking place, as well as of recent analyses of

72 Cover, "Violence and the Word."

modern societies, it is clear that there is a growing body of evidence suggesting that the traditional juxtaposition of violence and law—and, consequently, of traditional and modern societies—needs to be fundamentally reconsidered. The evidence scrutinized above reinforces the argument that they were strategic tools invariably applied in the process of conflict negotiations.

Applying the processual model of conflict negotiation, we have looked closely at the uses of justice and violence in a particular area at a particular time—East Central Europe in the later Middle Ages. Because the sources analyzed above were the products of the workings of universal canon law as applied by a central European institution instead of the local system of justice, their reading shed a particularly strong light on general patterns. My findings stress the significance of enmity as central to interpersonal conflicts and their multi-layered negotiations on a European scale. Moreover, the hypothesis that ordinary people appropriated the courts as arenas for vengeance seems to have gained further support from these examples.

CHAPTER 8

Tales of a Peasant Revolt

In the previous chapter we considered the involvement of lesser clergymen in local family feuds fought and represented in the language of honor. Violence, however, served as an alternative tool of negotiation, in addition to everyday interactions, not only in horizontal social relations, but also between subjects and their authorities.[1] In the present chapter we will investigate the role lesser clergymen played in the armed conflicts between peasants and overlords and the ways they subsequently interpreted events.

In April 1515, an ordinary priest from southern Hungary, Kelemen Canimich, submitted a pardon request to Pope Leo X confessing that:

> When he [Kelemen] was notary of a captain in the army of Tamás, the cardinal-primate and legate of the Holy See, and a crusade was declared [...] against the infidels, out of ignorance and because of the cowardice of the captain, he [Kelemen] forged letters in the name of the Hungarian King and the Cardinal which were sent to the Christian faithful so that they would join the fight against the Turks. When many Christians had gathered [...], out of fear of the captain, and since he could not escape the peril of death otherwise, he took part in numerous battles, fights, pillaging, rape, arson and the murder of laymen and even clerics, which they perpetrated against Christians with the captain's troops.[2]

This account is a personal recollection of events usually referred to as the greatest peasant revolt in Hungarian history. At first sight the story, as told by Kelemen six months after the event, seems incongruous: why and how did he and his captain end up fighting against Christians if they originally summoned an army to take up arms against Ottoman forces? Yet it nevertheless made sense. The revolt had developed in response to a call for a crusade in 1514, in which peasants were ordered by pope and king to fight the "infidel." When the nobility tried to stop their peasants from leaving during the busy summer season, the "*rustici cruciati*" turned against their "infidel" landlords. As events

1 With regard to the interpretation of armed collective resistance in the process of *Herrschaft*, see Blockmans, Holenstein and Mathieu, Introduction to *Empowering Interactions*, 17–18; Erdélyi, Introduction to *Armed Memory*, 23–24.

2 APA, vol. 59, fols 72r–v (April 7, 1515, Bachien. dioc.).

 | DOI 10.1163/9789004361263_009

unfolded, György Dózsa (in contemporary sources known as György Székely), a Sekler (*székely* in Hungarian) lesser nobleman and soldier in the anti-Ottoman border fortresses emerged—under unclarified circumstances—as the leader of the peasants. The rebellion was supported by many simple priests, who together with a new generation of Observant Franciscan friars had forged documents and used preaching as an ideological tool to turn the war against pagans into a war against nobility. Thus, the language of negotiating freedom between subjects and authorities was the language of religion in which traditional, heretical and revolutionary elements intermingled. To be sure, peasants fought for their "salvation" under the sign of the cross in the name of the pope, the king and God against "infidel" landlords and tax collectors with the battle cry "Jesus."[3] The uprising was squashed in August 1514 by royal forces and its military leaders were brutally and theatrically executed.[4]

Priest Kelemen was one of the thousands of ordinary priests who had joined the peasants and the first among fifteen who, in the decade preceding 1525, asked the Roman tribunal for the pope's absolution. The petitioners discussed here, all of them clergymen, needed papal clemency for their war crimes in order to exonerate their infringement of canonical rules to regain their clerical status.[5] In order to provide additional force to their requests, these lesser clerics went to Rome to personally present their petitions to the Curia. The fact that they were prepared to invest time and money to undertake such a trip suggests that their supplication was primarily a response to the risk that local competitors would report them to the diocesan authorities. As examined in greater detail in chapter 5, the rivalry among a growing mass of poor clerics for ecclesiastical benefices and offices was intense.

While the voices of the victors of the 1514 revolt are quite familiar to historians, these petitions to the pope provide a rare opportunity to hear the voices of the losing side. Research on collective violence often focuses on

3 Norman Housley stresses the role of orthodox crusade religion, which provided stimulus, social integration and symbolism to the social revolt. Housley, *Religious Warfare*, 20–22, 69–75. The Hungarian historian Jenő Szűcs called attention to Franciscan spiritualistic ideas expressed in texts produced by the rebels. See Szűcs, "Die Ideologie des Bauernkrieges." For more detail on this issue, see Erdélyi, Introduction to *Armed Memory*, 24–29.

4 On the political and military history of the revolt, see: C. Tóth, and Neumann, eds., *Keresztesekből lázadók;* Barta and Fekete Nagy, *Parasztháború.* With regard to the leader of the revolt, György Dózsa, see: Barta, "Georgius Zekeltől Dózsa Györgyig." For an examination of the manifold relations of the Hungarian province of Observant Franciscans to the revolt, see: Szűcs, "A ferences obszervancia" and Szűcs, "Die Ideologie des Bauernkrieges."

5 The so-called *irregularitas ex delicto* was an impediment to priestly ordination. Plöchl, *Geschichte des Kirchenrechts*, vol. 2, 290.

FIGURE 10 *Crusader with flag. Cover image of pamphlet* Ain gross wunderzaichen, das do geschechen ist durch das Creütz, das ain Cardinal hat aussgeben inn dem ganzten Hungerischen Land wider die Türcken.

the motivation of agents and the relation between social status and willingness to participate in a revolt.[6] Historical scholarship on the events of 1514 has also been primarily concerned with such issues.[7] Examining the requests of the participants, however, provides us with a different perspective and makes it possible to construct a "bottom up" narrative of the revolt.[8] The autobiographical narratives constructed after the events enable us to explore the processing

6 McPhail, *The Myth of the Madding Crowd.*

7 See the chapter on the social and economic standing of the peasantry in Barta and Fekete Nagy, *Parasztháború*, 42–59. Ferenc Szakály argues that Observant Franciscans joined the peasants because of their own peasant origins, *Mezőváros és reformáció*, 7–32.

8 See the landmark study by John Keegan, who first produced a battle narrative focusing on the experiences of common soldiers based on narrative sources. Keegan, *The Face of Battle.* More recently on the culture of total war, see Audoin-Rouzeau and Becker, *1914–1918.*

of collective violence of both individuals and social groups. How did individuals reflect upon and cope with the experience of partaking in and committing extreme violence? We can also examine the tools competing social groups applied in the war fought for the possession of justified violence and truth. It has been observed that in the twentieth century collective violence tended to be followed by silence, with violent events becoming a taboo subject that only much later was followed by a "wave of speech." Such a wave of speech can be interpreted either as a form of individual or collective therapy, or as an attempt to stake a claim to a monopoly over a "true" version of events. In the verbal battle to establish authority over the past, the "possession" of the dead and claims to martyrdom were essential weapons.[9]

Generally speaking, war memories of the late medieval and early modern period are difficult to access due to the limited availability of sources as well as to the different structure of the public sphere. Memories of the Thirty Years' War seem to have been an exception to this rule, perhaps because, in the war's immediate aftermath, the events became a major source of contention between Catholics and Protestants. Eventually, it was the Lutherans who succeeded in monopolizing the commemoration of the war: annual commemorations turned into a celebration of their victory over their Catholic opponents. By the nineteenth century, however, the military *Festkultur* that flourished in the multi-confessional cities of southern Germany was domesticated and turned into a celebration of peace. Framed as a cultural memory, the Thirty Years' War became a constitutive part of national identity.[10]

Memories of the 1514 revolt developed quite differently. Recently the rather robust claim has been made that the revolt constituted "the unspoken trauma of Hungarian history, which was turned into a taboo right after the event and has remained so ever since."[11] Instead of offering a historical-psychological evaluation of the type inherent in this statement, I will apply a sociological approach to cultural trauma by seeking to reconstruct the processes of remembering and forgetting that were used following the 1514 peasant revolt. This sociological approach rests on the premise that the events themselves might only have become traumatic under the impact of narratives forged by historical agents sharing an interest in the making of trauma.[12] To judge whether this

9 On the phase of repression followed by an outburst of speaking in the aftermath of the 1956 revolution in Hungary, see Kövér, "Források, értelmezések, történelmek," 391.

10 Sack, *Der Krieg in den Köpfen*. I use the distinction between communicative and cultural memory introduced by Assmann, *Das kulturelle Gedächtnis*, 48–55.

11 Péter, *A Reformáció*, 73.

12 Alexander, "Toward a Theory of Cultural Trauma"; and Kansteiner, "Finding Meaning in Memory," esp. 186–87.

is the case, we need to ask who were the agents of trauma (or the dramatization of memory) and what was at stake.

First, I will briefly outline the dynamics of the memory war that followed the dramatic events of the revolt, and address the question of how personal memory and identity formation interacted with public stories in petitions. In what ways did individual and collective memories shape representations of violence? In the second part, I will sketch the later memories of the uprising in early modern cultural memory in Hungary and abroad.

Two Competing Myths of Just War

The petition of priest Kelemen makes no mention of the revolt, instead isolating and portraying the events as the outcome of his exchange with the cardinal:

> Since, however, Holy Father, the petitioner was warned by the cardinal to desist from his acts [i.e., illegal recruiting], he was excommunicated for his obstinacy, [...] which he regretted and regrets now. [...] He therefore asks to be absolved for homicide and other excesses and sins in return for due penitence and also to be suspended from divine services for a time. He would like, though, to keep his priestly office and benefices under the condition that he exercise penitence before the cardinal and humbly requests his forgiveness.

As we have seen, the effort of Kelemen to conceal the uprising and his role in it involves an incongruous story, starting with a proclamation of a crusade against the Ottomans and ending with Christians killing Christians. It is so peculiar that one suspects that Kelemen may have been one of the illegal preachers of the crusade who organized the uprising. His dissimulation may reflect the defensive reorganization of his personal identity under the impact of the new social realities, which he must have perceived as menacing. He composed his story in the aftermath of the uprising in a very tense situation dominated by anger and fear. Inevitably, his version of events was grounded in the brutal execution of peasant leaders and the decree of the National Diet ordering the search for and execution of all rebels, who were called "public malefactors," murderers of noblemen and rapists of virgins.[13] Characterizing the reaction of the frightened nobility, one sixteenth-century chronicler noted that, "the

---

13 DRMH, vol. 4, anno 1514/paragraph 4, 13, 14, 33.

Hungarian landlords behaved ruthlessly toward the poor and oppressed the crusaders in many different ways."[14]

However, petitions from subsequent years reveal that rebel memories of the revolt were suppressed only temporarily. As the bloody wave of noble revenge came to an end and the anticipated mass executions did not ensue, former rebels were able to resurface and present themselves publicly in the emerging memory war over the monopoly of legitimate violence and just war. We can witness the fabrication of rebel myths penned by lesser priests from villages and market towns situated in the heartland of the rebellion. The war of interpretation evolved around the issue of who was responsible for the outbreak of the war and who acted in self-defense. "During the time of the crusaders" he raised arms together with other noblemen to defend himself, wrote István Deák, tutor of the son of Gergely Pöstyéni, steward of Várad.[15] In the clash between war and peace, the moral good was obviously on the side of the latter. In the dramatic story of Priest Benedek Nagyhatvani, written in 1519, the opposing protagonists are the crusaders and the nobility:

> When a crusade against the infidels was declared in Hungary and he himself took up the cross with many others, a conflict and quarrel erupted between the nobles and the crusaders, in the course of which the nobles attacked the crusaders. To defend themselves, he too needed to take up arms with his fellow crusaders.[16]

In the story of Miklós Bihari, the chantry priest of the parish church of the market town Bihar, he was still a layman when he recruited crusaders to gather for the

---

14 Bessenyei, ed., *1504–1566 Memoria Rerum*, 17.

15 "Cum alias dictus orator tempore cruciferorum in partibus illis tunc vigentium unacum nobilibus huiusmodi provincie in quodam illorum conflictu interesset et in huiusmodi cruciferorum vim vi repellendo et se necessarie defendendo nec alias mortis periculum evitare valens absque alia eiusdem oratoris culpa quandam religiosum et alterum secularem in eodem conflictu existentes percussit et vulneravit, quorum aliter videlicet secularis ab humanis decessit, si vero religiosus huiusmodi decesserit nec ne, ignorat." APA vol. 70, fol. 358v (1523). Gergely Pöstyéni governed the vacant bishopric of Várad and directed the fight against the rebels in Bihar County. His performance was rewarded by János Szapolyai, elected King of Hungary, who appointed him lord chief justice (*iudex curiae regiae*) in 1527. Márki, *Dósa György*, 357–58. The chronicler György Szerémi claimed to have been the tutor of Ferenc, son of Gergely Pöstyéni, following which he served as the court chaplain of Ferenc Perényi, bishop of Transylvania, in Várad after 1514 (Szerémi, *Magyarország romlásáról*, 17, 161). István Deák must have been the tutor of Ferenc before him.

16 APA vol. 64, ff. 111r–v (April 19, 1523).

"honorable campaign in order to hunt down the enemies of the Christian faith and their temerity," eventually thwarted by the assault of the nobility.[17] By attacking the crusaders as they were preparing to fight the natural enemies of Christianity, the nobles had taken the place of the Ottomans by themselves becoming *infidelis*. This chain of thought must have appeared familiar at the papal curia since it borrowed its central concepts from the papal bull declaring the crusade against the Turks. Both Pope Leo X and the crusaders spoke of a "holy" and "praiseworthy" crusade.[18] The pope had promised the remission of all sins for participants and supporters of the war, while threatening absentees and those obstructing the war with excommunication on earth and eternal damnation in hell. The peasants could thus interpret the revolt as the realization of the papal curse and replace *infidelis* Turks with *infidelis* landlords.[19] Of course, this version of events countermanded the plot in the official stories of the ruling élite, in which the label *infidelis* had connotations of rebellion and treason and was used to describe the peasantry.[20]

The voices of the verbal battle emerged in the geographical centers of the revolt (Abaúj and Zemplén Counties, the border region of Békés and Bihar Counties, the area around the town of Csanád, and Bodrog and Bács Counties). Parties disputed who had been the aggressors, who had been forced to defend themselves and which party had been the most ruthless. On both sides, the dramatization of events climaxed in a conspiracy theory:

> After he had recruited many crusaders against the enemies of the Christian faith and when they were ready for launching this honorable expedition—suddenly, at the instigation of the enemy of humankind—the nobles attacked the crusaders. When the crusaders realized the betrayal of the nobility, they bravely started to defend themselves in order to save their lives.

This quote is taken from one of the rebel narratives by the above-mentioned Miklós Bihari.[21] In this account, penned in 1523, the conflict is no longer attributed to the discord between the crusaders and the nobility, but rather to the treachery of the latter. A very different conspiracy theory is elaborated in the counternarrative of a noble participant, Dénes Kascach, in 1525:

---

17 APA, vol. 70, fols 358v–59r (April 2, 1523, Waradien. dioc.).

18 Fekete Nagy, Kenéz et al., eds., *Monumenta rusticorum*, 47.

19 Szűcs, "Die Ideologie des Bauernkrieges," 12–38.

20 For an exhaustive analysis of the characterization of the rebellious peasant in the different genres and sources produced in the sixteenth century, see Klaniczay, "Images and designations for rebellious peasants."

21 APA vol. 70, fols 358v–59r.

> When his most reverend eminence, Cardinal Tamás, was sent as legate to Hungary in order to launch a crusade with royal permission and apostolic authority, some ignorant rebels and troublemakers rebelled against him and his followers and took up the cross in order to kill his eminence and his followers. [...] Among them was the royal captain, György Székely, as well. [...] When he [the captain] discovered the fraud, he turned at once against the aggressors and rebels.[22]

The story of Kaschach is modeled on the plot developed in a humanist epic poem about a revolt, written in the cardinal's court shortly after the events and published in Vienna in 1519 under the title *Stauromachia id est Cruciatorum Servile Bellum.*[23] In Stephanus Taurinus's humanist tale, events, which had originally occurred in various locations and had very complex causes, were all subsumed in one easily comprehensible conspiracy theory. It presents the crusaders as determined from the outset to exterminate the entire nobility under the pretext of the crusade led by a fraudulent and power-thirsty leader, Dózsa, "who is hiding the fraud in his feigned smile [...] and incites the serfs to take arms."[24] Both in the humanist story and in the petition of the nobleman Dénes Kaschach, the honest and good crusaders, identified with ecclesiastical and secular authorities, fight against fraudulent crusaders. Even if it is difficult to ascertain the activities of Kaschach during the revolt, his narrative seems to have been forged in one of the centers of the memory war in 1525.

Representations of Violence: Private and Public Perspectives

The conspiracy theory on the noble side is repeated in an autobiographical account by another cleric, Gergely Koppándi, from the landed nobility of Transylvania, who wrote in 1520:

> Many peasants gathered under the pretext of a crusade in the Kingdom of Hungary and revolted against the nobility with the intention to destroy them totally. Then, on royal orders, he took up arms with the barons and

22 APA vol. 73, ff. 157r–58r (3 January 1525, Wesprimien. dioc.).

23 Taurinus, *Stauromachia*. In Hungarian translation: Taurinus, *Paraszti háború*. For an in-depth analysis, see Kiss, "Ambiguity and Paradox." Taurinus belonged to the entourage of Cardinal Bakócz, but later became the vicar of Ferenc Várdai, bishop of Transylvania, who was the vice-legate entrusted by Bakócz to gather the army in Transylvania for the crusade. See below Várdai's petition to the pope after the revolt.

24 Both Taurinus and Dénes Kaschach use the word *fraus*. Taurinus, *Stauromachia*, 12 (line 352).

> nobles to destroy this huge peasant army. After they had defeated the peasants, he imprisoned forty peasants by the law of war, and considering the brutality the peasants had committed against nobles and clergymen, he made a peasant sit on a trunk and nailed his genitals and his buttocks to the trunk with iron nails, so that by punishing him, others would be terrified and deterred.[25]

The narrator obviously derived a strange pleasure from the detailed account of the tortured peasant. Within the context of the memory war, such details may seem surprising since they run counter to usual practice. When petitioners claimed in their formal written statements that they had committed legitimate violence, they refrained from explicit, let alone literal, depictions of what they had done. Instead, the legitimacy of their acts was underpinned by brief references to the brutality of the enemy. The powerful, for their part, accounted for their bloody retribution simply with reference to their defense of the *patria* and their right to wage war.[26] Our noble cleric was more talkative: it was possible for him to speak about his own extreme violence. In the contemporary culture of honor there was much room for extreme, but legitimate violence. Koppándi depicted his acts of violence as enforcement of the law by arguing that he had taken part in a defensive war under royal orders and that he had captured and punished rebels in accordance with what was common wartime practice. In a similar vein, those who had fought against the infidel Turks readily and extensively recounted their savage deeds in subsequent petitions to the pope.[27] Sexual torture, mutilation and dehumanization of the enemy served to exert power over the rebels and symbolically restore social order.[28] Rather than being brutal, Koppándi was being just. His story is a textual representation of the late medieval theatre of horror in which public

25 APA vol. 66, ff. 52r–v (March 28, 1520, Transylvanien. dioc.). It is possible that Gergely described one of the last battles fought at the castle of Bihar (July 1514) with the army of his patron, Pál Tomori, castellan of Fogaras (Făgăras, Romania).

26 For example, Ferenc Móré, Canon of Vác argued that "Alias atrocissima rabie illius rusticane thyrannidis in Regno Hungarie vigente" he fought 'pro domestica libertate conservanda.' APA vol. 63, ff. 74r–v (1518). Ferenc Várdai, Bishop of Transylvania: "Conflictibus et bellis iustis pro defensione patrie [...] armatus interfuit." APA vol. 59, f. 424r (1515).

27 As did the Transylvanian nobleman Péter Berekszói: Once "exercitum penes mare contra infideles haberet dictus exponens in dicto exercitu fuit et ibidem quamplures turcos [...] viros et mulieres cum parvulis manu propria interfecit, quandam etiam mulierem puerum lactantem manu propria interfecit et puerum etiam mortuum exinde credit." APA vol. 3, ff. 397v–98r (1452).

28 Davis, "The Rites of Violence."

execution and the cruelties of warfare were regulated and accepted sites of the body in pain.[29] We read the naturalistic portrayal of the execution of the "peasant king" Dózsa in the humanist epos: "The lymph burst forth abundantly from his broken skull, his brain bubbling out through his ears, mouth and nose."[30] A pamphlet entitled *The Crusade of the Hungarians and the Extreme Cruelty Committed on Both Sides* was published in Rome in 1514.[31] In its pages, pious peasants who deemed themselves "followers of the cross" are transformed into "savage pagans" after they collectively rape noblewomen, but the climax of the story is the "brutal, but well-deserved" death of the peasant leaders:

> The leaders were immediately taken and their naked bodies tied with irons to long stakes and burned alive on fire, some of them put on the cross, others skinned and left alive for some days. Some were quartered and fed to the dogs.[32]

The staging of their torture had a moral, spiritual and aesthetic value in a communicative space distinct from the memory war. Reports such as these were trying to meet the increasing demand by an international public for news and entertainment.[33] A pamphlet series published in German cities as the events unfolded in 1514 ended with an image of the peasant king crowned with a red-hot iron crown, being roasted and eaten by his fellows while listening to a *Te Deum laudamus*.[34] The author promised a second issue to update readers on the continuing fight on the battlefield, but this never appeared, as—we might guess—the readership's appetite for horror was already well satisfied.

With regard to the Hungarian battle of words, we have seen how participants on both sides, rebels and the powerful alike, fabricated conspiracy theories, transforming very diverse individual motives and chaotic happenings into a linear and logical sequence of events. A process of smoothing personal and public memories into basic stories that made normative claims and aimed to shape the experience of those in the present and future alike seems to have been well underway, but was still tied to the original setting of events.

29 Tóth, "A fájdalom metaforái," with further literature.

30 Taurinus, *Paraszti háború*, 65.

31 Janus Vitalis Panormitanus, *De Ungarorum Cruciata facto anno 1514. et de infanda saevitia utrinque patrata*, Roma 1514. Edited in *Monumenta rusticorum*, 242–45.

32 Ibid., 245.

33 Tóth, "A lator teste," 150.

34 Zeckel Jorg, *Die auffrur so geschehen ist im Vngerlandt mit dem creutzern vnnd auch darbey wie man der creutzer haubtman hat gefangen vnnd getoedt* [1514]. Edited in *Monumenta rusticorum*, no. 227.

Accounts of participants who remained outsiders of the memory war, however, have a very different narrative structure. Since "outsider stories" were not influenced by retrospective schemes of explanation and communal myth making, they remained far closer to authentic individual experience. Incidents were portrayed through the lenses of participants drifting through the crowd with no idea of what was happening. This may be realistic in the sense articulated by some theorists of collective violence, who argue that the majority are in the dark and cannot foresee possible consequences.[35] In these accounts, the revolt is presented merely as a background for personal vicissitudes and as a cause of individual hardships. Imre Wolconz, a cleric student from the diocese of Zagreb, made the following assertion:

> When his adopted father was forced to join the formidable army of the crusaders [...], since he, driven by filial love and solicitude, did not want to leave his father, he also joined the army. As he was, however, a literate man, which the captain of the troops also knew, he was commissioned to compose letters of recruitment sent out to parish priests. In fear of death and not daring to deny compliance, he wrote these letters.[36]

References to men joining the crusaders under force are found six times in these accounts. They are further supported by episodes describing escapes from peasant troops, which enhance the credibility of the claim that they had joined the peasants out of fear. Cleric András Sokovich of Obedszentkereszt (Križ, Croatia) remembered:

> Some peasants in the market town of Halas, in the diocese of Csanád, where he was a student at the time, forced him and some of his fellows to join the peasant army under the threat of being impaled. As he could not evade death otherwise, he stayed with the peasants for three days, during which time the peasants impaled a lot of their enemies, in other words the noblemen of the kingdom.[37]

The participation of students (*scolaris*)—young clerics studying in parish and chapter schools—is a plausible circumstantial detail: the retributive legislation

35 This is called the irrational theory of collective violence. See McPhail, *The Myth of the Madding Crowd.*

36 APA vol. 66, fols 24v–25r (1520).

37 APA, vol. 63, fols 206v–7r (May 9, 1518, Zagrabien. dioc.). Halas is a village in Keve County (modern day Serbia).

of the National Diet prohibited not only peasants and *hajduks* from bearing arms, but unbeneficed clergy and students too.[38] The severity of the *cruciati* with people reluctant to join them, based on the papal bull, is also richly evidenced. Refusal to join the crusaders was punished by death and demolition of the offender's house.[39] Dominican friar György Bodonyi decided to fight with the peasants in order to avoid being impaled:

> He lived as a true friar in the convent of Boró, where he earned the title of the prefect, when a crusade erupted which turned into a rift and conflict between the nobility and the people (*plebei*). In this turmoil, he was forced by the commoners to join them, otherwise he would have been impaled and executed with brutality.[40]

After joining the peasant army, a long sequence of Friar György's vicissitudes began:

> As he could not dodge the perils otherwise, he stayed with them for eight days without killing anyone with his own hands and since he saw their cruelty and was unable to take part in their horrible manslaughters, he escaped secretly and returned to his convent. The peasants got so enraged by his escape that they led their troops against the friary in order to impale him anonymously and execute him brutally. The friars of the convent realized the imminent danger and secured a little boat for him, with which he fled on the river Danube during the night. When the *cruciati* broke into the convent and the sacristy searching for him in vain, they tied and detained the provost instead. Finally, they killed another friar instead of him.[41]

Similar fugitive adventures formed the backbone of the hardships of another clergyman from southern Hungary, Priest Benedek Pellérdi. "He served once in the village of Kétsoprony, in the diocese of Várad, when some crusaders led him by force to the infamous György Székely, the head and captain of the tyranny of peasants, [...] and he was ordered to fight with them or else die."[42] He

38 DRMH, vol. 4, anno 1514/paragraph 60.

39 Szűcs, "Die Ideologie des Bauernkrieges."

40 APA vol. 62, fols 57v–58r (5 April, 1517, Quinqueecclesien. dioc.). Boró (Borovo, Croatia) was the site of a well-known Augustinian mendicant friary. The Dominican cloister has not yet been identified.

41 Ibid.

42 Ibid., vol. 63, fols 38r–39r (March 27, 1518).

followed them to Nagylak (Nădlac, Romania), but after the crusaders had captured the castle, he escaped and joined the nobility, with whom he defended the chapter of Arad (located in modern-day Romania). "When they had to give up fighting and leave the chapter fortress due to famine and lack of food, he once again fell into the hands of the crusaders."[43]

The authors of these "outsider accounts" were all active participants in the revolt one way or the other: they had joined the war on either side usually under pressure, as they confessed, then fled or remained, shooting or composing letters. The biographical framework and life-like perplexity of their accounts compared to the narratives constructed by the *cruciati* and the powerful cannot be accounted for by the fact that they were written closer in time to the events themselves. Their narratives were not so much influenced by the events of the revolt, but by the circumstances of the narrators at the time of storytelling, in this case by the fact that they were outsiders to the memory war. Slavonian clerics András Sokovich and Imre Wolconz were only temporarily players in the revolt during their studies. Sokovith was a student in the village of Halas in Keve County, where the revolt seems to have spread to from Csanád, Bács and Szerém Counties, although afterwards he probably returned to Slavonia. Benedek Pellérdi, from the town of Pécs, which had been untouched by the war, was serving as priest in the village of Mezőkétsoprony in Békés County, one of the well-known centers of the conflict. Friar György Bodonyi, who also came from the eastern regions of Baranya, was continually on the move after 1514: he tried to escape his involuntary past as a crusader by fleeing to the friary in Győr in western Hungary, before moving on to Vienna. He returned to western Hungary a year later in 1515 or 1516, thinking that the turmoil had been settled; however, his plan was thwarted when the Dominicans of Vasvár refused his entry "due to the fear of the crusaders." When the friars of Németújvár (Güssing, Austria) also closed their gate to him, György went to the bishop of Veszprém, who gave him license to remove his friar's habit and minister as a secular priest for two years. When the episcopal license expired in April 1517, he asked the Pope personally to prolong it. The scenes of György's wanderings, Vienna and western Hungary, lay far from the centers of the revolt. In sum, all of these narrators participated in the military conflict, yet remained outsiders in the battle of words aimed at legitimizing the acts of war.

---

43 Nagylak was besieged by the Dózsa-led army from May 22 to May 24, 1514. From this location, the peasant army proceeded eastwards along the banks of the Maros (Mureș) River to Arad, where the residents of this market town surrendered to them, though the clergy of the local chapter took up arms. Barta and Fekete Nagy, *Parasztháború*, 85, 97.

In contrast, the revolt myths of the rebels emerged at locations where the revolt had broken out: in Bács (the story of Priest Kelemen Canimich), Bihar (the story of Priest Miklós Bihari) and the region of Eger (the story of Priest Benedek Nagyhatvani). The myths of the ruling élite, on the other hand, emerged in the territories where military conflicts unfolded, which coincided with the headquarters and fields of action of the bishop-generals responsible for putting down the revolt. The Transylvanian cleric and nobleman Gergely Koppándi, who had been with the army of General Pál Tomori that had defeated the peasant army at Bihar, served as the parish priest of Ludas (Luduș, Romania) near Torda (Turda, Romania) a few months following his petition, and in 1522 he was canon of Gyulafehérvár (Alba Iulia, Romania). In other words, he was a member of the court of Ferenc Várdai, the bishop of Transylvania (1512–24),[44] where Taurinus wrote his epic poem about the revolt, in which the bishop featured as a hero suppressing the rebellion.[45] Another example of this is the priest Dénes Kaschach, who wrote his petition to the pope from the surroundings of the town of Veszprém, from where Péter Beriszló, the bishop of Veszprém and ban of Slavonia, commanded the noble troops against the insurgents.

In conclusion, a comparison of accounts by neutral outsiders as opposed to public stories of the memory war permits some generalizations about their representations of violence. Outsiders of the war remembered participating in collective violence but denied having killed anyone, which suggests that it was possible to preserve personal identity at the expense of making a taboo of interpersonal violence (a memory practice that has also been observed in individual memories of the First World War).[46] The denial of committing interpersonal violence resulted in rather absurd and incredible narratives. Priest Benedek Pellérdi argued that although he had shot crusaders from the besieged chapter of Arad, he had not killed anyone. After he was captured by the crusaders, he killed no noblemen, because he had intentionally aimed at walls or into the air.[47] As the above story by Gergely Koppándi demonstrates, interpersonal violence resurfaced in the memory war in which competing group identities were at stake and when there were political arguments to justify the use of extreme violence outside the context of the normal suspension of everyday wartime norms.

---

44 MNL OL DL 36402; DL 36400; DL 67263.

45 Taurinus was active as vicar (1517–18) in the same episcopal court. See his lines about Várdai: Taurinus, *Paraszti háború*, 61–62.

46 Audoin, Rouzeau and Becker, *1914–1918*, 39.

47 APA, vol. 63, fols 38r–39r (March 27, 1518).

Given the barbarity of the enemy, war was frequently idealized and presented as a fight of civilization against barbarity.[48] In the bloodthirsty "public history" found in pamphlets, however, both parties were portrayed as extremely cruel. The centers of the memory war overlap with the intellectual and military centers of the revolt. Interestingly, these were exactly the same regions that in earlier decades had produced the bulk of long-distance pilgrims and where evangelical teachings met with a quick and intense response.[49] These paradoxical coincidences can most probably be explained, as Jenő Szűcs has proposed, by the presence of Observant Franciscans, whose friaries show a similar geographical distribution.[50] This finding suggests that the popular public sphere of the late fifteenth and the early sixteenth centuries was strongly shaped by the activities and preachings of Observant Franciscan friars, from exhortations to take up the cross to anti-noble sermons and the spreading of spiritualist, messianic ideas.

György Dózsa, the Martyr

In the 1520s the first investigative campaigns against "heretics" began in the same locations where the memory war about the 1514 Revolt had occurred. As noted by Katalin Péter, it is remarkable that the charge of heresy was never enforced by identifying the accused as rebels during the inquests.[51] This decoupling is all the more remarkable since, during the time of the bloody retribution following the 1525 German Peasants' War, the figure of the rebel and the Lutheran were totally fused. A Würzburg pastor was imprisoned by a landowner in 1525 because "he preached the tenets of Luther and a rebellion" and was therefore considered a dangerous person "liable to make the ordinary folk rebel in the future."[52] From the perspective of Catholic and Lutheran authorities alike, the German Lutheran was considered an insubordinate subject.

In Hungary, by contrast, the identity of rebel and Lutheran were not coterminous because the revolt was not instrumentalized in the construction of Catholic and Protestant identities. Instead of personifying rebels, the

48 For the modern analogue see again ibid., 116.

49 The regions in question are Abaúj and Zemplén counties in northeastern Hungary, Csanád, Békés and Bihar Counties in the Great Hungarian Plain, and Bács-Bodrog County in southern Hungary along the Danube. Cf. Csukovits, *Középkori magyar zarándokok*, 188; and Szűcs "Ferences ellenzéki áramlat," 426.

50 Szűcs, "A ferences obszervancia," 243–44.

51 Péter, *A reformáció*, 72–73.

52 Scribner and Scott, eds., *The German Peasants' War*, document no. 149.

extreme brutality of the death of the "peasant king" Dózsa came to epitomize memories of the revolt. By that time, they were already disconnected from the sites on which the events had occurred. Miklós Istvánffy, an early seventeenth-century chronicler at the court of the Habsburg king, introduced his lengthy description of Dózsa's execution as follows:

> I shudder at the thought of enumerating the horrible, extreme and unprecedented punishments of these miserable people. Since even if they deserved this terrible torture and death, it would nevertheless have rather suited pious Christians to subdue such a cruel massacre by piety and compassion.[53]

Looking at it from the distance of a century, the theater of horror of public executions appears to have undergone a profound shift, but the image of the peasant leader sitting with a red-hot crown on his head watching the execution of his brother while waiting to be quartered and devoured by his starved fellow rebels continued to be reproduced in words and images.

It seems that this image persisted in the consciousness of the aristocracy and nobility since they were familiar with historical chronicles of the revolt and occasionally commissioned such texts.[54] The memory of the revolt could thus be used to mobilize the paralyzed nobility in times of crisis. In 1632 the aristocratic political leader, Palatine Miklós Esterházy (1625–45), exhorted the nobility with the following words:

> You should remember the peasants' attack in the time of King Ladislaus, which caused huge bloodshed and the country's devastation. Those who have ever read the chronicles about it, will possibly know [...] that we will have to follow the example of John Szapolyai [who put down the revolt and ordered the executions] when acting against the peasants, not letting the traitors go and searching for them all possible ways.[55]

Palatine Esterházy was a man of his word. The leader of the 1632 peasant revolt, Péter Császár, was tortured and quartered.[56] From the sixteenth to the eighteenth

---

53 Nicolaus Istvánffy, *Historiarum de rebus Ungaricis libri XXXIV* (Colonia Agrippina, 1622). In Hungarian translation: Benits, ed., *Istvánffy Miklós*, vol. I/1, 141–42.

54 Monok, *A művelt arisztokrata*, passim.

55 Letter of Esterházy to the nobility of Sáros County, March 31, 1632. Published in Reizner, "A Császár-féle," 128.

56 Makkai, *A felsőtiszavidéki parasztfelkelés*.

FIGURE 11 *The execution of peasant leader György Dózsa on the front page of Stephanus Taurinus,* Stauromachia (*Vindobonae, 1519*).

century, ritual retributions for peasant revolts and other political rebellions became public occasions for remembering 1514.[57] The public execution of early modern rebels reminded spectators of the sacralized death of Dózsa staging the passion of Christ, and the ritual of Holy Communion.[58] I would go so far as to speculate that the nobility's perceptions included even the Dózsa-Christ analogue.[59]

57 For further examples see Tóth, "A fájdalom metaforái," 352–53, 359–60.

58 On the parallels between the iconography of Christ's Passion and that of the Dózsa execution, see Birnbaum, "A Mock Calvary." See also Freedman, "Representations of Peasant and Seigneurial Fury."

59 On the reading of contemporary mock passion narratives and of humanist narratives of Dózsa's death, see Kiss, "Ambiguity and Paradox."

For them, the sufferings of the peasant rebel must have represented the deserved penance for the sins of his fellows, whose redemption in the afterlife must have also seemed natural to them. The contemporary chronicler, György Szerémi, a native of the region where the execution happened, recorded that György Dózsa, soon after his death, was venerated as the "second St. George of Macedonia, the martyr," and the place of his execution became a site of pilgrimage.[60] The above-mentioned chronicler Istvánffy commented on the execution of the leader of the Croatian peasant revolt in 1573, Matija Gubec:

> Tearing dreadfully with burning pliers and crowned with a burning iron-crown and finally cut into four in the manner of thieves, he received the due punishment for his crime and usurpation of the royal title; he was punished with such severity so that the elderly, who are still alive, would remember with horror the unfortunate assault of György Sekler Dózsa who had wanted to extirpate the nobility.[61]

The ruling elite, who had learned to fear the peasants in 1514, engineered the staging of the dramatic memorialization of the Revolt and its stigmatization in subsequent centuries. Public executions were designed to deter crime and to legitimize power by reminding people of the consequences of rebellion, making them recoil from thoughts of repetition. We do not know how ordinary folk responded. If early modern spectators remembered, identified with and experienced pain when it was performed on stage, as several scholars have suggested, they must have felt that this suffering contributed to purification and salvation.[62] In terms of the psychological concepts current today, the repeated recollection and staging of such painful events would have hindered mental healing, and we would expect the pre-modern practice of public execution as a commemorative ritual to have worsened collective traumas. If "nations can [freely] repress [and forget] with psychological impunity,"[63] as has been recently argued, we may have to conclude that the self-image of early modern society in Hungary was, in fact, stabilized by the cultivation in text, image and ritual of the martyr Dózsa and his crown of thorns.[64]

60 Georgius Sirmiensis, *De Perditione Regni Hungariae*, 68. The association of Christ's martyrdom with Dózsa's death was suggested by István Nemeskürty in his 1983 book *Önfia vágta sebét*, 164–66.

61 Benits, ed., *Istvánffy Miklós*, 485.

62 See, for example, Groebner, *Defaced*, 99–104.

63 Irwin-Zarecka, *Frames of Remembrance*, 116.

64 For this definition of cultural memory, see Assmann, "Collective Memory and Cultural Identity," 132.

FIGURE 12 *The execution of György Dózsa in Paul Ricaut,* Die Neu eröffnete Ottomanische Pforte *(Augsburg, 1694) vol. 2, p. 106.*

In this chapter, we have investigated issues related to the experiences of collective violence and the ways in which individuals and groups used remembering and forgetting as means of forging identities for themselves. In the following chapter, we will explore how those individuals, who had crossed the seemingly greatest divide—the one between the Muslim and Christian worlds—also sought to construct coherent life stories for themselves.

CHAPTER 9

Shifting Identities in the Christian-Muslim Contact Zone

Mátyás, son of Lőrinc Antusui, started his adventurous career in an Observant Franciscan friary in Transylvania. He claimed in his remission request in 1510 that he had professed his vow as a child and continued to live in the cloister for years until he reached the age of fourteen. Then, instead of confirming his vow, he decided to leave, though he did not specify the reasons for his decision. Because his fellow friars tried to prevent Mátyás from leaving the friary, he had to escape in secret:

> He went among the pagans, where passing himself off as one of them he married Axpianna, a pagan woman of another religion. They consummated the marriage conducted according to the customs and rituals of his wife's religion. However, the fear then overtook him that it might become known that he was, in fact, a Christian and they would therefore try to take his life. His conscience also inspired him to leave his pagan wife and come to Rome.[1]

In Rome, Mátyás asked the pope to annul his vows both as a friar and as a husband because he wanted to marry a Christian woman. While he allegedly sought refuge among "pagans" in his flight from his Christian fellows, another apostate friar from the southern regions of the kingdom, Bertalan Seres, fled in the opposite direction from the Ottoman Turks to the security of the cloister:

> When the Turks and other enormous masses of infidels invaded the regions of the Kingdom of Hungary, [...] they savagely slaughtered many Christians and priests in particular, whom they tortured to death in many different ways. Since he, being scared, hoped to evade death by taking on the habit of the preaching friars, driven by fear he entered their St. Nicholas cloister in the town of Szeged."[2]

1 APA vol. 55, fol. 196r (1510, Transylvanien. dioc.).

2 Ibid., vol. 2, fol. 221v (Quinqueecclesien. dioc.).

 | DOI 10.1163/9789004361263_10

Bertalan traveled to Rome in 1441 so that the pope would permit and legalize his career as a secular priest. Notwithstanding their differences, both accounts suggest that dissimulation and change of identity were routine strategies of survival during moments of crisis. More precisely, self-interested narrators deemed such episodes credible and reckoned that tricksters ready to reshape their identities to match the politics of the moment would earn the sympathies of their audiences. Just as in previous chapters we examined crossing from the cloister to the outside world as a means of negotiating social status, we will now consider traversing the boundary separating Christians from Muslims as another tactic.[3]

Runaway friars faced difficulties that inspired them to navigate astutely in the frontier regions between the Kingdom of Hungary and the Ottoman Empire. The main political consequence of the military conflict between Hungarians and Ottoman Turks is common knowledge: the middle regions of Hungary were under Ottoman suzerainty until the end of the seventeenth century. Ottoman rule in Hungary is portrayed by traditional historical narratives as a period of war and devastation resulting from the presence of an alien and destructive Muslim culture. These narratives provide an elaborate picture of mass killings, deserted and depopulated areas, refugees and the captivity and enslavement of huge numbers of people or, at best, the payment of taxes to both Ottoman and Hungarian authorities.[4] Instead of the familiar image of fierce Christian-Muslim rivalry in the form of crusades and *jihads*, this chapter will focus on individual careers in order to illuminate, at the level of social practices, the coexistence and intersection of the Muslim and Christian worlds. This new perspective makes it possible to conceive traditionally imagined "conflict zones" as "contact zones."[5] Applying the perspective of those who voluntarily crossed the Christian-Muslim boundary through marriage, we will draw out connections between the violent and intimate domains of Ottoman rule in Hungary and thus offer a more nuanced picture of the daily coexistence—previously conceived as sharp antagonism—of Christians and Muslims.[6]

---

3 On the concept of everyday "tactic," see Certeau, *The Practice of Everyday Life*, passim.

4 See, for example, Engel, "A török dúlások"; Sz. Simon, "Flight or Submission"; Dávid, *Pasák és bégek*; and Fodor and David, eds., *Ransom Slavery*.

5 Contact zones have been defined as spaces of cross-cultural encounters in which historically separated peoples established ongoing relations involving coercion, unequal power relations and conflict. Pratt, *Imperial Eyes*, esp. 7–8.

6 I promote the approach of recent colonizing literature, which engages in the study of the intimate in a colonizing context, not to turn away from the structure of dominance, but to discern transfer points of power relations. Stoler, "Intimidation of Empire," esp. 13–16.

The already familiar image of Hungarian-Ottoman wars and of "Turkish" invaders bringing devastation and captivity appears in petitions addressed to the pope. Parish priest Mihály from the village of Kravarszko (Kravarsko, Croatia) remembered one of the many Ottoman incursions as follows: "When the inhuman Turks, the enemies of Christ, invaded the town of Kravarszko, its inhabitants, being frightened by the news of their approach, deserted the town" and took refuge in the surrounding countryside.[7] Because the audience of these stories was the head of Latin Christendom, the armed conflict was emphatically depicted as a defensive war of Christian religion and culture against the barbarity and brutality of pagans. In 1521, the year in which Belgrade fell to the Turks, another Slavonian priest, Johannes Dugonosics, related that "the undefeatable Turks, the perfidious enemies of the name of Christ and the persecutors of true belief, do not cease to harass the neighboring province with raiding, pillaging the population, dragging away many and keeping them in miserable captivity."[8]

The brutality of the "pagans" served as a narrative device to legitimize the guilt of the petitioner: paradoxically, clergymen also needed absolution for partaking in war and committing violence against infidels.[9] Péter Nogneres, a layman from the town of Kalocsa, used the same charge to justify being too weak to resist: when he was fighting in 1463 "for the defense of true religion"—probably as part of the royal army besieging the castle of Jajca (Jajce, Bosnia and Herzegovina)—"he was captured by the Turks and imprisoned, where he was handled so unmercifully that under the impact of force and fear he denied his faith and lived with the Turks, eating, drinking and conversing with them."[10] Apparently, the claim of forced conversion was an effective tool for fabricating an exculpatory story. To this end, he must have condensed a series of more complicated and messy events into a brief narrative in order to attain the pope's clemency.

The narrative tradition of *Turcica* literature provided more extensive space for a realistic depiction of the experiences of Christians coming under Ottoman domination.[11] György of Hungary (better known as Georgius de Hungaria) had

7 APA, vol. 28, fol. 214rv (1479).

8 Ibid., vol. 68, fol. 231v–2r (1521).

9 Gáspár Back, the archdeacon of Szepes, fought against the Turks during the Siege of Jajca, while Kelemen Garai, the canon of Zagreb, confessed to hiring laymen to kill a captive Turk. APA vol. 17, fol. 255v–6r (1469, Chanadien. dioc.); vol. 3, fol. 173v (1450).

10 "A dictis Thurcis captus et diris carceribus mancipatus ita, quod per vim et metum, qui cadere potuit in constantem virum, suam fidem abnegavit et cum ipsis cibo, potu, loquela conversatus est." APA vol. 15, fol. 80r (1467, Colocen. dioc.).

11 See, for example, Fügedi, ed., *Kimondhatatlan nyomorúság*.

been captured as a boy by Turkish marauders in Transylvania in 1438 and had spent twenty-one years as a slave in the heartlands of the Ottoman Empire. After his escape, he went directly to the center of Latin Christendom, where he entered the Dominican order (perhaps thus fulfilling a vow made in captivity). He described his experiences among the Ottomans in a treatise published in 1480, which served as a warning to his fellow Christians regarding the spiritual vulnerability that had led many of them to accept Islam.[12] In this treatise, György wrote:

> This evil sect does not resort to force, but divests people of their free will: breaks the steadiness of the heart, defeats any endurance and blurs and infects the mind so much that one cannot help but to ignominiously deny his religion, for which he was earlier ready to die.[13]

A cleric from Slavonia, András Kunics, described in his pardon request the years he had spent in slavery among the Turks as having been an unwanted interlude on his path to the priesthood. According to Kunics, he was taken to Turkey around 1460 (*extra patriam in Turchiam ductus*), where he became a slave of an Ottoman soldier of Croatian origin with whom he had fought against Christians.[14]

The protagonists of this chapter did not bend under pressure, but voluntarily crossed the Christian-Muslim border. They are the less familiar figures who opted to travel from Christian regions to lands occupied by Turks, typically fleeing from a Christian marriage into the arms of a Muslim spouse and converting. The liberty inherent in their decision-making cannot be compared to the circumstances of the renegades described above, who were subjected to the Ottomans, either voluntarily or by force, while living under their suzerainty. This chapter aims to better understand the rationality underlying their free and exceptional choices.[15]

---

12 The treatise of the Spanish converso Juan Luis Vives entitled *De Conditione Vitae Christianorum sub Turca* (published in 1529) is a very similar piece, fraught with an anxiety of current Christian spiritual frailty. See George, "Juan Luis Vives," 663–68.

13 "Magyarországi György barát értekezése a törökök szokásairól, viszonyairól és gonoszságáról" [The Treatise of Friar George of Hungary about the Customs, Ways and Evil Nature of the Turks] in Fügedi, ed., *Kimondhatatlan nyomorúság*, 23, 60–61.

14 APA vol. 32, fol. 136r (1483, Zagrabien. dioc.).

15 Klára Hegyi outlined the general reasons for which the majority of Hungarians did not embrace Islam: Hegyi, "Kereszténység és Iszlám." For the perspective of the Ottomans see Fodor, "A kincstár."

With regard to other contact zones such as the Mediterranean, historians have recently become interested in tricksters who forged and maintained Christian-Muslim dual identities.[16] The evidence of a number of fabulous careers and a rich variety of deceits (inventing identities or fraudulently assuming the identity of others) allowed for the thesis of the "fluidity of identities" in the early modern period,[17] an age teeming with impostors.[18] More recently, historical narratives of Christian women converting to Islam at court or opting for marriages with Muslim men have highlighted their gendered strategies of subverting hierarchical social relations.[19]

Here I will put on center stage the forgotten tricksters, both male and female, who exploited the Hungarian-Ottoman encounter. I will explore situations that facilitated their strategic use of religious conversion.[20] In other words, I will portray these ordinary men and women as active agents striving to take control of their lives, thus rendering their voluntary conversions as a mode of operating in everyday life rather than as deviant or abnormal behavior. What previous experiences and resources supported their adaptation to another religion and culture? Who turned the perils and possibilities inherent in the plurality of norms in contact zones to their own advantage, and when and how did they do so? Do their actions and representations allow us to interpret late medieval and early modern religious identity as situative?[21]

"Apostate" Spouses

Ferenc Csiszár ("Gunsmith") who lived in the diocesan town of Várad, was deserted by his wife for a Turkish man living in Buda. He narrated the events in his supplication to the pope: his wife, the mother of his child, "instigated by diabolic inspiration, during the time he was away from his homeland, sold

16 Davis, *Trickster Travels.*

17 Kafadar, *Between Two Worlds*, 28.

18 Eliav-Feldon, *Exposing Impostors*; Eliav-Feldon, "Invented Identities," with further literature.

19 See, for example, Peirce, *Morality Tales*; and Dursteler, *Renegade Women.*

20 Sándor Takáts was the only historian writing at the turn of the nineteenth and twentieth centuries who took an interest in the lives of ordinary men living in Ottoman Hungary, and presented voluntary renegades—spies, guides, henchmen, scribes working in the service of the Turks, Hungarian wives of several pashas and beys—as characteristic figures of their time. See most importantly Takáts, *Rajzok a török világból.*

21 On theories of identity, see Hall and du Gay, eds., *Questions of Cultural Identity*, esp. 3–17.

all their goods and ran away. She went to the city of Buda, in the regions of infidels, where she married a Turk." Csiszár was unable to divert her from this intention, although "he sent many of his men after her, calling her back, some of whom were killed by the Turk, which put him to huge expenses."[22] We have no reason to doubt his words. It was uncharacteristic of men to accept being cuckolded (an issue raised by slanderers); moreover, Ferenc appears to have been a man of strict morals. In 1548 he turned to the pope, not to obtain permission to remarry, but for authorization to receive the sacraments despite his disordered marital affairs. Obviously there must have been many people in similar situations who never sought to restore their legal and spiritual status.

While the described events suggest that a dramatic conflict of interest and emotion lay in the background of this episode, we are forced to make inferences with regard to the incentives of the runaway wife.[23] What enticed her to leave Várad, the thriving episcopal town of the Partium region, for Buda, the former capital of the Kingdom of Hungary, which, after its Ottoman occupation, became a melting pot of Latin and Orthodox Christians, Jews, and Muslims, and where the muezzin called people to prayer and church bells were silenced?[24] Was she trying to escape an unpleasant husband, or did she seek security and socioeconomic prosperity in the bed of the enemy, who may have been a garrison soldier or a civil servant of the new administration? Regardless of whether emotion, necessity or cold calculation served as the motive for her flight, her conversion for the purpose of marriage renders the question even more pressing: what made it possible for ordinary Christian women and men to adapt to another culture with such apparent ease?

Similar stories from abandoned husbands about runaway wives freely marrying "Turks" must be read with circumspection. The manner in which they described their first, broken marriages most often functioned to negotiate the validity of their second marriages with Church authorities. A prerequisite was to have their first marriage declared void, so the alleged "apostasy" of their spouses and their rejection of Christianity served as a credible and legal argument to achieve this end.[25]

---

22 APA, vol. 121, fol. 64rv (1548, Waradien. dioc.).

23 On the underlying material component of such conflicts, see Butler, "Runaway Wives," 342–43.

24 See Dávid, *Pasák és bégek*, 79–84; and Káldy-Nagy, *Harács-szedők*, 106–10.

25 In canon law, difference of religion was not an impediment to marriage, though it could serve as the basis for invalidating one (without the possibility for remarriage). Plöchl, *Geschichte des Kirchenrechts*, 294–96.

The Slavonian nobleman István Velikei ("from Velike") of Radovanc was also portrayed as a trickster who moved freely and deliberately across religious and ethnic boundaries. His abandoned wife, Fruzsina, daughter of the nobleman János Kasztellánfi of Szentlélek (Sveti Duh, Croatia), presented two versions of a request narrative to two different papal offices in order to be licensed to remarry. Her first petition, submitted to the Penitentiary during the first half of 1541, rested upon two pillars: first, that she had been betrothed to István Velikei of Radovanc at only nine or ten years of age, and had never confirmed the vow after reaching the age of majority (very reminiscent of the routine reasoning of apostate friars who claimed that they had professed their religious vow as children); and second, that following their betrothal, her fiancé had "gone to the Turks, donned their clothing and together with them attacked and plundered the settlements of the Christians and perhaps even delivered his own castle into the hands of the Turks."[26] Fruzsina therefore claimed that she was not bound to her marital vow because Velikei had "committed adultery, keeping a Turkish woman as a concubine who had borne him daughters." However, her arguments of having been betrothed as a minor and the "apostasy of faith" of her fiancé proved to be insufficient. As Fruzsina related in her request to the Penitentiary, she had turned before to the papal nuncio at the Viennese royal court with the same request, but the nuncio had refused to invalidate her betrothal.[27]

Her second petition, submitted to the Apostolic Dataria, the office that issued more prestigious and costly licenses, increased her chances of gaining the decision she sought. The social standing of the Slavonian Kasztellánfis made such a judicial maneuver feasible. They were an old and locally distinguished noble family that owned a couple of castles, while Fruzsina's father had successfully increased familial assets and prestige through royal military service.[28] This second appeal employed a totally different rhetoric, probably due to the fact that Fruzsina's father had died in the meantime and the architect of her next petition must have been her widowed mother,

26 APA vol. 106, fol. 667v–68r (Zagreb, August 27, 1541). The date indicates when the office approved the petition, not when it was submitted.

27 Johannes de Morono (Giovanni Morone), bishop of Modena (1536–42) and, beginning in 1542, cardinal. HC, vol. 3, 252.

28 On the history of the family, see Pálosfalvi, *The Noble Elite*, 179–89, where several details of a previous reconstruction of the family history are corrected: Maček and Jurković, *Rodoslov*, 152–61. The father served as a royal tax collector, as well as as a member of the light cavalry attached directly to the royal court during the reign of King Louis II (1516–26) and King Ferdinand I (1526–64). Pálosfalvi, *The Noble Elite*, 189.

Barbara Ősi.[29] She chose not to portray the marriage as a union between two individuals in accordance with the ideal propagated by the Church, opting instead to depict the matrimony in a more down-to-earth fashion as a mere family matter.

The mother's narrative stated that it had been the responsibility of the head of the family to arrange his daughter's marriage (her status as a minor was not mentioned) to a neighboring nobleman from Pozsega (Požega, Croatia). Related archival data highlights that the Kasztellánfi-Velikei marriage had served to strengthen the alliance between two families of relatively equal status who had neighboring estates and ties of affinity.[30] Naturally it was also the father who, according to the petition, had "wanted to defend the honor of his daughter and give her in marriage to another" following the apostasy and betrayal of the husband he had selected for her. The necessity of her daughter's second marriage was also dictated by family dynamics. Barbara Ősi was an old, widowed mother, she claimed, who could not take care of six young children and defend three castles—in Szentlélek, Bikszád and Zelnyak (Sveti Duh, Bisag and Sirač, Croatia)—under threat from the Turks, which, if lost, would gravely undermine the security of the region. She had therefore needed a forceful and energetic son-in-law to be the husband of her seventh child and eldest daughter, Fruzsina. The self-assertive widowed mother, who oversaw the affairs of her large family with extraordinary skill, cleverly exploited the popular image of the "miserrima orphana."[31]

29 The Ősi and the Kasztellánfi families were bound by many marriages. Pálosfalvi, *The Noble Elite*, 186, 189.

30 On István Velikei's descent and the ties of affinity that the Velikeis maintained with the county nobility and the family holdings, see MNL OL DL 74679 (1507, 1519), DL 88551. I would like to thank Tibor Neumann for sharing his collection of data regarding the Velikeis. For the medieval family tree (the Velikeis of Zsadán clan), see Engel, *Magyar középkori adattár* (*CD-ROM*). See also Pálosfalvi, *The Noble Elite*, 328, 448, 466–67. Fruzsina's paternal grandmother was of aristocratic descent and the Velikeis were distantly related through marriage to the Bosnian royal family. Ibid., 188.

31 Her success in governing family affairs is reinforced by the fact that in 1569 her then eldest son, Péter, earned the baronial title for the family through courtly and military services. MNL OL, P 1314, A herceg Batthyány család levéltára [Archives of the Batthyány family], Missiles, no. 24255–24260: Letters of Barbara Ősi between 1542 and 1552 to Kristóf Battyhány and his wife, Erzsébet Svetkovics; Pálffy, *A Magyar Királyság*, 170. According to Maček and Jurković, Ősi had eight children—five boys and three girls, the oldest of whom was twenty-one-year-old Fruzsina. In her petition, Ősi specified seven children—four girls and three boys. Fruzsina presumably died soon thereafter, because she is not listed among her siblings designated as beneficiaries of property endowments that the family received in the 1540s and 1550s. MNL OL, A 57, Libri Regii, for example vol. 2, 122–23 (1546) and vol. 3, 649 (1559).

Widow Ősi's reasoning implied that beyond the survival of the family, that of Latin Christendom depended upon the marital affairs of her eldest daughter. Amid the trauma connected to Buda's fall to the Turks in August 1541 and the prevailing desperation in Europe regarding the "Turkish threat," this must have been the decisive argument that finally warranted the Pope's decision to approve the petition, thus overriding the canon law to which the papal nuncio in Vienna had earlier adhered.[32] The fate of the Slavonian region in which this episode took place became a matter of European importance and István Velikei, who had "removed his Christian clothing and dressed as a Turk" and maintained a Turkish concubine, was deemed unworthy of marriage to a Christian woman. They also made sure to embellish the story of the fiancé becoming Turk: yielding to the temptation of the Turks, István had abandoned not only the Catholic faith, but, when they had invaded the territory in which Pozsega was located in 1536, he had delivered provisions to the attackers and ceded his well-fortified Velike castle to them in a betrayal of the relatives with whom he shared possession. Furthermore, István adopted a Turkish voivode as his brother and maintained friendly relations with many Turks.[33]

We can only surmise the motives that inspired István Velikei to leave his family and property behind in order to stand among the Turks. The Slavonian nobleman's deserted fiancée seems to have suggested that he hoped to gain social and economic advantages. He had obviously weighed his prospects at the frontier of the Christian world while facing the advancing Ottoman Empire, and determined that he had better career opportunities as a Turk. Velikei had had two choices: to flee to a territory better defended from the Ottomans, thus abandoning his lands in Pozsega; or to remain.[34] Unlike the majority of nobles, he had chosen the latter. Family memory may have also played a role in Velikei's decision to collaborate with the conquerors rather than resist: two generations previously, one of his distant relatives, Katalin Velikei, had been the wife of Prince Radivoj, the illegitimate brother of King Stephen Thomas

32 This second petition survives in the form of the apostolic response to it: in March 1542, Pope Paul III instructed Simon Erdődy, bishop of Zagreb, to invalidate the betrothal. This decision was exceptionally favorable for the petitioner, because it did not call for further examination of the case, as was customary.

33 ASV, Dataria Apostolica, Brevia Lateranensia, vol. 33, fol. 76r–77v, March 20, 1542.

34 With regard to the movement of the Croatian nobility to northern territories protected from the Turks, see Pálffy, *Miljenko Pandžić and Felix Tobler.* For such movement away from the Zala border zone, see Sz. Simon, "Flight or Submission." On fleeing in general: Szakály, *Magyar adóztatás*, 44–45.

of Bosnia and claimant to the throne.[35] Following the Ottoman occupation of Jajca in 1463, which brought the Kingdom of Bosnia to an end, Radivoj had been executed. By ceding the ancient family residence to the Turks, he may have hoped to regain it from his brothers-in-law, whose share of the residence had grown uncomfortably over the preceding years. Unfortunately, we do not know whether István Velikei's decision to join the Turks, whom he correctly estimated to be the stronger party, promoted his interests in the Ottoman Sanjak of Pozsega.[36]

We have more clues regarding factors that impelled Velikei to convert to Islam. Both the words of his abandoned fiancée and historical scholarship claim that the Ottoman concept of conversion had an integrative attitude to converts. In Velikei's case, as in others, contemporary witnesses perceived individual conversions in terms of external influences. In both of her petitions, Fruzsina mentioned that Velikei "dressed as a Turk, abandoning his Christian clothing." Another usual device to describe conversion was the changing of names.[37] Taking a Muslim name constituted part of the formal, though very simple rite of religious conversion: after declaring the one-sentence confession of faith, assuming a Muslim name symbolized a break with the past and a rebirth in the true religion. The newly converted then received gifts, among which, according to long-established custom, were clothes.[38] The perception of outsiders actually offers a clear reflection of the process of conversion, which manifested in external factors. Contrary to the ideals and practices of Christian conversion, inner transformation of oneself was not expected of new Muslims. The Muslim community was not interested in the motives or sincerity of converts, but was content if they followed their customs.[39] Ottoman Muslims sought rather to socially integrate newcomers by providing them with

35 Pálosfalvi, *The Noble Elite*, 220, 276.

36 Ferenc Pribék, alias Bey Huszein, was also a voluntary renegade who orchestrated the transfer of a castle located in Fülek (Fil'akovo, Slovakia) to the Turks in 1562 and in return was appointed to serve as one of the commanders of another castle. In the 1570s, Pribék lived in Buda as the influential head of the Turkish spy network (Szakály, *Mezőváros és reformáció*, 271–72). Very few of the high dignitaries and administrative and military leaders in Ottoman Hungary can be identified as Hungarians. Cf. Szakály, "Magyar diplomaták," 45–47.

37 With regard to the nobleman Gergely Bakó of Körmend: "His wife similarly dropped the name Erzsébet hoping that her husband would be promoted to pasha." Letter of vice-*comes* István Keserű to Ferenc Batthyány, September 11, 1605. MNL OL, P 1314, A herceg Batthyány család levéltára, Missiles, no. 26397.

38 Minkov, *Conversion to Islam*, 152–53, 156–57.

39 Dutton, *Conversion to Islam*, 151–65; Radishev, "The Spread of Islam."

clothing, monetary gifts and even a spouse and livelihood.[40] The complaints of the Kasztellánfis regarding the converted Velikei also reflect the receptive behavior of the Ottomans: "He adopted as his brother (*in fratrem sibi iuravit*) a voivoide, a leader of the Turks, and to such an extent behaves on friendly terms with him and other Turks."[41]

The authentic figures of Muslim converts in petitions of papal pardon suggest that there must have been more familiar figures in the Ottoman-Hungarian contact zone than traditional historical scholarship leads us to believe. We will continue below to describe some of the further "structural" aspects that rendered conversion to Islam a viable and attractive choice for agile individuals, whose diverse personal motives remain inaccessible. Following upon Fruzsina's perspective, we will look at how and why the institution of Christian marriage in the Ottoman-Hungarian contact zone became too constricted as a result of the dogmatic attitude of Church authorities. Second, we will look more closely at the religious and ethnic characteristics of the eastern and southern regions of the Kingdom of Hungary inhabited by our "apostate" protagonists.

Christian "Bigamists"

According to Jesuit missionaries in Ottoman Hungary, the flight of women and men from ruined marriages frequently led them across the Christian-Muslim frontier.[42] A native observer, the Reformed pastor of a market town under Ottoman rule, was perhaps biased and moralizing when he indicated that voluntary renegades were typically women seeking a more luxurious lifestyle or escaping violent husbands.[43] King Matthias drew the attention of the Roman Curia to another kind of destabilizing impact of the Ottoman-Hungarian encounter on marriages:

> There are several inhabitants of the various parts of our country whose spouse had been dragged away by the Turks. Husbands mourn their wives and wives lament over the unhappy fate of their husbands; they do not

40 Bulliet, *Conversion to Islam*, 33–64.

41 On the custom of adopting Turkish-Hungarian brothers in Ottoman Hungary, see Takáts, *Rajzok*, vol. 1, 315; and Hegyi, "Kereszténység és iszlám," 33–34.

42 Molnár, "Jezsuiták," 236, 257.

43 See Pál Farkas Thuri's humanist epistle "Idea Christianorum Hungarorum in et sub Turcismo [1556–57]," printed first in 1613. Edited by Kathona, *Fejezetek*, 61–69.

> live in a marriage anymore, but they are left in uncertainty concerning the life or death of their spouse, which makes them unwilling to remarry. [...] Many, losing hope of ever being able to give birth to children, leave or ruin their inheritance and go to other regions, often to those held by the enemy, while others give rise to scandals.[44]

In the opinion of the authorities, the people who caused scandals were those attached to their old homes, villages and kin and—just as Fruzsina Kasztellánfi wished to do—remarried locally. Thus, the king requested the pope to give licenses to remarry to those who had lost their spouses and had looked for them in vain among the infidels. According to the king, some of those who had lost spouses had left their homes for foreign lands, often those under Ottoman dominion, in order to start new families. When Illés Klokocsi returned home to Zagreb following seven years of captivity in Turkey, he was unable to find his wife, who must have tired of waiting for him and moved away to find another spouse.[45] In 1500 Klokocsi wrote a petition to the Pope to legalize his second marriage.

Set within the context of everyday life in the Ottoman-Hungarian border zone, the actions of Mrs. Csiszár, the runaway wife from Várad, do not seem extraordinary or hazardous. She might have left in order to escape an undesirable husband, but it is also possible that she believed that her "husband absent from the homeland" had been lost forever, and she wished to remarry. Local Catholic authorities might not have officially recognized a remarriage—just as Fruzsina Kasztellánfi's bid for remarriage was initially refused—and could have charged her with bigamy if her husband's death could not be proven.[46] From her perspective, marriage to a Muslim was less risky and more desirable than life as a lonely Christian woman.

---

44 Letter of King Matthias, written in 1480, addressed to Cardinal John of Aragon, protector of Hungary at the papal curia. Kovács, ed., *Mátyás*, no. 61.

45 APA vol. 48, fol. 536r (Helias de Clokocz laicus habitator opidi Grecz Zagrabiensis diocesis). For a parallel case of moving abroad and remarrying, see Csukovits, "Miraculous Escapes," 7.

46 Several men from Slavonia requested that the Church regard their second marriages and resulting children to be legitimate after their first wives had fallen into Turkish captivity. These petitioners lived undisturbed in their second marriages for decades, which illuminates the general social acceptance of remarriage as well as the meager degree of official control. *Petrus de Podagaris*: APA vol. 48, fol. 485rv; *Valentinus Piscete laic. de villa Toplice*: ibid., vol. 48, fol. 490r.

Várad was the most important town in eastern Hungary at the beginning of the sixteenth century. Many women living in the town decided to take the risk of remaining in the city to remarry, thus placing themselves in a difficult position. The curial lawyer commissioned to submit Ferenc Csiszár's petition was also responsible for another case: Anna Vadasi and Máté Agasi had been reported to the court of the diocesan vicar because Anna had become betrothed to Máté while still married to her previous spouse.[47] Her first husband may well have been the person who reported her to the vicar's court. The decision of Anna and Máté to marry was rather heedless, entailing the foreseeable consequence of a legal separation and prohibition against living together again; however, their supplication reveals that they continued to reside under the same roof and produce children. They were excommunicated from the Church on the grounds of bigamy and forbidden to attend holy mass at their parish church or take the sacraments, none of which bothered them as much as the fact that their children were considered illegitimate. When Anna's first husband died, they requested papal absolution, the legitimation of their children and permission to legally remarry. The vicar of Várad, István Ilosvai, may have prompted Anna and Máté to address their petition to the pope, though it is also possible that they simply decided to bypass the local court that had passed judgment against them, and to turn directly to Rome.[48] In the end they were not able to avoid the Várad court, since, prior to their absolution, the vicar had been commissioned by the pope to conduct an examination to verify their statements; that is, the court questioned local residents about the death of Anna's first husband and the related circumstances.

György Korláth's daughter, Anna, belonged to an entirely different social group—the distinguished urban nobility. Anna found herself in a more difficult position when, as an adult, she balked at living in marriage with the man to whom she had been betrothed as a child—or so she claimed.[49] Several factors provide an indication of the family's social standing. The girl had become an orphan at an early age, and had as her guardian the canon of the cathedral chapter and archdeacon of the diocese. He engaged five-year-old Anna to Pál Szabó, whose name suggests that he was a master artisan, a member of the tailor's guild. Following her engagement, Anna was placed under the tutelage

47 In both cases the lawyer was named Aspra and the petitions were approved by the Penitentiary on January 15, 1548. APA vol. 121, fol. 63v–64r. There is little chance that petitioners from Várad can be identified, since in 1660 Janissaries destroyed the town's medieval cathedral, chapter and municipal archives. See Jakó, "Váradi siralmas krónika."

48 Bunyitay, *A váradi püspökség*, vol. 2, 55–57.

49 APA vol. 93, fols 162rv (1536).

of Poor Clare nuns at the St. Anne cloister in Várad. According to Anna, the nuns persuaded her to formally confirm her engagement to Pál Szabó at the age of ten (more likely to have happened when she reached the age of twelve, the legal age of adulthood), which probably means that the betrothal and the marital vow took place. However, the betrothed couple was never united in matrimony, because either Anna or her canon guardian presumably reconsidered the betrothal a few years later in view of a more favorable match.[50] Likely at the instigation of the forsaken fiancé, the case was heard at the court of the vicar of Várad and, in the second instance, at that of the archbishop of Esztergom, and both Anna and her guardian were excommunicated. The noble origin of Anna Korláth can be proven by the fact that this matter was also brought to the royal court of appeal, which decided that she had to marry Pál Szabó. According to the customary law of the nobility, breaching the marriage vow constituted high treason and entailed the forfeiture of property.[51] Being outlaws from the perspective of both state and church, Anna and her guardian looked to the Papal Court for support.

Regardless of the outcome of the above cases, they clearly demonstrate that both Church and secular control over the local residents of Várad operated efficiently even during the Ottoman wars and the concomitant civil conflicts. Local authorities had more trouble with those who were geographically mobile.[52] Mrs. Csiszár was quite aware of this situation and acted smartly and rationally: in order to live legitimately and free of official harassment with her chosen husband, she moved from Christian Várad to Ottoman-governed Buda. It appears that the possibility of remarriage mattered more to her than a difference in religion; but how much did she and fellow Christians perceive the religion and culture of the Ottoman Turks living in Hungary to be contrasting and foreign?

Latin and Orthodox Christian Intermarriages

In a supplication aimed at legalizing his second marriage, Tamás Tót claimed that his first wife, Magdolna Rachaz, had "left him and, guided by an evil spirit and forgetting about the salvation of her soul, run off to a pagan and schismatic

50 Her petition reads: *ad pubertatem deveniens dictis sponsalibus et confirmationi contradixit et dictum Paulum in virum suum habere nolle asserit.*

51 As testified by the case: MNL OL DL 99775.

52 Synodal decrees urging the lower clergy to proclaim the banns because many husbands were leaving their wives and remarrying abroad serve to substantiate this. Solymosi, ed., *A veszprémi egyház*, 67; Alberigo et al., eds., *Conciliorum Oecumenicorum Decreta*, 758.

with whom she united in marriage, which they consummated."[53] Who might Magdolna's "pagan and schismatic" husband have been? In the southeastern diocese of Csanád in which Magdolna and Tamás lived, particularly in the southern parts of the district, an increasing number of Romanians lived with Orthodox South Slavs (Bulgarians, Serbs and Bosnians) who had moved northward to escape the Turks. Hussite "heretics" had also taken refuge in this area together with Patarenes and Bogomils.

As a result of Catholic missionary activity, there was a considerable number of converted Latin Christians among the new immigrants.[54] "Turkish" soldiers who made incursions across the Hungarian-Ottoman border along the lower Danube were either Orthodox Christians or newly converted Muslims. In Roman terminology, the Orthodox were referred to as "schismatics," but in ordinary usage they were called "heretics" and "pagans."[55]

Magdolna Rachaz's new "pagan and schismatic" husband may well have been a South Slav conqueror who had converted from Orthodoxy to Islam, though it seems more probable that he was an Orthodox Romanian or South Slav. The surname of Magdolna's first husband, Tót, was used in Hungarian to refer to Slovaks, Slovenes and Croats, indicating that he might also have been a South Slav who had converted to the Roman Church. Although her deserted husband accused her of "apostasy," Magdolna may simply have returned to her original religion and ethnic community. In a similar vein, the runaway friar, Mátyás Antusui, whose case opened this chapter, may not have fled from Transylvania to Ottoman lands, but simply have moved to a Romanian-inhabited territory within Transylvania or to one of the adjacent Romanian principalities. In this case, the *paganus* that Mátyás had married after his escape from the cloister might have been an Orthodox Christian Romanian rather than a Muslim.[56]

---

53 APA vol. 57, fol. 697v (1512, Chanadien. dioc.).

54 For an overview of South Slav immigration in the period before 1526, see Szakály, "Remargues sur l'armée de Jovan Tcherni." For the religious affiliation of the population, see Juhász, *A csanádi püspökség*, 16–17.

55 For instances in which "pagan" refers to Orthodox Christians, see: Mályusz and Borsa, eds., *Zsigmondkori oklevéltár*, vol. 5, 65, no. 33. (1415–16); and Lukcsics, *XV. századi pápák*, no. 833.

56 The ex-friar reported that he had entered into a marriage that had been celebrated "according to the customs and rituals of his wife's religion." However, this is surprising, since both Orthodox and Muslim marriages were secular contracts (kalugers and kadis played no roles in the celebrating of marriages) that were possible to dissolve. For information regarding Islamic marital rites, see Fekete, *Budapest*, 267, 292; On Orthodox Christian rites, see Levin, *Sex and Society*, 83–85.

Although further research will be needed to determine the frequency of interfaith marriages between Latin and Orthodox Christians in Transylvania and southern Hungary, such unions certainly served to ease the shifting boundaries between religious and ethnic groups and reshape individual identities and how the "other" was perceived. An example reflecting this point is provided by Margit, daughter of the late János Nadabori of Hunyad, who traveled from Transylvania to Rome in 1517 in order to submit a request to the Penitentiary for permission to marry Nan, the son of Dan Török of Bérc (*Naan filio Daan Thererk de Beercz*). Nan was not only a distant cousin, but also a "schismatic" who, based on his Christian name, was likely Romanian. Margit requested that the marriage be permitted despite their kinship because Nan would thus convert to the Catholic faith and Jesus Christ (*orthodoxe fidei et Domino nostro Jhesu Christo lucrifacto*); that is, he would be baptized as a Latin Christian.[57] When Margit promised that her schismatic fiancé would be rebaptized, she was conforming to canonical prescriptions. The Roman Church did not recognize the validity of marriages to non-Christians, the category to which Orthodox Christians belonged.[58]

In addition to the Church, secular authorities also expected Margit's fiancé to be rebaptized as a Roman Christian. Fifteenth-century rulers repeatedly issued decrees prohibiting Orthodox priests from celebrating baptisms and requiring Orthodox Christians to be baptized according to Roman ritual upon marriage to a Latin Christian.[59] Repeated royal efforts signal that religiously mixed marriages were common and consciously used by authorities as a means of converting Orthodox peoples. The Nadaboris of Hunyad and the Töröks of Bérc were distantly related Romanian families, or *kenéz* (*cneaz* in Romanian, meaning distinguished) owning adjacent lands in Hunyad County. The Nadaboris had previously become Magyarized through marriage and converted to the Roman Church, which facilitated their social rise, as indicated by their land acquisitions.[60] The marriage between the Nadaboris and the ambitious *kenéz* Töröks

57 APA vol. 61, fol. 20r (1517).

58 Plöchl, *Geschichte des Kirchenrechts*, 294–96.

59 Royal decree issued in 1428: Batthyány, ed., *Leges Ecclesiasticae*, vol. 3, 405–408. The same decree issued in 1478: MNL OL DF 275475. See also Juhász, *A csanádi püspökség*, 130–131. With regard to the existence of Roman Christian Romanian nobility beginning in the fifteenth century, see Molnár, "Jezsuita misszió Karánsebesen."

60 I would like to thank Géza Hegyi for his help in charting the Nadabori family. Csánki, *Magyarország*, vol. 5. 211–12, 241. The village of Nadabor (Nădrap, Romania) belonged to the Vajdahunyad estate until the fifteenth or sixteenth centuries. Pataki, *Domeniul Hunedoara*, 133, 142, 158, 215.

again entailed the conversion of the Orthodox partner. István Vajda's 1510 petition from the diocese of Várad records an instance in which Romanians living in the Partium were Catholicized through marriage. Vajda, whose name suggests that he was a Catholic Romanian noble, married his "schismatic" lover following the death of his first wife. His new wife, Margaret of Wallachia (*Margaretha Valache*), was rebaptized as a Roman Christian at the time of their marriage.[61] Shifting religious and ethnic identities of the Orthodox population from the Balkans and their mixed religion as new Muslims must have contributed to the declining perception of "pagans" or "schismatics." Even the runaway woman from Várad, located in the Partium region—where, by the sixteenth century, Hungarians, Romanians, Serbs and Bosnians had long lived together and in which she could regularly meet Ottoman soldiers—may not have been able to make a clear distinction between Muslims and Orthodox.[62] Her chosen "Turk" was most likely a South Slavic new Muslim, as were most of the soldiers and civil servants stationed in Buda.[63] I would venture, however, to argue that religious affiliations mattered much less to her than social status and power. The essential difference between the second husbands of the runaway wives, Mrs Csiszár from Várad and Magdolna Rachaz from the South Regions, lay not in their religions (new Muslim and Orthodox Christian) and ethnic affiliations (presumably either Bosnian or Serb), but in the radical disparity in social status.

The above narratives about religiously mixed marriages and conversions highlight that these were social practices which facilitated the shift of boundaries and the reshaping of individual identities in regions of religious and ethnic coexistence.

Conclusion

Historians reconstructing Mediterranean renegade life stories argue that women usually converted to Islam for familial reasons, while men were most often driven by socioeconomic opportunities.[64] My reading of the pardon

61 APA vol. 55, fol. 532v (1510).

62 Kristó, *Nem magyar népek*, 81–120, 191–218.

63 On the South Slavic (from Bosnia, Hercegovina, northern Serbia, the regions of Sirmium, Posega and Vidin) ethnic origin of the military forces in the Vilayet of Buda, see Hegyi, "Etnikum." With regard to the religious indifference and syncretism of new Muslims in the Balkans, see, with further literature cited, Fodor, "A kincstár," 260–61.

64 See Dursteler, *Renegade Women*, 13; and Rothman, *Brokering Empire*.

requests concerning people converting for the purpose of marriage in the Ottoman-Hungarian contact zone does not conform to this gendered dichotomy, but suggests that individual strategies were more complex. I contend that for both men and women, the change of religious identity represented a pragmatic tactic: to promote their survival and increase their sense of security. This feeling of safety and well-being stemmed from having a secure livelihood as well as an opportunity to live as part of a family with a spouse and children. People in ruined or broken marriages, a common experience in contact zones, were ready to transgress religious and cultural boundaries for the sake of having a new legally recognized spouse and family, which Christian authorities, constrained by canon law, tended to obstruct.

The encounter of different cultures offered greater opportunities for those capable of discerning and utilizing the plurality of norms and institutions for their own purposes. Their increased agency and power is perhaps more conspicuous in the cases of women, who are traditionally regarded as having been subjugated and passive. We observed some of their experiences that enabled individuals living in Christian-Muslim contact zones to reshape their religious identities. Ethnic and religious diversity in the eastern and southern regions of the Kingdom of Hungary during the Late Middle Ages, primarily the coexistence of Latin and Orthodox Christians and the integrative attitude of the Ottoman Turks, eased the way for many to cross Christian-Muslim boundaries and transform their personal identities.

CHAPTER 10

Conclusion

> Legal interpretation takes place in a field of pain and death. This is true in several senses. Legal interpretative acts signal and occasion the imposition of violence upon others. A judge articulates his understanding of a text, and as a result, somebody loses his freedom, his property, his children, even his life. Interpretations in law also constitute justifications for violence which has already occurred or which is about to occur. When interpreters have finished their work, they frequently leave behind victims whose lives have been torn apart by these organized, social practices of violence. Neither legal interpretation nor the violence it occasions may be properly understood apart from one another.[1]

This milestone assessment of the twentieth-century U.S. legal theorist Robert Cover reassesses the relationship between law, violence and narrative. From the perspective of modern judicial practice, he challenges the traditional concept of a binary division between violence and law, and argues that the practice of the judge not only generated, but also legitimized and institutionalized violence.[2]

Our analysis of the self-narratives framed in pardon requests confirmed the earlier observation that fifteenth and sixteenth century courts performed totally different social functions than they do today. The episodes presented here highlighted that lawsuits rarely reached a formal judicial judgment and, if they did, the sentence passed was often not executed. Courts, just as elsewhere in Europe were arenas for publicly debating private hostilities. In a world where satisfying damages and publicly reconciling and forgiving was the norm, whoever allowed authorities to execute a capital punishment against his enemy was considered a murderer, as demonstrated by the tales of several pardon seekers.

We have also seen that reports of violent acts followed a "conflict" script in the language of honor and shame. Narrators eager to prove their innocence portrayed their enemies as perpetrators who had triggered conflict through insults and aggression. Violence has remained "faceless" in the portrayal of

1 Cover, "Violence and the Word," 203.

2 See also the central thesis of the study: "Legal interpretation is (1) a practical activity (2) designed to generate credible threats and actual deeds of violence, (3) in an effective way." Ibid., 214.

 | DOI 10.1163/9789004361263_11

interpersonal violence and in the narratives of collective fights, since petitions were designed to legitimize the violence committed by the narrators rather than accurately depict facts.

Neighborhood conflicts were debated in the language of emotion. Petitioners represented their feelings as rightful anger triggered by the insults they had suffered, while their enemies, they argued, had been motivated by malevolent hatred. People made a clear division between legitimate and illegitimate violence, which differed from the official perspective that made a distinction between purposeful and random acts. In the private memories of collective violence, earlier participants defended their innocence by exposing the brutal and thus unjustifiable actions of their enemies. Those who had acted in self-defense had an exclusive claim on waging a just war in return, a universal memory and narrative practice.

The criminalization of the other party helped construct legitimacy for both the individual and the collective battlefield as well as in memory. We have been witness to how late medieval petitioners presented their personal adversaries as unidentifiable malefactors and rogues. The facelessness of the foe served to validate spontaneous violent responses. From this perspective, violence between individuals signaled disruption in the flow of routine reciprocity that characterized social relationships. People were used to being familiar with everyone in their surroundings, and seem to have perceived strangers as threats to whom they reacted violently out of fear, explained retrospectively as self-defense.

An impersonal representation of an adversary made it possible to narrate violence in much the same way as twentieth-century war memories. Circumstances rendered collective violence nameless: mass manslaughters, in which faceless groups confronted each other, were more easily forgiven than killing someone with a face and a name. Interestingly, the representation of extreme violence renders its victims anonymous: media anonymously offers news consumers images of distorted bodies of people executed or killed in war.[3] The tragedies of real flesh and blood people are transformed into anonymous *exempla* of horror, arousing both fear and excitement. Late medieval public executions were not only "the theatres of horror," they also dramatized the route to salvation and mercy. As Valentin Groebner has claimed, public executions reminded contemporaries of the sufferings of Christ that made their own redemption possible.[4]

3 Sontag, *Regarding the Pain*. There is a collective memory practice that has a contrary aim: when a community that remembers tries to identify and name its martyrs, it returns their lives to them. Audoin, Rouzeau and Becker, *1914–1918*, 150.

4 Groebner, *Defaced*, 99–104.

FIGURE 13 *Calvary. Probably Central Panel of Tryptich. Artist with a Bavarian learning (?), 1450–60.*

This argument is convincing in light of recent scholarly findings regarding the Christocentric devotional culture of the time,[5] and is further supported by the portrayal of the thieving rascal in the priest's petition, who beseeched onlookers to pray for his salvation as he climbed the scaffold. Similarities between past and present also manifest in the justification of twentieth-century wars before the public began to "objectively" represent the enemy as cruel and brutal. In light of the genuine wickedness and barbarity of the enemy, violence levied against them could be presented as a crusade defending civilization.[6]

During the memory war fought to monopolize "just" war, the grounds for war and the faces of its victims could remain obscured. Violence in war was justified by the treachery or deceit of the enemy, and violence in neighborhood disputes was justified by the need to uphold honor. The faces of the enemy and the reality of violence rarely surfaced.

Petitions designed to earn the pope's clemency are testimonies to the long battle for justice. By besieging the papal curia with written appeals and asking the pope to absolve them of the spiritual and legal consequences of their violent deeds, petitioners facilitated, albeit unconsciously, the growth of Church authority by defining the lawfulness of violence. This occurred at the same time that state control over violence was expanding. As Robert Cover has argued, the judge's interpretation and judgment legitimized both the violence that had already taken place as well as the violence that was to follow in terms of punishment, in a manner similar to modern judicial practice. The tribunal of the Apostolic Penitentiary not only took part in the process of defining legitimate violence, it also justified violent acts.

Even though violence continued to be nameless and faceless, flesh and blood individuals occasionally emerged from the anonymous masses as protagonists of conflicts: students, schoolmasters, unbeneficed priests and vagabond clerics as well as chantry priests, village parish priests and their chaplains. Students, who we have discovered existed in astonishingly great numbers in the Hungarian countryside, attended parish schools and lived separately from their families making a stir primarily by their tendency to move about in groups, make noise and be exceptionally mobile. Through an examination of the papal petitions, we have shed light on intense late medieval student mobility between villages and small towns facilitated by a strikingly dense network of rural parish schools. We have also encountered clerics participating in tavern squabbles, and men insulting one another at dinners; we have

5 Peters, *Patterns of Piety;* Rubin, *Corpus Christi.*

6 Audoin—Rouzeau—Becker, *1914–1918*, 78–86, 94–108.

witnessed fights among students at their lodgings or in cemeteries, and seen friars pulling each other's hair in cloisters. We have witnessed priests turning the wheels that broke the limbs of rogues, and parish priests disciplining lazy pupils with sticks as commonly as schoolmasters trying to control insolent students with their fists. These lower strata of clergymen were the constant social elements in the public and semi-public spheres of village life, and they lived in close daily coexistence with villagers, participating in their leisure activities and festivals. They also appeared as agents in the routine acts of spontaneous violence as well as as performers of symbolic violence by attending to carnivalesque rituals. Unbeneficed, vagabond clerics and poor priests also occasionally mingled in the world of criminals, and their desperate search for incomes and livelihoods seems to have played a role in compelling them to join the Christian army against the Turks, transforming them into rebels in the anti-establishment uprising of the peasants.

Due to their level of education, renegade friars in search of smaller Church benefices had fairly good prospects; for a time, at least, many of them shared the insecure fortunes of wage-earning clerics and priests. Young men of humble social origin even considered the career of the unbeneficed clergy to be appealing and to represent a viable springboard for gaining advancement in the world. Many took the habit of mendicant friars in order to gain entrance into the privileged estate of the priesthood, since friars were routinely ordained without having a benefice. The fact that this route to the priesthood, via mendicant orders, became widely used in the 1510s possibly signals a growing social demand for the traditional function of the Church as a means of upward social mobility.[7] Another possibility for the poor was provided by irregular consecrations (on fictitious benefices) in Italy, especially in the papal curia, and its legalization by papal dispensations at the Penitentiary and other curial offices.

The high number of rural youths leaving the peasantry in order to enter friaries for the purpose of studying in preparation for ecclesiastical careers can be interpreted as a symptom of growing attention being paid to schools and students. In the 1520s and 1530s, "good manners" as well as the importance of schooling became a central issue of public discourse. Civilized behavior did not entail any kind of specialized knowledge, requiring only the most elementary gestures such as facial expression and mimicry, dress, posture and movement, in addition to table manners and cleanliness in public. We can assume that the shifting divide between propriety and impropriety encoded in everyday behavior played a role in the increased interest of youth in schools.

7 On this function of the early modern Churches, see: Reinhard, "Kirche als Mobilitätskanal."

Cloister schools offered novices a standard curriculum and consistent quality of education contrary to the random character of rural parish schools, where both the content and quality of education depended on the learning and interests of the schoolmaster. Notwithstanding its changing profile and standard, the existence of a dense network of parish schools in the Hungarian-Croatian countryside at the end of the Middle Ages testifies to a general social demand for elementary and grammar education.

Renegade friars, who returned to the outside world after having led strictly regulated lives in the cloister or studied in distant regions, returned to their native villages to make a living and model forms of proper behavior. Even if villagers did not learn to read and write from them, they must have observed and acquired the rudiments of good manners. The lively interactions between the laity and the growing number of pastoral lesser clergy resulted not only from the peasant origin of rural priests, but also from the fact that they remained "local boys" with regard to their lifestyle: village incumbents who formed the upper layer of the lower clergy continued to farm and govern their households and their extended *familia*, and were tied to the local community through blood, affinity and spiritual kinship ties, compelling them to participate in communal and familial festivities. After years of temporary social disintegration while studying away, the embeddedness in village life of the parish clergy, notwithstanding their diverse levels of education, facilitated their role as mediators between popular and learned culture in contrast to the professionalized clergy of the approaching confessional era, the members of which remained outsiders.

Vagabond clerics, renegade friars and students, who stand out among the transgressors of canon law who sought the pope's forgiveness, did not rebel or swindle, but attempted to change their lifestyles via education. In the eyes of fearful ecclesiastical and secular authorities interested in the preservation of the social order, vagabonds were transgressors, false priests or dissenters, whose social, geographical and intellectual mobility had led them to involvement in the peasant uprising of 1514. In addition, a contemporary observer mentioned their presence among the first propagators of the evangelical teachings in Hungary. In 1546, András Szkhárosi Horvát, the Lutheran preacher of the small town of Tállya in northeastern Hungary, wrote, "You cannot say that you do not know the will of the Lord, for both priest, pupil, child and minstrel cry it out openly."[8] Historians and literary scholars unanimously claim that

8 "Az istennek irgalmasságáról és ez világnak háládatlanságáról (1546)" [On the mercy of God and the ungratefulness of the world] in: Szilády, ed., *16. századbeli magyar költők művei*, vol. 1, 207.

Szkhárosi had been referring to the social groups that belonged to the first generation of evangelical reformers; in other words, to his own colleagues.[9] The preacher from Tállya seems a reliable source, as his knowledge was based on personal experience. In another song, he referred to himself as "a friar turned into a priest," and as a result is usually regarded as having been one of the renegade Franciscans who became evangelicals.[10]

The first evangelicals Szkhárosi mentions, that is priests, pupils, children and minstrels, seem to coincide with the protagonists of the late medieval episodes that unfolded on the pages of this book.

People who traveled a great deal and kept open minds were the first to learn about Luther's ideas. It is therefore very improbable that among the proclaimers of the new teachings Szkhárosi would have thought under the term *priest* of the beneficed clergy, the parish priests with local ties, but rather of the unbeneficed vagabonds and renegades of which he himself was one. The term "pupil" (*deák* in Hungarian, *litteratus* in Latin), as used by Szkhárosi, referred to the members of the growing group of lettered men educated in schools within Hungary (which had no university at the time). We met Imre Litteratus of Bélc, who earned his living as a literate professional after escaping from the cloister. Several among the hundreds of petitioners to Rome who were vagabond clerics, upper-level students, school rectors and manorial officials used "Litteratus" as their surname.[11] Szkhárosi, in his mention of children among the first generation of evangelical preachers, must have meant the "young students" or "child students" who served the "big students" at parish and chapter schools and enjoyed, in return, their protection. *Puer scolaris* was the Latin term for this group. Szkhárosi may well have come into contact with such pupils on a daily basis in his friary, since Franciscan (and Pauline) friars taught children how to read and write, as suggested by the repeated prohibitions against religious superiors doing so.[12] Finally, the song-writer mentions "violin

9 Klaniczay, "A magyar reformáció irodalma," 20–21. More recently, it has been proposed that Szkhárosi had formulated, in his own way, Luther's concept of the priesthood of all believers. Csepregi, *A reformáció nyelve*, 236.

10 András Szkhárosi Horvát, "Emberi szerzésről" [On Human inventions] in: Szilády, ed., *16. századbeli magyar költők művei*, vol. 1, 227–30. On Szkhárosi's career: Klaniczay, "A magyar reformáció irodalma," 20–21.

11 There were approximately twenty *litterati* among the *clerici* and *scolares*. APA, passim.

12 See the repeated proscription by the Franciscan provincial assembly in the 1530s against teaching children (*pueri scolares*) in the cloisters or allowing students to sleep in the cloisters. ETE vol. 2, 473, 482, 515. On the Paulines, see: Gyöngyösi, *Vitae fratrum*, a decree passed between 1516–19, 172.

players" who can be identified as itinerant minstrels entertaining audiences encountered along their routes; they were also called "lute players."[13] Earlier in this book we encountered students fighting over a lute, not for use by their church choir, but to accompany performances of their worldly songs at village festivities where they joined other groups of popular entertainers.

At the beginning of this book I refrained from embracing the idea that renegade friars in Hungary had continued their careers among evangelical preachers and schoolmasters as had the Augustinian renegade Martin Luther and the ex-Dominican Martin Bucer. My initial assumption was certainly formed under the influence of my first encounter with the friars: I saw them making painstaking efforts to recover their priestly status within the Roman Church. However, after following them through their conjectured careers and looking more closely at their desires, fears, choices and pitfalls, I can easily imagine how at least some of these ordinary runaway friars would have followed a route from the cloister via the secular ministry to the evangelical pulpit and schoolmaster's desk.

Vagabond clerics, renegade friars and students who, in the first two decades of the sixteenth century, appear to have been violators of canon law despite their requests for papal absolution for their trespasses, became rebels over the following decades. They figured among intellectual leaders as captains, crusade preachers, scribes, pastors and teachers of the common man during the peasant revolt and evangelical movement. Their position required them to play the role of mediator between popular and learned cultures.

In Hungary, the reception of evangelical ideas by the rural population seems not to have taken place by domination, unlike in the German territories. German peasant resistance and Protestant Reformation, due to a chronology that was the inverse to events in Hungary, were closely intertwined. For decades now it has been a unanimously held view that the German Peasants' War of 1525 signified the reformation of the common man: the norm of scripture provided universal legitimation to the previously fragmented, local and secular agendas of small communities, and thus galvanized social movements.[14] By contrast, in Hungary, after the open conflict between lords and peasants in the 1514 peasant revolt, the issue of religion seems to have been neither a tool used to elicit the obedience of subjects nor a means of inciting peasant resistance. In short, the rural reformation was a predominantly religious event in Hungary:[15] landlords expressed little or no interest in the religious practices of

13 The Lutheran pastor and author Gáspár Heltai is quoted with regard to contemporary terminology by Ács, "'hegedűsök, néktek szólok.' Hegedűs Márton éneke (1580)," 135.

14 Scribner, *The German Reformation*; Blickle, *Die Reformation im Reich*, 122–23.

15 Péter, *A reformáció*, 108–17.

their serfs (what kind of services they attended and who performed them); the latter were able to freely choose their religion. This left ample room for capable clergymen to influence the common men at individual and communal levels.

Vagabond priests and ex-friars must have participated in this exciting process all the more willingly as a result of the professed reform ideas and endeavors including, in Hungary as well as in Germany, the idea that schools should be opened for lay society.[16] As young men they had experienced, more than others, religious orders that did not aspire to meet the increasing lay demand for education. They therefore donned the habit, which paved the way for free further education and the privileged order of the clergy. However, in 1524, a good number of years after leaving the cloister, a young German former friar called upon secular authorities to close the old educational institutions in their towns and cities, that is, the cloisters, in the interest of the education of youth, and to establish new Christian schools accessible to all poor children, both boys and girls.[17] The leaders of the mendicant orders resisted this change,[18] whereas by the middle of the sixteenth century the entire intellectual and political elite agreed that the operation of schools was not primarily the mission of the Church, but of secular authorities. In Transylvania, the Protestant estates at the 1557 Diet of Torda decreed that Queen Isabella, who had adhered to her Catholic faith, was to transform the cloisters of the friars into schools at which teachers would instruct youth in a suitable way. They also stipulated that schools were to be established at the Dominican friaries in Kolozsvár and Várad and the Franciscan friary in Marosvásárhely (Târgu Mureș, Romania). The Catholic queen was not deaf to the demands of her subjects; in Transylvania, the founding of schools became the official program of secular powers regardless of religious affiliation.[19]

---

16 On the clerical orientation of city schools in German territories prior to the Reformation, see Kintzinger, *Wissen Wird Macht*, 139.

17 "An die Ratsherren aller Städte deutschen Lands." WA 15, 27–53, 28–29.

18 This theme represented a source of contention before consensus was finally reached. Earlier, the viewpoint prevailed that public schools operated in the cloisters were attended by both secular clerics and lay students. This notion spread as a result of the unproven claim that Dante Alighieri had acquired his philosophical education via Franciscan lectures held in Florence. Oediger, *Über die Bildung der Geistlichen*, 62–63; Sheffer, *Schools and Schooling*, 52–53; On the Dominicans Hasenbrink, "Latinität als Bildungsfundament," 62–64. On mendicants in general: Kintzinger, *Wissen Wird Macht*, 163.

19 Szilády, ed., *Erdélyi Országgyűlési Emlékek*, vol. 2, 79. The Catholic queen made this stipulation in order that two cloisters remain in Várad in which Franciscan friars would continue to reside. Cf. Péter, "Az erdélyi magyar iskolázás," 101. For more examples: the *schola reformata* moved into the Beguine house in the town of Sárospatak in the 1530s. Gömöri,

A significant difference between the old cloister and chapter schools and the new schools was that the latter were expected to educate first the laity and then later the clergymen and teachers who emerged from among the gifted students. As school rector Lénárt Stöckel of Bártfa stated in the school regulations he composed in the 1540s, they educated within the walls of their school not friars and priests, but good politicians and farmers.[20] The words of Stephanus Pannonius, the school rector in the town of Nagyszombat in Habsburg Hungary, reflect the enormous desire to study among youth of this era. In 1549, Pannonius reported to the town council that "the number of children [...] is growing so much day by day that the school can hardly accommodate them."[21] The same situation was recorded in a market town under Ottoman rule: Pál Thuri Farkas, the school rector in Tolna, wrote that he could hardly satisfy the thirst for knowledge among his pupils; they barely fit into two rooms as the younger students were numerous and students in the upper grade numbered an even fifty.[22] If the runaway friars and other poor priests had been unable to attend such schools as students, they may have all the more enthusiastically undertaken the instruction of youth from the pulpit and in the classroom as members of the new Churches in their mature years.

Just as the everyday forms and meanings of law and violence were not in direct opposition to each other, the walls that divided "civilized life" from acts of violence, laity from clergy, peasants from noblemen and Christians from Muslims did not crumble in a holy year when the pope struck the Holy Door with the golden hammer, but rather over time, day by day and brick by brick.

"A sárospataki középkori plébániai iskola," 69–86. The Dominican cloister in Nagyszeben (Sibiu, Romania) became a Lutheran municipal school, while that in Kolozsvár became a Unitarian school (1568): Lupescuné, "A Domonkos Rend," 379.

20 Mészáros, *XVI. századi városi iskoláink*, 153–58, 156.

21 Békefi, *A népoktatás*, 472.

22 Pál Thuri Farkas, "Idea Christianorum Hungarorum in et sub Turcismo [1556–57]," Printed first in Kassa, 1613 (RMNY 2 1054), edited in Latin and Hungarian by Kathona, *Fejezetek*, 61–70, 65.

Bibliography

Archival Sources

APA — Sacra Poenitentiaria Apostolica (Citta di Vaticano), Registra Matrimonialium et Diversorum
ASV Arm. — Archivio Segreto Vaticano (Citta di Vaticano), Armadio
ASV, Dataria Apostolica, Brevia Lateranensia
MNL OL — Magyar Nemzeti Levéltár Országos Levéltára [The National Archives of Hungary], Budapest:
Q szekció: Mohács előtti gyűjtemény [Q Section: Pre-Mohács Collection]
- DL — Diplomatikai Levéltár[Arhives of Original Charters]
- DF — Diplomatikai Fényképgyűjtemény [Photo Collection of Medieval Charters].
A 57 Libri Regii
P 1314 A herceg Batthyány család levéltára [Archives of the Batthyány family], Missiles

Printed Primary Sources

Apáczai Csere, János. "*De summa scholarum necessitate earumque inter Hungarorus barbariei causis.*" In *Apáczai Csere János válogatott pedagógiai művei* [The Selected Pedagogical Works of János Apáczai Csere], edited by Orosz Lajos. Budapest: Tankönyvkiadó, 1976.

Batthyany, Ignatius, ed. *Leges ecclesiasticae regni Hungariae et provinciarum adiacentium*. 3 vols. Albae Carolinae–Claudipoli: Typis Episcopalibus, 1785–1827.

Bessenyei, József, ed. *1504–1566 Memoria Rerum*. Budapest: Magyar Helikon, 1981.

Bunyitay, Vince, ed. *Monumenta Vaticana historiam regni Hungariae illustrantia, vol. I/5. Liber confraternitatis S. Spiritus de Urbe. 1446-1523*. Budapest: Szent István Társulat, 1889.

Bucko, Vojtech, ed. *Reformné hnutie v arcibiskupstve ostrihomskom do r. 1564 Reformatio in archidioecesi Strigoniensi ad a. 1564*. Bratislava: Unia, 1939.

CIC = *Corpus Iuris Canonici*, edited by Aemilius Friedberg. 2 vols. Graz: Akademische Druck- u. Verlagsanstalt, 1955–1959.

COD = *Conciliorum Oecumenicorum Decreta*, edited by J. Alberigo, J. A. Dosetti Perikle, P. J. Claudius Leonardi, and P. Prodi. Bologna: Istituto per le scienze religiose, 1973.

Dienes, Dénes, ed. *Református egyházlátogatási jegyzőkönyvek, 16–17. század* [Reformed ecclesiastical visitation records from the sixteenth and seventeenth centuries]. Budapest: Osiris, 2001.

DRMH = *Decreta Regni Mediævalis Regni Hungariæ. The Laws of the Medieval Kingdom of Hungary*. 5 vols. Idyllwild, CA, and Budapest: Schlacksand CEU Press, 1989–2012.

Erdélyi, Gabriella, ed. *The Register of a Convent Controversy, 1517–1518*. Collectanea Vaticana Hungariae I. Budapest–Rome: PPKE Egyháztörténeti Kutatócsoport, 2006.

ETE = *Egyháztörténelmi Emlékek a Magyarországi Hitújítás korából* [Sources on Church history at the time of the Reformation], edited by V. Bunyitay, R. Rapaics, J. Karácsonyi, F. Kollányi, and J. Lukcsics. 5 vols. Budapest: Szent István Társulat, 1902–12.

Fekete Nagy, Antal, Viktor Kenéz, László Solymosi, and Géza Érszegi, eds. *Monumenta rusticorum in Hungaria rebellium anno MDXIV*. Publicationes Archivi Nationalis Hungarici II. Fontes 12. Budapest: Akadémiai Kiadó, 1979.

Fügedi, Erik, ed. *Kimondhatatlan nyomorúság. Két emlékirat a 15–16. Századi oszmán fogságról* [Misery beyond description. Two memoirs on Ottoman captivity in the fifteenth and sixteenth centuries]. Budapest: Európa, 1976.

Gyöngyösi, Gregorius. *Vitae fratrum eremitarum Ordinis Sancti Pauli Primi Eremitae*, edited by Franciscus L. Hervay. Bibliotheca Scriptorum Medii Recentisque Aevorum, Series Nova XI. Budapest: Akadémiai Kiadó, 1988.

HC = Eubel, Konrad, *Hierarchia Catholica Medii et Recentioris Aevi*. 6 vols. Regensburg: Monasterii, Sumptibus et Typis Librariae Regensbergianae, 1913–1967.

Heltai, Gáspár. *Krónika az magyaroknak dolgairól* [Chronicle about the Deeds of the Hungarians], edited by Kulcsár Margit, foreword by Kulcsár Péter. Bibliotheca Historica. Budapest: Magyar Helikon, 1981.

Istvánffy, Nicolaus. *Historiarum de rebus Ungaricis libri XXXIV*. Cologne: Sumptibus Antonii Hierati, 1622. In Hungarian: Benits, Péter, ed. *Istvánffy Miklós magyarok dolgairól írt históriája Tállyai Pál XVII. századi fordításában* [The history of Nicolaus Istvánffy in the seventeenth-century translation of Pál Tállyai]. Vol. 1. Budapest: Balassi, 2001.

Kollányi, Ferenc. "*Visitatio Capituli* E. M. Strigoniensis Anno 1397." *Magyar Történelmi Tár*, New Series II. 1–2 (1901): 71–106, 239–72.

Komlovszki, Tibor, ed. *Széphistóriák* [Novels]. Budapest: Helikon, 1975.

Luther, Martin. "An die Ratsherren aller Städte deutschen Lands." WA 15, 27–53.

Luther, Martin. "De votis monasticis iudicium." WA 8, 573–669.

Mályusz, Elemér and Borsa Iván, eds. *Zsigmondkori oklevéltár* [Charters of the Sigismund era]. Vol. 5. Budapest: Magyar Országos Levéltár, 1997.

MREV = *Monumenta Romana Episcopatus Vesprimiensis*, edited by Collegio Historicorum Hungarorum Romano. 4 vols, Budapest: Franklin, 1896–1908.

Radó, Polycarpus, ed. *Libri liturgici manuscripti bibliothecarum Hungariae et limitropharum regionum*. Budapest: Akadémiai Kiadó, 1973.

Sarbak, Gábor, ed. *Declarationes constitutionum. Gyöngyösi Gergely és a pálos rend alkotmánya (Editio critica cum commentariis)* [Declarationes constitutionum.

Gergely Gyöngyösi and the constitution of the Pauline order]. Budapest, 2014. Manuscript DSc Dissertation.

Sarbak, Gábor, Bellus Ibolya and Lorenz Weinrich, eds. *Gyöngyösi Gergely OSPPE: Epitoma et Directorium.* Res Libraria Hungariae, Fragmenta Codicum Kutatócsoport. Budapest, 2011.

Schmugge, Ludwig, Béatrice Hersperger, and Patrick Wiggenhauser, eds. *Die Supplikenregister der päpstlichen Pönitentiarie aus der Zeit Pius' II: 1458–1464.* Bibliothek des Deutschen Historischen Instituts in Rom 84. Tübingen: De Gruyter, 1996.

Sirmiensis, Georgius. *De Perditione Regni Hungariae.* Translated by László Juhász. Monumenta Hungarica 5. Budapest: Magyar Helikon, 1961.

Solymosi, László, ed. *A veszprémi egyház 1515. Evi zsinati határozatai* [Decrees of the 1515 Synod of Veszprém Diocese]. Budapest: Argumentum, 1997.

Szilády, Áron, ed. *XVI. Századbeli magyar költők művei* [Works of Hungarian poets of the sixteenth century]. Régi Magyar Költők Tára 2. Budapest: Akadémiai, 1880.

Szilágyi, Sándor, ed. *Erdélyi Országgyűlési Emlékek*: Történeti bevezetésekkel. [Memories of Transylvanian Diets: with Historical Introductions.] Budapest: Akadémia, 1876, vol. 2.

Szmollény, Nándor. *A középkori Szeged műveltsége. Caspar Fraxinus (Körösi) de Zegedienus levelezése Nádasdi Tamás nádorral (1553–1562)* [The Culture of Medieval Szeged: The Correspondence of Caspar Fraxinus (Körösi) de Zegedienus and Palatine Tamás Nádasdi (1553–1562)]. Szeged: Endrényi Nyomda, 1910.

Taurinus Olomucensis, Stephanus. *Stauromachia id est cruciatorum servile bellum. Servilis belli pannonici libri V [1519]*, edited by Ladislaus Juhász. Budapest: Egyetemi Nyomda, 1944. In Hungarian translation: Taurinus, István *Paraszti háború* [Peasant War]. Translated by László Geréb. Budapest: Magyar Helikon, 1972.

Thuri, Pál Farkas. "Idea Christianorum Hungarorum in et sub Turcismo [1556–57]." In *Fejezetek a török hódoltsági reformáció történetéből* [Chapters from the history of the Reformation in Ottoman Hungary], edited by Kathona Géza, 61–69. Budapest: Akadémiai Kiadó, 1974.

V. Kovács, Sándor, ed. *Temesvári Pelbárt válogatott írásai* [Selected writings of Pelbárt Temesvári]. Budapest: Helikon, 1982.

V. Kovács, Sándor, ed. *Mátyás király levelei 1460–1490* [Letters of King Matthias 1460–1490]. Budapest: Szépirodalmi Könyvkiadó, 1986.

Veress, Endre. *Olasz egyetemeken járt magyarországi tanulók anyakönyve és iratai 1221–1864.* [The register of matriculation of Hungarian students at universities in Italy, 1221–1864]. Budapest: MTA, 1941.

WA = Martin Luther, *Werke: Kritische Gesamtausgabe.* 73 vols, Weimar: Böhlau, 1883–2009.

Secondary Sources

Ács, Pál. "Katolikus irodalom és kultúra a reformáció századában" [Catholic literature and culture in the century of the Reformation]. *Vigilia* 5 (1995): 360–74.

Ács, Pál. "Hegedűsök, néktek szólok": Hegedűs Márton éneke (1580)—folklór vagy paródia?" ["I am speaking to you, violinists": The song of Márton Hegedűs—folclore or parody?]. In idem *"Az idő ósága": Történetiség és történetszemlélet a régi magyar irodalomban*, 577–87. Budapest: Osiris, 2001.

Alexander, Jeffrey C. "Toward a Theory of Cultural Trauma." In *Cultural Trauma and Collective Identity*, edited by Jeffrey C. Alexander, Ron Eyerman, Bernard Giesen, Neil J. Smelser, Piotr Sztompka, 1–30. Berkeley: University of California Press, 2004.

Appold, Kenneth G. *The Reformation. A Brief History*. Chichester: Wiley-Blackwell, 2011.

Arnaude, Peter and Walter Prevenier. *Honor, Vengeance and Social Trouble: Pardon Letters in the Burgundian Low Countries*. Ithaca and London: Cornell University Press, 2015.

Assmann, Jan and John Czaplicka. "Collective Memory and Cultural Identity." *New German Critique* 65 (1995): 125–33.

Assmann, Jan. *Das kulturelle Gedächtnis: Schrift, Erinnerung und politische Identität in frühen Hochkulturen*. Munich: C. H. Beck, 2007.

Audoin-Rouzeau, Stephane and Annette Becker, eds. *1914–1918: Understanding the Great War*. London: Profile Books, 2002.

Bácskai, Vera. "Small Towns in Eastern Central Europe." In *Small Towns in Early Modern Europe*, edited by Peter Clark, 77–89. Cambridge: Cambridge University Press, 1995.

Baer, Marc. "Islamic Conversion Narratives of Women: Social Change and Gendered Religious Hierarchy in Early Modern Ottoman Istanbul." *Gender and History* 16 (2004): 425–58.

Bakhtin, Mikhail. *Rabelais and His world*. Translated by Hélene Iswolsi. Bloomington: Indiana University Press, 1984.

Bálint, Sándor. *Szeged reneszánsz kori műveltsége* [Renaissance education in Szeged]. Humanizmus és reformáció. Budapest: Balassi, 1975.

Balogh, Jolán. *Varadinum: Várad Vára* [Varadinum: The castle of Várad]. 2 vols. Budapest: Akadémiai Kiadó, 1982.

Barnes, Andrew. "The Social Transformation of the French Parish Clergy, 1500–1800." In *Culture and Identity in Early Modern Europe (1500–1800): Essays in Honor of Natalie Zemon Davis*, edited by Barbara B. Diefendorf and Carla Hesse, 139–58. Ann Arbor: University of Michigan Press, 1993.

Barta, Gábor. "Georgius Zekeltől Dózsa Györgyig" [From Georgius Zekel to György Dózsa]. *Századok* 109 (1975): 63–88.

Barta, Gábor and Antal Fekete Nagy, *Parasztháború 1514-ben* [Peasant war in 1514]. Budapest: Gondolat, 1973.

Bartlett, Robert. *"Mortal Enmities": The Legal Aspects of Hostility in the Middle Age.* Aberystwyth: T. Jones Pierce Lecture, 1998.

Békefi, Remig. *A káptalani iskolák története Magyarországon 1540-ig* [The history of chapter schools in Hungary until 1540]. Budapest: MTA, 1910.

Ben-Amos, Ilana Krausman. *Adolescence and Youth in Early Modern England.* New Haven, Conn.: Yale University Press, 1994.

Benda, Borbála. *Étkezési szokások a 17. Századi főúri udvarokban Magyarországon* [Eating customs in seventeenth-century aristocratic courts in Hungary]. Szombathely: Vas Megyei Levéltár, 2014.

Birnbaum, Marianna D. "A Mock Calvary in 1514? The Dózsa-Passion." In *European Iconography East and West: Selected Papers of the Szeged International Conference,* edited by Szőnyi György E., 91–108. Brill: Leiden, 1996.

Blickle, Peter. *Gemeindereformation: Die Menschen des 16. Jahrhundert auf dem Weg zum Heil.* Munich: Oldenbourg Verlag, 1985.

Blickle, Peter. *Die Reformation im Reich.* Stuttgart: UTB Ulmer, 1992.

Blickle, Peter, ed. *Resistance, Representation and Community.* Oxford: Clarendon Press, 1997.

Blockmans, Willem, André Holenstein and Jon Mathieu eds. *Empowering Interactions: Political Cultures and the Emergence of the State in Europe, 1300–1900.* London: Routledge, 2009.

Blockmans, Willem, André Holenstein and Jon Mathieu. *Introduction: Empowering Interactions: Looking at Statebuilding from Below to Empowering Interactions: Political Cultures and the Emergence of the State in Europe, 1300–1900*, edited by Wim Blockmans, André Holenstein and Jon Mathieu, i–xxxi. Farnham: Ashgate, 2009.

Bónis, György. "Men Learned in the Law in Medieval Hungary." *East-Central Europe* 4, no. 1 (1977): 181–191.

Boockmann, Hartmut. *Die Stadt im späten Mittelalter.* Munich: C. H. Beck, 1986.

Bossy, John. *Disputes and Settlements: Law and Human Relations in the West.* Past and Present Publications. Cambridge: Cambridge University Press, 1983.

Bouza, Fernando. *Communication, Knowledge, and Memory in Early Modern Spain.* Pennsylvania: Pennsylvania University Press, 1999.

Brecht, Martin. *Martin Luther.* Vol. 1. *Sein Weg zur Reformation (1483–1521).* Stuttgart: Calwer, 1983.

Broomhall, Susan and Sara Finn, eds. *Violence and Emotions in Early Modern Europe.* Abingdon, Oxon: Routledge, 2016.

Brundage, James A. *Medieval Canon Law.* London: Longman, 1995.

Brundage, James. A. "Professional Canon Lawyers: Advocates and Proctors." In idem, *The Medieval Origins of the Legal Profession: Canonists, Civilians, and Courts*, 344–70. Chicago and London: The University of Chicago Press, 2008.

Brunner, Otto. *Land and Lordship: Structures of Governance in Medieval Austria.* Philadelphia: University of Pennsylvania Press, 1992.

Bryson, Anna. *From Courtesy to Civility: Changing Codes of Conduct in Early Modern England.* Oxford: Oxford University Press, 1998.

Bulliet, Richard W. *Conversion to Islam in the Medieval Period: An Essay in Quantitative History.* Cambridge–London: Harvard University Press, 1979.

Bunyitay, Vincze. *A váradi püspökség káptalanai s monostorai a püspökség egyházai a püspökség alapításától 1566. évig* [The chapters, monasteries and churches from the foundation of the diocese of Várad until 1566]. Vol. 2 of *A váradi püspökség története* [The history of the diocese of Várad]. Nagyvárad: Franklin Nyomda, 1883.

Bünz, Enno. "Thüringen und Rom: Die systematische Erschließung der vatikanischen Quellen des Mittelalters und ihre Bedeutung für die mitteldeutsche Landesgeschichte." *Zeitschrift für Thüringische Geschichte* 51 (1997): 187–211.

Bünz, Enno. "Thüringens Pfarrgeistlichkeit vor der Reformation." *Historisches Jahrbuch* 124 (2004): 45–74.

Burgess, Clive. *The Parish, the Church and the Laity in Late Medieval Bristol.* The Bristol Branch of the Historical Association, Local History Pamphlets, 80. Bristol: Bristol Branch of the Historical Association, 1992.

Burghartz, Susanna. "Disziplinierung oder Konfliktregelung? Zur Funktion städtischer Gerichte im Spätmittelalter: Das Züricher Ratsgericht." *Zeitschrift für Historische Forschung* 16 (1989): 385–408.

Burke, Peter. *Popular Culture in Early Modern Europe.* 3rd ed. Farnham: Ashgate, 2009. First published in 1978.

Butler, Sara M. "Runaway Wives: Husband Desertion in Medieval England." *Journal of Social History* 40 (2006): 337–59.

C. Tóth, Norbert. *Az esztergomi székeskáptalan a 15. században* [The cathedral chapter of Esztergom in the fifteenth century]. 2 vols. Budapest: MTA, 2015.

C. Tóth, Norbert and Neumann Tibor, eds. *Keresztesekből lázadók: Tanulmányok 1514 Magyarországáról* [Crusaders turned into rebels: Studies on Hungary in 1514]. Budapest: MTA BTK, 2015.

Carroll, Stuart. *Blood and Violence in Early Modern France.* Oxford: Oxford University Press, 2006.

Carroll, Stuart. *"Introduction." In Cultures of Violence: Interpersonal Violence in Historical Perspectives*, edited by Stuart Carroll, i–xlvi. Basingstoke: Palgrave Macmillan, 2007.

Castan, Nicole. "The Arbitration of Disputes under the Ancient Regime." In *Disputes and Settlements: Law and Human Relations in the West*, edited by John Bossy, 229–60. London and New York: Cambridge University Press, 1983.

Castel, Robert. *From Manual Workers to Wage Laborers: Transformation of the Social Question.* New Brunswick: Transaction Publishers, 2003.

Castel, Robert. "The Roads to Disaffiliation: Insecure Work and Vulnerable Relationships." *International Journal of Urban and Regional Research* 24, no. 3 (2000): 519–35.

Chartier, Roger. *Lectures et lecteurs dans la France d'Ancien Régime.* Paris: Editions Seuil, 1987.

Chartier, Roger. "Phantasie und Disziplin. Das Fest in Frankreich vom 15. bis 18. Jahrhundert." in *Volkskultur. Zur Wiederentdeckung des vergessenen Alltags (16.–20. Jahrhundert)*, edited by Richard von Dülmen and Norbert Schindler, 153–177. Frankfurt am Main: Fischer, 1984.

Chartier, Roger and Guglielmo Cavallo, eds. *The History of Reading in the West.* Massachusetts: University of Massachusetts Press, 2003.

Clark McPhail. *The Myth of the Madding Crowd.* New York: Walter de Gruyter, 1991.

Clarke, Peter D. "Central Authority and Local Powers: The Apostolic Penitentiary and the English Church in the Fifteenth Century." *Historical Research* 84 (2011): 416–42.

Cohen, Thomas V. and Elizabeth S. Cohen, *Words and Deeds in Renaissance Rome: Trials before the Papal Magistrates.* Toronto: University of Toronto Press, 1993.

Comerford, Kathleen M. "Clerical Education, Cathecesis, and Catholic Confessionalism: Teaching Religion in the Sixteenth and Seventeenth Centuries." In *Early Modern Catholicism: Essays in Honour of John O'Malley, S.J.*, edited by Kathleen M. Comerford and Hilmar M. Pabel, 241–65. Toronto: University of Toronto Press, 2001.

Condorelli, Orazio. *Clerici peregrini. Aspetti guiuridici della mobilità clericale nei secoi XII–XIV*, Roma: Il cigno Galileo Galilei, 1995.

Connerton, Paul. *How Societies Remember*. Cambridge: Cambridge University Press, 1989.

Cooper, Tim. The Last Generation of English Catholic Clergy: Parish Priests in the Diocese of Coventry and Lichfield in the Early Sixteenth Century. Studies in the History of Medieval Religion (Book 15). Suffolk: Boydell Press, 1999.

Cover, Robert. "Violence and the Word." In idem, Narrative, Violence, and the Law: The Essays of Robert Cover, edited by Marta, Minow, Michael Ryan and Austin Sarat, 203–38. Ann Arbor: University of Michigan Press, 1995.

Csánki, Dezső. *Magyarország történelmi földrajza a Hunyadiak korában* [Historical geography of Hungary in the Hunyadi era]. Vol. 5. Budapest: Állami Könyvterjesztő Vállalat, 1985.

Csepregi, Zoltán. "A magyarországi iskolázás a reformáció századában (1540–1610) a wittenbergi ordinációs anyakönyvek tanúsága alapján." [Schooling in Hungary in the century of Reformation (1540–1610) Based on evidence from Wittenberg Ordination Registers] In *Teológia és oktatás: Az Evangélikus Hittudományi Egyetem oktatóinak tanulmánykötete* [Theology and education: Collective volume of the professors at the Lutheran Theological University], edited by Szabó Lajos, 53–70. Budapest: Luther Kiadó, 2015.

Csepregi, Zoltán. *A reformáció nyelve: A magyarországi reformáció első negyedszázadának vizsgálata* [The language of the Reformation: Investigation of the first 25 years of the Reformation in Hungary]. Budapest: Balassi, 2013.

Csukovits, Enikő. "Bűn és büntetés a középkori városi gyakorlatban" [Crime and punishment in medieval towns]. In *Bártfától Pozsonyig: Városok a 13–17. században* [From Bártfa to Pozsony: Towns from the fourteenth to the seventeenth centuries], edited by Csukovits Enikő and Lengyel Tünde, 199–222. Budapest: MTA Történettudományi Intézet, 2005.

Csukovits, Enikő. *Középkori magyar zarándokok* [Medieval Hungarian pilgrims]. História Könyvtár, Monográfiák 20. Budapest: MTA Történettudományi Intézete, 2003.

Csukovits, Enikő. "Miraculous Escapes from Ottoman Captivity." In *Ransom Slavery along the Ottoman Borders*, edited by Fodor Pál and Dávid Géza, 1–18. Leiden: Brill, 2007.

Danto, Arthur C. "The Decline and Fall of the Analytical Philosophy of History." In *A New Philosophy of History*, edited by Frank Ankersmit and Hans Kellner, 70–85. Chicago: University of Chicago,1995.

Dávid, Géza. *Pasák és bégek uralma alatt* [Under the rule of pashas and beys]. Budapest: Akadémiai Kiadó, 2005.

Davis, Natalie Zemon. *Fiction in the Archives: Pardon Tales and—Their Tellers in Sixteenth-Century France*. Stanford: Stanford University Press, 1987.

Davis, Natalie Zemon. "The Reasons of Misrule." In idem *Society and Culture in Early Modern France: Eight Essays*, 97–123. Stanford: Stanford University Press, 1988.

Davis, Natalie Zemon. "The Rites of Violence." In idem *Society and Culture in Early Modern France: Eight Essays*, 152–188. Stanford: Stanford University Press, 1975.

Davis, Natalie Zemon. *Trickster Travels: A Sixteenth-century Muslim between Worlds.* New York: Hill and Wang, 2006.

Davis, Natalie Zemon. "Women on Top." In idem *Society and Culture in Early Modern France: Eight Essays, 124–151*. Stanford, California: Stanford University Press, 1975.

Davis, Virginia. "Irish Clergy in Late Medieval England." *Irish Historical Studies* 32 (2000): 145–60.

Davis, Virginia. "Rivals for Ministry? Ordinations of Secular and Regular Clergy in Southern England, c. 1300–1500." In *The Ministry, Clerical and Lay: Papers Read at the 1988 Summer Meeting and the 1989 Winter Meeting of the Ecclesiastical History Society*, edited by W. J. Sheils and Diana Wood, 99–109. Cambridge: Blackwell, 1989.

de Certeau, Michel. *The Practice of Everyday Life*. Berkeley: University of California Press, 1984.

de Cevins, Marie-Madeleine. *Az egyház a késő-középkori magyar városokban* [The Church in late Medieval Hungarian Towns]. Budapest: Szent István Társulat, 2003.

de Cevins, Marie-Madeleine. *Les Franciscains Observants Hongrois de l'Expansion à la débâcle* (vers 1450–vers 1540). Rome: Istitutio Storico dei Cappuccini, 2008.

Delumeau, Jean. *Angst im Abendland. Die Geschichte kollektiver Ängste im Europa des 14. bis 18. Jahrhunderts.* Hamburg: Rowohlt, 1998.

Dinges, Martin. "Die Ehre als Thema der Stadtgeschichte: Eine Semantik am Übergang vom Ancien Regime zur Moderne." *Zeitschrift für Historische Forschung* 16 (1989): 419–40.

Dinges, Martin. "Formenwandel der Gewalt in der Neuzeit: Zur Kritik der Zivilisationstheorie von Norbert Elias." In *Kulturen der Gewalt: Ritualisierung und Symbolisierung von Gewalt in der Geschichte*, edited by Rolf Peter Sieferle and Helga Breuninger, 171–94. Frankfurt am Main: Campus Verlag, 1998.

Dinges, Martin. "Usi della giustizia come elemento di controllo sociale nella prima etá moderna." In *Criminalità e giustizia in Germania e in Italia: pratiche giudiziarie e linguaggi giuridici tra tardo medioevo ed età moderna*, edited by Marco Bellabarba, Gerd Schweroff and Andrea Zorzi, Annali dell'Istituto storico italo-germanico in Trento 11, 285–327. Bologna: FBK Press, 2001.

Dixon, C. Scott. *Contesting the Reformation.* Chichester: Wiley-Blackwell, 2012.

Dixon, C. Scott and Luise Schorn-Schütte. "The Protestant Clergy of Early Modern Europe." In *The Protestant Clergy of Early Modern Europe*, edited by C. Scott Dixon and Luise Schorn-Schütte, 1–38. New York: Palgrave Macmillan, 2003.

Dömötör, Tekla. "Erscheinungsformen des Charivari im ungarischen Sprachgebiet." *Acta Ethnographia* 6 (1957): 73–89.

Dömötör, Tekla. *Naptári ünnepek, népi színjátszás* [Calendar holidays, popular theater plays]. Budapest: Akadémiai Kiadó, 1964.

Du Boulay, F. R. H. *An Age of Ambition. English Society in the Late Middle Ages.* London: Avery, 1970.

Duffy, Eamon. *Stripping of the Altars: Traditional Religion in England, 1400–1580.* New Haven and London: Yale University Press, 1992.

Duggan, Charles. "Papal Judges Delegate and the "New" Law." In *Cultures of Power: Lordship, Status and Process in Twelfth-Century Europe*, edited by Thomas N. Bisson, 172–99. Philadelphia: University of Pennsylvania Press, 1995.

Dursteler, Eric. *Renegade Women: Gender, Identity, and Boundaries in the Early Modern Mediterranean.* Baltimore: Johns Hopkins University Press, 2011.

Dutton, Yasin. "Conversion to Islam: The Qur'anic Paradigm." In *Religious Conversion: Contemporary Practices and Controversies*, edited by Lamb, Christopher and M. Darroll Bryant, 151–65. London: Cassel, 1999.

Eckhart, Ferenc. *A földesúri büntetőbíráskodás a XVI–XVII. században* [Seigneurial criminal courts in the sixteenth and seventeenth centuries]. Budapest: Akadémiai Kiadó, 1954.

Eddie, S. A. *Freedom's Price: Serfdom, Subjection and Reform in Prussia, 1648–1848.* Oxford: Oxford University Press, 2013.

Eisenbichler, Konrad, ed. *The Premodern Teenager, Youth in Society 1150–1650*. Toronto: Centre for the Reformation and Renaissance Studies, 2002.

Elias, Norbert, *The Civilizing Process: Sociogenetic and Psychogenetic Investigations*. Revised Edition. Translated by Edmund Jephcott, edited by Dunning, Eric, Johan Goudsblom and Stephen Mennel. Oxford: Blackwell, 2000; first German edition in 1939.

Eliav-Feldon, Miriam. *Exposing Impostors: Invented Identities in Early Modern Europe*. Basingstoke: Palgrave Macmillan, 2012.

Eliav-Feldon, Miriam. "Invented Identities: Credulity in the Age of Prophecy and Exploration." *Journal of Early Modern History* 3 (1999): 204–32.

Elliott, Dylan. *Fallen Bodies: Pollution, Sexuality, and Demonology in the Middle Ages*. Philadelphia: University of Pennsylvania Press, 1998.

Elm, Kaspar. "Die Franziskanerobservanz als Bildungsreform." In *Lebenslehren und Weltentwürfe im Übergang vom Mittelalter zur Neuzeit*, edited by Hartmut Boockmann, Bernd Moeller and Karl Stackmann, 201–13. Abhandlungen der Akademie der Wissenschaften in Göttingen, Phil.-hist. Kl. III, 179. Göttingen: Vandenhoeck & Ruprecht, 1989.

Endrei, Walter and Zolnay László. *Társasjáték és szórakozás a régi Európában* [Board games and entertainment in Old Europe]. Budapest: Corvina, 1986.

Engel, Pál. *Magyar középkori adattár: Középkori magyar genealógia* [Medieval Hungarian Databank: Medieval Hungarian genealogy]. CD-ROM, Budapest: Arcanum, 2001.

Engel, Pál. *The Realm of St. Stephen: A History of Medieval Hungary*. London and New York: I. B. Tauris, 2005.

Engel, Pál. "A török dúlások hatása a népességre: Valkó megye példája" [The effect of Turkish raids on the population: The case of Valkó County]. *Századok* 134 (2000): 267–321.

Erdélyi, Gabriella. *A Cloister on Trial: Religious Culture and Everyday Life in Late Medieval Hungary*. Burlington: Ashgate, 2015.

Erdő, Péter. *Egyházjog a középkori Magyarországon* [Canon law in medieval Hungary]. Budapest: Osiris, 2001.

Esch, Arnold. *Die Lebenswelt des europäischen Mittelalters: Kleine Schicksale selbst erzählt in Schreiben an den Papst*, Munich: C. H. Beck Verlag, 2014.

Evans, Robert John Weston. *The Making of the Habsburg Monarchy 1550–1700*. Oxford: Clarendon Press, 1991.

F. Romhányi, Beatrix. "A koldulóbarátok szerepe a XV–XVI. századi vallási megújulásban" [The role of mendicant friars in the religious renewal of the fifteenth and sixteenth centuries]. In *Szentírás, hagyomány, reformáció: Teológia- és egyháztörténeti tanulmányok* [The Bible, tradition, Reformation: Essays in theology and church history], edited by F. Romhányi Beatrix and Kendeffy Gábor, 143–55. Budapest: Gondolat, 2009.

F. Romhányi, Beatrix. "Egy régi-új forrás az erdélyi domonkosok történetéhez" [An old-new source with regard the history of Transylvanian Dominicans]. *Communicationes Archeologicae Hungariae* (2004): 235–47.

F. Romhányi, Beatrix. Kolostorhálózat—településhálózat—népesség [Monastery network—settlement network—population]. *Történelmi Szemle* 57, no.1 (2015): 1–49.

F. Romhányi, Beatrix. *Kolostorok és társaskáptalanok a középkori Magyarországon* [Monasteries and collegiate chapters in Medieval Hungary]. Budapest: Pytheas, 2000.

Faber, Riemer A. "Humanitas as Discriminating Factor." In *Educational Writings of Erasmus and Luther, in the Formation of Clerical and Confessional Identities in Early Modern Europe*, edited by Weim Janse and Barbara Pitkin, 25–37. Dutch Review of Church History 85. Leiden: Brill, 2005.

Farge, Arlette. *The Allure of the Archives*. New Haven: Yale University Press, 2015.

Fazekas, István. *Szerzetesrendek Kelet-Magyarországon a XVII. században* [Religious orders in Eastern Hungary in the seventeenth century]. Acta Collegii Evangelici Presoviensis 7. Pressburg, 2000.

Febvre, Lucien. *The Problem of Unbelief in the Sixteenth Century*. Translated by Beatrice Gottlieb. Cambridge: Harvard University Press, 1982.

Fedeles, Tamás, Sarbak Gábor and Sümegi József, eds. *A pécsi egyházmegye története* [History of the Diocese of Pécs]. Vol. 1. of *A középkor évszázadai (1009–1543)*. [The centuries of the Middle Ages (1009–1543)]. Pécs: Fény Kft., 2009.

Fekete, Lajos. *Budapest a török korban* [Budapest under Ottoman rule]. Budapest: Királyi Magyar Egyetemi Nyomda, 1944.

Fenster, Thelma and Lord Daniel Smail. Introduction to *Fama: Politics of Talks and Reputation in Medieval Europe*, edited by Thelma Fenster and Lord Daniel Smail, I–XI. Ithaca and London: Cornell University Press, 2003.

Fodor, Pál. "'A kincstár számára a hitetlen a leghasznosabb': Az oszmánok magyarországi valláspolitikájáról" ["The infidel is the most useful for the Treasury": On the religious policy of the Ottomans in Hungary]. In idem *Szülejmán szultántól Jókai Mórig. Tanulmányok az oszmán-török hatalom szerkezetéről és a magyar–török érintkezésekről* [From Sultan Süleyman to Mór Jókai: Studies on the structure of Ottoman Turkish power and Hungarian–Ottoman encounters], 258–71. Budapest: MTA BTK, 2014.

Fodor, Pál and Dávid Géza, eds. *Ransom Slavery along the Ottoman Borders*. Leiden: Brill, 2007.

Földesi, Béla. "Adalékok a magyarországi gergelyjárás történetéhez" [Data on the Gergely name day folk custom in Hungary]. In Folklór tanulmányok [Folclore studies], edited by Hoppál Mihály, 119–176. Előmunkálatok a Magyarság Néprajzához. Budapest: MTA Néprajzi Kutatócsoport, 1981.

Forster, Marc. *The Counter-Reformation in the Villages: Religion and Reform in the Bishopric of Speyer 1560–1720*. Ithaca and London: Cornell University Press, 1992.

Fraknói, Vilmos. "II. Lajos király számadási könyve: 1525. január 12–július 16" [The account books of King Louis II: January 12–July 16, 1525]. *Magyar Történelmi Tár* 22 (1877): 45–236.

Frank, Isnard W. O.P. *Hausstudium und Universitätsstudium der Wiener Dominikaner bis 1500*. Vienna: Böhlau, 1968.

Fredriksen, Paula. "Paul and Augustine: Conversion Narratives, Orthodox Traditions, and the Retrospective Self." *Journal of Theological Studies* 37, no.1 (1986): 3–34.

Freedman, Paul. "Representations of Peasant and Seigneurial Fury in Late Medieval and Early Modern Europe." *Temas Medievales* 19 (2011): 79–82.

Frenz, Thomas. *Die Kanzlei der Päpste der Hochrenaissance (1471–1527)*. Bibliothek des Deutschen Historischen Instituts in Rom, Band 63. Berlin: De Gruyter, 1986.

Fuchs, Ralf-Peter and Winfried Schulze, eds. *Wahrheit, Wissen, Erinnerung: Zeugenverhörsprotokolle als Quellen für soziale Wissensbestände in der Frühen Neuzeit*. Wirklichkeit und Wahrnehmung in der Frühen Neuzeit, 1. Münster, Hamburg and London, 2002.

Fügedi, Erik, "A XV. századi magyar püspökök" [Hungarian bishops in the fifteenth century]. In idem *Kolduló barátok, polgárok, nemesek. Tanulmányok a magyar középkorról* [Mendicant friars, burghers, noblemen. Studies on the Hungarian Middle Ages], 89–113. Budapest: Magvető, 1981.

Gauvard, Claude. *"De grace especial": Crime, État et société en France à la fin du moyen âge*, vol. 2. Paris: Publications de la Sorbonne, 1991.

Gauvard, Claude. "Le roi de France et l'opinion publique à l'époque de Charles VI. "In *Culture et idéologie dans la genèse de l'État moderne: Actes de la table ronde de Rome (15–17 Octobre 1984)*, edited by Charles Pietri and Jean-Claude Maire Vigueur, 353–66. Paris and Rome: École Française de Rome, 1985.

George, Edward. "Juan Luis Vives." In *Western Europe 1500–1600*. Vol. 6 of *Christian-Muslim Relations: A Bibliographical History*, edited by David Thomas and John Chestworth, 663–68. Leiden and Boston: Brill, 2014.

Geremek, Bronisław. *The Margins of Society in Late Medieval Paris*. Translated by Jean Birrell, Cambridge: Cambridge University Press, 1991.

Gerevich, László, ed. *Towns in Medieval Hungary*. Boulder: Social Science Monographs, 1990.

Ginzburg, Carlo. *The Cheese and the Worms: The Cosmos of a Sixteenth Century Miller*. Baltimore: Johns Hopkins University Press, 1980.

Ginzburg, Carlo and Carlo Poni. "The Name and the Game: Unequal Exchange and the Historiographic Marketplace." In *Microhistory and the Lost Peoples of Europe*, edited by Edward Muir and Guido Ruggiero, 1–10. Baltimore: Johns Hopkins University Press, 1991.

Gömöri, János. "A sárospataki középkori plébániai iskola" [The Medieval parish school in Sárospatak]. In *A magyar iskola első évszázadai: 996–1526* [First centuries of

Hungarian schooling], edited by G. Szende Katalin and Szabó Péter, 69–86. Győr: Xántus Múzeum, 1996.

Goodale, Jay. "Die Pfarrer als Außenseiter. Landpfarren und religiöses Leben in Sachsen zur Reformationszeit." *Historische Antropologie* 7, no. 2 (1999): 197–211.

Gordon, Bruce. "Preaching and the Reform of the Clergy in the Swiss Reformation." In *The Reformation of the Parishes: The Ministry and the Reformation in Town and Country*, edited by Andrew Pettigree, 63–85. Manchester: Manchester University Press, 1993.

Gowing, Laura. *Domestic Dangers: Women, Words, and Sex in Early Modern London*. Oxford: Clarendon, 1996.

Gramsch, Robert. "Erfurter Juristen im Spatmittelalter: Karrieremustere und Tätigkeitsfelder einer gelehrten Elite in 14. und 15. Jahrhunderts." In *Education and Society in the Middle Ages and Renaissance*, edited by Jürgen Miethke, William Courtenay, Jeremy Catto and Jacques Verger, 561–66. Leiden: Brill, 2003.

Grendi, Edoardo. "Micro-analisi e storia sociale." *Quaderni Storici* 35 (1977): 506–520.

Grendler, Paul F. "Le scuole della dottrina cristiana nell'Italia del Cinquecento." In *Cittá italiane del '500 tra Riforma e Controriforma*, edited by Martin Kroener, 299–312. Lucca, 1988.

Grendler, Paul F. "Schooling in Western Europe." *Renaissance Quarterly* 43 (1990): 775–87.

Greschat, Martin. *Martin Bucer: A Reformer and his Times*. Westminster: John Knox Press, 2004.

Groebner, Valentin. Defaced. The Visual Cultures of Violence in the Late Middle Ages. New York: Zone Books, 2004.

Hal, Sutart and Paul du Gay, eds. Questions of Cultural Identity. London: Sage, 1996.

Harrington, Joel F. The Unwanted Child: The Fate of Foundlings, Orphans, and Juvenile Criminals in Early Modern Germany. Chicago: University of Chicago Press, 2009.

Hasebrink, Burkhard. "Latinität als Bildungsfundament. Spuren subsidiärer Grammatikunterweisung in Dominikanerorden." In *Schulliteratur im Späten Mittelalter*, edited by Klaus Grubmüller, 49–76. Münsterische Mittelalter Schriften 69. Munich: Fink, Wilhelm, 2000.

Házi, Jenő. *Sopron középkori egyháztörténete* [The medieval Church history of Sopron]. Sopron: Székely Nyomda, 1939.

Hegyi, Klára. "Etnikum, vallás, iszlamizáció: A budai vilájet várkatonaságának eredete és utánpótlása" [Ethnicity, religion and Islamization: The origins and reserves of the garrison of the Eyalet of Buda]. *Történelmi Szemle* 40 (1998): 229–56.

Hegyi, Klára. "Kereszténység és iszlám az Oszmán birodalom balkáni és magyar tartományaiban" [Christianity and Islam in the Hungarian and Balkan provinces of the Ottoman Empire]. *Korunk* 7 (1996): 32–42.

Heinrich, Gerd. "Klosterflucht und Klosterzucht im 15. Jahrhundert. Zur Geschichte Chorins." *Jahrbuch für die Geschichte Mittel-und Ostdeutschlands* 12 (1963): 195–206.

Horváth, János. *A reformáció jegyében: A Mohács utáni félszázad magyar irodalomtörténete* [In the spirit of Reformation: History of Hungarian Literature in the half century following Mohács]. Budapest: Gondolat, 1957.

Housley, Norman. *Religious Warfare in Europe, 1400–1536.* Oxford: Oxford University Press, 2002.

Hyams, Paul. "Due Process versus the Maintenance of Order in European Law: The Contribution of the *ius commune.*" In *The Moral World of the Law,* edited by Peter Coss, 62–90. Cambridge: Cambridge University Press, 2000.

Illés, Pál Attila and Zágorhidy Czigány Balázs, eds. *A domonkos rend Magyarországon* [The Dominican order in Hungary]. Piliscsaba: Művelődéstörténeti Műhely—Rendtörténeti konferenciák, 2007.

Irwin-Zarecka, Iwona. *Frames of Remembrance: The Dynamics of Collective Memory.* New Brunswick: Transaction, 1994.

Jakó, Zsigmond. "Váradi siralmas krónika: Könyvtár- és levéltárügy Nagyváradon a múltban és a jelenben" [Miserable chronicle of Várad: The issue of libraries and archives in Nagyvárad, in the past and in the present]. *Magyar Egyháztörténeti Vázlatok* 16, no. 1–2 (2004): 93–7.

James D. Tracey. *Erasmus of the Low Countries.* Berkeley, Los Angeles and London: University of California Press, 1997.

Jennings, Donald C. "Women in the Early Seventeenth-Century Ottoman Judicial Records: The Sharia court of Anatolian Kayseri." *Journal of the Economic and Social History of the Orient* 18 (1975): 53–114.

Juhász, Kálmán. *A csanádi püspökség története 1434–1500* [History of the Diocese of Csanád]. Makó: 1947.

Kafadar, Cemal. *Between Two Worlds: The Construction of the Ottoman State.* Berkeley: University of California Press 1995.

Kagan, Richard L. *Lawsuits and Litigants in Castile, 1500–1700.* Chapel Hill: Books on Demand, 1981.

Kagan, Richard L. *Students and Society in Early Modern Spain.* Baltimore: Johns Hopkins University Press, 1974.

Kansteiner, Wulf. "Finding Meaning in Memory: A Methodological Critique of Collective Memory Studies." *History and Theory* 41, no. 2 (2002): 179–97.

Karras, Ruth Mazo. *From Boys to Men: Formations of Masculinity in Late Medieval Europe.* Philadelphia: University of Pennsylvania Press, 2003.

Kathona, Géza. *Fejezetek a török hódoltsági reformáció történetéből* [Chapters from the history of the Reformation in Ottoman Hungary]. Humanizmus és reformáció 4. Budapest: Akadémiai Kiadó, 1974.

Kaufmann, Thomas. "*The Clergy and the Theological Culture of the Age: The Education of Lutheran Pastors in the Sixteenth and Seventeenth Centuries.*" In *The Protestant clergy of early modern Europe,* edited by C. Scott Dixon and Luise Schorn-Schütte, 120–36. Basingstoke: Palgrave Macmillan, 2003.

Keegan, John. *The Face of Battle: A Study of Agincourt, Waterloo, and the Somme.* London: Penguin, 1976.

Kintzinger, Martin. "A profession But Not a Career? Schoolmasters and the Artes in Late Medieval Europe." In *Universities and Schooling in Medieval Society*, edited by William Courtenay and Jürgen Miethke, 167–81. Leiden: Brill, 2000.

Kintzinger, Martin. *Wissen wird Macht: Bildung im Mittelalter.* Stuttgart: Jan Thorbecke Verlag, 2007.

Kisbán, Emil. *A magyar pálosrend története* [History of the Hungarian Pauline order]. Budapest: Fráter György Alapítvány, 2012.

Kisbán, Eszter. "Az étkezések napi rendjének újkori átalakulása és az ebéd" [The modern transformation of the daily order of meals and the concept of lunch]. *Magyar Nyelv* 71 (1975): 177–85.

Kiss, Farkas Gábor. "Ambiguity and Paradox in the Humanistic Literature of the Jagiellonian Age." In *Armed Memory: Agency and Peasant Revolts in Central and Southern Europe* (1450–1700), edited by Erdélyi Gabriella, 171–89. Göttingen: Vandenhoeck & Ruprecht, 2016.

Kiss, Farkas Gábor. "Latin és népnyelv a késő-középkori magyarországi domonkos kolostorokban in Leonhard Huntpichler ed.: *Directio pedagogorum*" [Latin and vernacular language in Medieval Dominican monasteries in Hungary—Leonhard Huntpichler: *Directio pedagogorum*]. *Irodalomtörténeti Közlemények* 120, no. 2. (2016): 225–47.

Kiss, Réka. "Református egyházfegyelmi iratok elemzési lehetőségei: kora újkori példák" [Possibilities for analyzing Reformed Church disciplinary documents: Examples from the early modern period]. In *Történeti forrás—néprajzi olvasat: Gazdaság-, társadalom- és egyháztörténeti források néprajzi értelmezésének lehetőségei* [Historical source—ethnographical interpretation: Possibilities for the ethnographical interpretation of economic, social and church historical sources], edited by Fülemile Ágnes and Kiss Réka, 316–38. Documentatio Ethnographica 23. Budapest: L'Harmattan, 2008.

Klaniczay, Tibor. "A magyar reformáció irodalma" [The literature of the Hungarian Reformation]. *Irodalomtörténeti Közlemények* 71, no. 1–2 (1957): 12–47.

Klaniczay, Tibor. "A reformáció szerepe az anyanyelvű irodalmak fejlődésében" [The role of reformation in the development of vernacular literatures]. In idem *Hagyományok ébresztése* [Awakening Traditions], 296–310. Budapest: Szépirodalmi Kiadó, 1976.

Klaniczay, Gábor. "Hungary: The Accusations and the Universe of Popular Magic." In *Early Modern European Witchcraft: Centres and Peripheries*, edited by Bengt Ankarloo and Gustav Henningsen, 219–25. Oxford: Clarendon Press, 1990.

Klaniczay, Gábor. "Images and Designations for Rebellious Peasants in Late Medieval Hungary." In *The Man of Many Devices, Who Wandered Full Many Ways ... Festschrift in Honor of János M. Bak*, edited by Nagy Balázs and Sebők Marcell, 115–27. Budapest: CEU Press, 1999.

Körmendy, Kinga. "Literátusok, magisterek, doktorok az esztergomi káptalanban" [Literates, magisters and doctors of philosophy at the Esztergom Cathedral Chapter]. In *Művelődéstörténeti tanulmányok a magyar középkorról* [Essays on the Cultural History of the Hungarian Middle Ages], edited by Fügedi Erik, 176–202. Budapest: Gondolat, 1986.

Kövér, György. "Források, értelmezések, történelmek" [Sources, interpretations, histories]. In idem *A felhalmozás íve: társadalom- és gazdaságtörténeti tanulmányok* [The arch of accumulation: Essays in economic and social history]. Budapest: Új Mandátum, 2002.

Kristó, Gyula. *Nem magyar népek a középkori Magyarországon* [Non-Hungarian people in medieval Hungary]. Budapest: Lucidus, 2003.

Kristóf, Ilona. *Egyházi középréteg a késő középkori Váradon 1440–1526* [The middle layers of ecclesiastical society in late medieval Várad 1140–1526]. Pécs: Pécsi Történettudományért Kulturális Egyesület, 2014.

Krug-Richter, Barbara. "Das Privathaus als Wirthaus. Zur Öffentlichkeit des Hauses in Regionen mit Reihebraurecht." In *Zwischen Gotteshaus und Taverne. Öffentliche Räume in der Frühen Neuzeit*, edited by Susanne Rau and Gerd Schwerhoff, 99–117. Norm und Struktur. Cologne, Weimar, and Vienna: Böhlau, 2004.

Kubinyi, András. "A királyi udvar élete a Jagelló-korban" [The life of the royal court under the Jagiellos]. In *Kelet és Nyugat között: Történeti tanulmányok Kristó Gyula tiszteletére* [Between East and West: Historical essays in honor of Gyula Kristó], edited by Koszta László, 309–35. Szeged: Szegedi Középkorász Műhely, 1995.

Kubinyi, András. "Budai és pesti polgárok családi összeköttetései a Jagelló korban" [The family connections of the citizens of Buda and Pest in the Jagiello period]. *Levéltári Közlemények* 37 (1967): 228–291.

Kubinyi, András. "Die Bevölkerung des Königreichs Ungarns am Ende des 15 Jahrhunderts." In *Historische Demographie Ungarns 896–1896*, edited by Kristó Gyula, 66–93. Herne, 2007.

Kubinyi, András. "Írástudás és értelmiségi foglalkozásúak a Jagelló korban" [Literacy and literate professionals in the Jagiello era]. *Magyar Herold* 1 (1984): 186–208.

Kubinyi, András. "Magyarország és a pálosok a 14–15. században." In *Decus solitudinis - Pálos Évszázadok*, edited by Gábor Sarbak, 40–56. Budapest: Szent István Társulat, 2007.

Kubinyi, András. "Orvoslás, gyógyszerészek, fürdők és ispotályok a késő középkori Magyarországon" [Healing, pharmacists, baths and hospitals in late medieval Hungary]. In *Főpapok, egyházi intézmények és vallásosság a középkori Magyarországon* [Prelates, church institutions and piety in medieval Hungary], edited by Várszegi Asztrik and Zombori István, 253–68. Budapest: METEM, 1999.

Kubinyi, András. "Polgári értelmiség és hivatalnokréteg Budán és Pesten" [Intellectuals and clerks in Buda and Pest]. In idem *Tanulmányok Budapest középkori történetéről* [Essays on the medieval history of Budapest], 599–620. Vol. 2. Budapest: BFL, 2009.

Kubinyi, András. *Változások a középkor végi Magyarországon* [Changes in late medieval Hungary]. História Könyvtár. Előadások a történettudomány műhelyeiből 2. Budapest: MTA Történettudományi Intézet, 1993.

Kubinyi, András. *Városfejlődés és városhálózat a középkori Alföldön és az Alföld szélén* [Urban development and network in the medieval Great Plain and its edge]. Szeged: Csongrád Megye Önkormányzata, 2000.

Kuehn, Thomas. *Law, Family, and Women: Toward a Legal Anthropology of Renaissance Italy*. Chicago: University of Chicago Press, 1991.

Kümin, Beat. *Drinking Matters. Public Houses and Social Exchange in Early Modern Central Europe*. Basingstoke: Palgrave Macmillan, 2007.

Kümin, Beat. *The Shaping of a Community: The Rise and Reformation of the English Parish c. 1400–1560*. Farnham: Ashgate, 1996.

Kurze, Dietrich. *Gesammelte Aufsätze*. Warendorf: Fahlbusch Verlag, 1996.

Laslett, Peter. *Family Life and Illicit Love in Earlier Generations: Essays in Historical Sociology*. New York and London: Cambridge University Press, 1977.

Lassonde, Stephen. "Age, Schooling and Development." In *The Routledge History of Childhood in the Western World*, edited by Paula S. Fass, 211–28. London and New York: Routledge, 2013.

Le Roy Ladurie, Emmanuel. *Le Carnaval de Romans*, Paris: Gallimard, 1979.

Levin, Eve. *Sex and Society in the World of the Orthodox Slavs 900–1700*. Ithaca: Cornell University Press, 1995.

Lindner, Andreas. "Martin Luther im Augustinerkloster." In *Luthers Erfurter Kloster. Das Augustinerkloster im Spannungsfeld von monastischer Tradition und protestantischem Geist*, edited by Lothar Schmelz and Michael Ludscheidt, 59–74. Erfurt: Burkhardt, René, 2005.

Logan, Francis Donald. *Runaway Religious in Medieval England (c. 1240–1540)*. Cambridge: Cambridge University Press, 1996.

Lortz, Joseph. *Die Reformation in Deutschland*. 2 vols. Freiburg: Herder, 1939.

Lukcsics, Pál. *XV. századi pápák oklevelei* [Breves of fifteenth-century popes]. Vol. 2. *IV. Jenő pápa és V. Miklós pápa* [Pope Eugene IV and Nicholas V]. Budapest: MTA, 1938.

Lupescuné Makó, Mária. "A Domonkos Rend középkori erdélyi kolostorainak adattára" [The register of the Transylvanian cloisters of the Dominican order]. *Történelmi Szemle* 46, no. 3–4 (2004): 339–84.

Lupescuné Makó, Mária. "Domonkos oktatás a középkori Erdélyben" [Dominican education in Medieval Transylvania]. *Református Szemle* 96, no. 6 (2003): 844–53.

Lupescuné Makó, Mária. "Két erdélyi domonkos kolostor a reformáció hajnalán" [Two Dominican cloisters at the dawn of Reformation in Transylvania]. In *Szentírás, hagyomány, reformáció: Teológia- és egyháztörténeti tanulmányok* [The Bible, tradition, Reformation: Essays in theology and church history], edited by F. Romhányi Beatrix and Kendeffy Gábor, 203–23. Budapest: Gondolat, 2009.

Lutton, Robert. *Lollardy and Orthodox Religion in Pre-Reformation England. Reconstructing Piety*. Woodbridge: Boydell Press, 2006.

Maček, Pavao and Ivan Jurković, *Rodoslov Plemića I Baruna Kaštelanovića od Svetog Huda (od 14. do 17. stoljeća)* [The genealogy of the Szentléleki Kasztellánfi family between the fourteenth and the seventeenth centuries]. Slavonski Brod: n.p., 2009.

Madas, Edit. "Esztergomi iskoláskönyv a 15. század első negyedéből" [Esztergom school book from the first quarter of the fifteenth century]. In *Művelődéstörténeti tanulmányok a magyar középkorról* [Essays on the cultural history of the Hungarian Middle Ages], edited by Fügedi Erik, 157–75. Budapest: Gondolat, 1986.

Maddern, Philippa. "Between Households: Children in Blended and Transitional Households in Late Medieval England." *Journal of the History of Childhood and Youth* 3 (2010): 65–86.

Maddern, Philippa. "Social Mobility." In *A Social History of England 1200–1500*, edited by Rosemary Horrox and W. Mark Ormrod, 113–33. Cambridge: Cambridge University Press, 2006.

Majorossy, Judit. "Church in Town: Urban Religious Life in Late Medieval Pressburg in the Mirror of Last Wills." PhD diss., Central European University, 2006.

Makkai, László. *A felsőtiszavidéki parasztfelkelés 1631–1632* [The Peasant uprising in the Upper Tisza Region, 1631–1632]. Budapest: Művelt Nép, 1954.

Mályusz, Elemér. "A pálosrend a középkor végén" [The Pauline order at the end of the Middle Ages]. *Egyháztörténet* 3 (1945): 1–53.

Mályusz, Elemér. *Egyházi társadalom a középkori Magyarországon* [Ecclesiastical society in medieval Hungary]. Budapest: Akadémiai, 1971.

Margolin, Jean-Claude. *Erasme, Précepteur de l'Europe*. Paris: Julliard, 1995.

Márki, Sándor. *Dósa György 1470–1514* [György Dózsa 1470–1514]. Budapest: Magyar Történelmi Társulat, 1913.

Mayali, Laurent. "Du vagabonde à l'apostasie. La moine fugitif dans la société médiévale." In *Religiöse Devianz. Unterschungen zu sozialen, rechtlichen und theoloischen Reaktionen auf religiöse Abweichungen im westlichen und östlichen Mittelalter*, edited by Dieter Simon, 121–42. Studien zur europäischen Rechtsgeschichte 48. Frankfurt: Klostermann, Vittorio, 1990.

Mayes, David. *Communal Christianity: The Life and Loss of a Peasant Vision in Early Modern Germany*. Leiden: Brill, 2004.

Medgyesy-Schmikli, Norbert and Őze Sándor, eds. *A ferences lelkiség hatása az újkori Közép-Európa történetére és kultúrájára* [The impact of Fransiscan spirituality on the history and culture of Central Europe]. Piliscsaba: Művelődéstörténeti Műhely—Rendtörténeti Konferenciák, 2005.

Mennel, Stephen. *Norbert Elias: Civilization and the Human Self Image*. Oxford: Blackwell, 1989.

Mészáros, István. *XVI. századi városi iskoláink és a "studia humanitatis"* [Our fifteenth-century municipal schools and the "studia humanitatis"]. Humanizmus és reformáció 11. Budapest: Akadémiai Kiadó, 1981.

Meyer, Andreas. *Arme Kleriker auf Pfründensuche. Eine Studie über das in forma pauperum—Register Gregors XII. von 1407 und über päpstliche Anwartschaften im Spätmittelalter.* Forschungen zur kirchlichen Rechtsgeschichte und zum Kirchenrecht 20. Cologne und Vienna: Böhlau, 1990.

Meyer, Andreas. "Der deutsche Pfründenmarkt im Spätmittelalter." *Quellen und Forschungen aus Italienischen Archiven und Bibliotheken* 71 (1991): 266–79.

Mezey, Barna, ed. *Magyar Jogtörténet* [A history of Hungarian law]. Budapest: Osiris, 2004.

Mezey, László. *Deákság és Európa: Irodalmi műveltségünk alapvetésének vázlata* [Literate men and Europe: Outline of the establishment of our literary culture]. Budapest: Akadémiai Kiadó, 1979.

Mezey, László. "Ország 'egyetem nélkül': A magyarországi felsőoktatás a középkor végén" [Country "without a university": Higher education in Hungary at the end of the Middle Ages]. In *A 600 éves jogi felsőoktatás történetéből, 1367–1967* [From 600 years of judicial higher education, *1367–1967*], edited by Csizmadia Andor, 75–88. Studia Iuridica Auctoritate Universitatis Pécs Publicata 60. Pécs: Pécsi Szikra Nyomda, 1968.

Mező, András. *Várdai-birtokok jobbágynevei a XV. század közepén* [Várdai-estate serf names in the middle of the fifteenth century]. Kisvárda: Járási Tanács, 1970.

Millet, Hélène, ed. *Suppliques et requêtes: gouvernement par la grâce en Occident (XIIe–XVe siècle).* Rome: École française de Rome, 2003.

Minkov, Anton. *Conversion to Islam in the Balkans: Kisve Bahas Petitions and Ottoman Social Life, 1670–1730.* Leiden: Brill, 2004.

Moačanin, Nenad. "Mass Islamization of Peasants in Bosnia: Demystifications." In *Melanges Prof. Machiel Kiel*, edited by Abdeljelil Temini, 353–58. Zaghouan: Fondation Temimi pour la Recherche Scientifique et l'Information, 1999.

Moeller, Bernd. "Die frühe Reformation in Deutschland als neues Mönchtum." In *Die frühe Reformation in Deutschland als Umbruch. Wissenschafltiches Symposiumdes Vereins für Reformationsgeschichte 1996*, edited by Stephen E. Buckwalter and Bernd Moeller, 76–91. Gütersloh: Gütersloher Verlagshaus, 1998.

Molnár, Antal. "Jezsuita misszió Karánsebesen (1625–1642)" [Jesuit mission in Karánsebes]. *Történelmi Szemle* 47 (1999): 127–56.

Molnár, Antal, "Jezsuiták a hódolt Pécsett (1612–1686)" [Jesuits in Pécs under Ottoman rule (1612–1686). In *Pécs a törökkorban,* [Pécs in Ottoman times], edited by Szakály Ferenc, 171–264. Pécs: Pécs Története Alapítvány, 1999.

Monok, István. *A művelt arisztokrata: A magyarországi főnemesség olvasmányai a XVI–XVII. században* [The erudite aristocrat: The readings of the Hungarian aristocracy in the sixteenth and seventeenth centuries]. Budapest and Eger: Kossuth Kiadó, 2012.

Moran, Jo Ann Hoeppner. *The Growth of English Schooling and Literacy 1340–1548: Learning, Literacy and Laicization in Pre-Reformation York Diocese.* Princeton: Princeton University Press, 1985.

Muchembled, Robert. "Die Jugend und die Volkskultur im 15. Jahrhundert." In *Volkskultur der europäischen Spätmittelalters*, edited by Peter Dinzelbacher and Hans-Dieter Muck, 35–58. Stuttgart: Kröner Verlag, 1987.

Muchembled, Robert. "Les jeunes, les jeux et la violence en Artois au XVIe siècle." In *Les jeus à la Renaissance*, edited by Philippe Ariès and Jean-Claude Margolin, 563–79. Paris: Librairie Philosophique J. Vrin, 1982.

Muir, Edward. "Carnival and the Lower Body." In *Ritual in Early Modern Europe*, 85–116. Edited by Edward Muir. New York: Cambridge University Press, 2005.

Mulchahey, Marian Michèle and Timothy B. Noone. "Religious Orders." In *A Companion to Philosophy in the Middle Ages*, Jorge J. A. Gracia and Timothy B. Noone, 45–54. Oxford and Malden: Blackwell, 2002.

Müller, Wolfgang P. "Die Gebühren der päpstlichen Pönitentiarie (1338–1569)." *Quellen und Forschungen aus italienischen Archiven und Bibliotheken* 78 (1998): 189–261.

Müller, Wolfgang P. "The Price of Papal Pardon. New Fifteenth-Century Evidence." In *Päpste, Pilger, Pönitentiarie. Festschrift für Ludwig Schmugge zum 65. Geburtstag*, edited by Andreas Meyer, Constanze Rendtel, Maria Wittmer-Butsch, 457–81. Tübingen: De Gruyter, 2004.

Müller-Wirthmann, Bernhard. "*Raufhändel.* Gewalt und Ehre im Dorf." In *Kultur der einfachen Leute*, edited by Richard van Dülmen, 79–111. Munich: C.H. Beck, 1983.

Nemeskürty, István. *Önfia vágta sebét* [Wounded by his own son]. Budapest: Magvető, 1983.

Orme, Nicholas. *Education and Society in Medieval and Renaissance England.* London: Hambledon Press, 1989.

Orme, Nicholas. *Medieval Schools: From Roman Britain to Renaissance England.* New Haven and London: Yale University Press, 2006.

Ortutay, Gyula, ed. *Magyar Néprajzi Lexikon.* [Hungarian ethnographic lexicon]. 5 vols. Budapest: Akadémiai Kiadó, 1977–1982.

Ozment, Steven. *When Fathers Ruled: Family Life in Reformation Europe. Cambridge and London: Harvard University Press*, 1983.

Pálffy, Géza. "*Koronázási lakomák* a 15–17. századi Magyarországon: Az önálló magyar királyi udvar asztali ceremóniarendjének koraújkori továbbéléséről és a politikai elit hatalmi reprezentációjáról" [Coronation feasts in Hungary between the fifteenth and seventeenth centuries: The preservation of the table ceremony order of the independent Hungarian royal court and the political representation of the power elite]. *Századok* 138, no. 5 (2004): 1005–101.

Pálffy, Géza. *A Magyar Királyság és a Habsburg Monarchia a 16. században* [The Kingdom of Hungary and the Habsburg Monarchy in the sixteenth century]. Budapest: MTA BTK TTI, 2011.

Pálffy, Géza. *Miljenko Pandžić and Felix Tobler, Ausgewählte Dokumente zur Migration der Burgenländischen Kroaten im 16. Jahrhundert.* Eisenstandt/Željezno: HKDC, 1999.

Pálosfalvi, Tamás. *The Noble Elite of the County of Körös (Križevci), 1400–1526.* Budapest: MTA BTK TTI, 2014.

Papp, Sándor. "Die Verleihungs-, Bekräftigungs- und Vertragsurkunden der Osmanen für Ungarn und Siebenbürgen. Eine quellenkritische Untersuchung." *Schriften der Balkan-Kommission der Österreichischen Akademie der Wissenschaften* 42 (2003): 91–107.

Pastor, Ludwig. *Die Geschichte der Päpste*. vol. 3, London: J. Hodges, 1894.

Pásztor, Lajos. *A magyarság vallásos élete a Jagellók korában* [Religious life of Hungarians in the Jagiello era]. Budapest: Egyetemi Nyomda, 1940.

Pataki, Iosif. *Domeniul Hunedoara la începutul secolului al XVI-lea* [The Hunyadi estates at the beginning of the sixteenth century]. București: Editura Academiei Republicii Socialiste România, 1973.

Peirce, Leslie. *Morality Tales: Law and Gender in the Ottoman Court of Aintab*. Berkeley and Los Angeles: University of California Press, 2003.

Pennington, Kenneth. *The Prince and the Law, 1200–1600: Sovereignty and Rights in the Western Legal Tradition*. Berkeley: University of California Press, 1993.

Péter, Katalin. "A reformáció és a művelődés a 16. században" [Reformation and literate culture in the sixteenth century]. In *Magyarország története 1526–1686* [History of Hungary 1526–1686], edited by Ágnes R. Várkonyi. Magyarország története tíz kötetben [The history of Hungary in ten volumes]. Vol. 3/1, 475–604. Budapest: Akadémiai Kiadó, 1985.

Péter, Katalin. *A reformáció: kényszer vagy választás?* Budapest: Nemzeti Tankönyvkiadó, 2004.Forthcoming in English: "Coercion or Choice? The Early Reformation in Hungary." In idem, *Studies on the history of the Reformation in Hungary and Transylvania*. Göttingen: Vandenhoeck und Ruprecht, 2017.

Péter, Katalin. "Az erdélyi magyar iskolázás a 16. és 17. században" [Hungarian schooling in Transylvania in the sixteenth and seventeenth centuries]. In idem *Papok és nemesek: Magyar művelődéstörténeti tanulmányok a reformációval kezdődő évszázadból* [Priests and noblemen: Studies on the cultural history of Hungary in the century of the Reformation], 98–108. A Ráday Gyűjtemény Tanulmányai 8. Budapest: Ráday Gyűjtemény, 1994. Forthcoming in English in idem, *Studies on the history of the Reformation in Hungary and Transylvania*.

Péter, Katalin. "Bibellesen. Ein Programm für jedenmann in Ungarn des 16. Jahrhunderts." In *Iter Germanicum. Deutschland und die Reformierte Kirche in Ungarn im 16–17. Jahrhundert*, edited by András Szabó, 7–38. Budapest: Kálvin Kiadó, 1999.

Péter, Katalin. *Házasság a régi Magyarországon* [Marriage in Old Hungary]. Budapest: L'Harmattan, 2008.

Péter, Katalin. "Il Rinnovamento cattolico e la Reforma protestante. In: *Storia Religiosa dell'Ungheria*, edited by Adriano Caprioli and Luciano Vaccaro, 185–99. Milano and Gazzada: La casa di Matriona and Fondazione ambrosiana Paolo VI, 1992.

Péter, Katalin. "Jobbágycsaládok életvitelének különbözőségei az örökös jobbágyság korában, 16–17. század" [Differences in the train of life of serf families at the time of perpetual serfdom in the sixteenth and seventeenth centuries]. *Századok* 137 (2003): 549–78.

Péter, Katalin. "The Other Way: Negotiating Freedom in a Gutsherrschaft Country, the Kingdom of Hungary in the Sixteenth and Seventeenth Centuries." In *Armed Memory, Agency and Peasant Revolts in Central and Southern Europe (1450–1700)*, edited by Gabriella Erdélyi, 59–82. Göttingen: Vandenhoeck&Ruprecht, 2016.

Péter, Katalin. "Társadalom és gazdálkodás a kora újkori Sárospatakon: A patakiak csendes ellenállása" [Society and farming in early modern Sárospatak: The silent resistance of the people of Sárospatak]. *Századok* 131 (1997): 809–56.

Peters, Christine. *Patterns of Piety. Women, Gender and Religion in Late Medieval and Reformation England.* Cambridge: Cambridge University Press, 2003.

Pilvousek, Josef. "Askese, Brüderlichkeit und Wissenschaft: Die Ideale der Erfurter Augustiner-Eremiten und ihre Bemühungen um eine innovative Umsetzung." In *Luther und das monastische Erbe*, edited by Christoph Bultmann, Volker Leppin, and Andreas Lindner, 39–56. Spätmittelalter, Humanismus, Reformation 39. Tübingen: Mohr Siebeck, 2007.

Plattard, Jean. *The Life of François Rabelais*, translated by Louis Peter Roche. London: Frank Cass and Co. Ltd, 1968.

Plöchl, Willibald M. *Geschichte des Kirchenrechts.* Vienna and Munich: Verlag Herold, 1955.

Po-Chia Hsia, Ronnie. *Social Discipline in the Reformation: Central Europe, 1550–1750.* London: Routledge, 1989.

Pócs, Éva. *Between the Living and the Dead: A Perspective on Witches and Seers in the Early Modern Age.* Budapest: CEU Press, 1999.

Pratt, Mary Louise. *Imperial Eyes: Travel Writing and Transculturation.* London: Routledge, 2008.

Quéniart, Jean. *Les hommes, l'église et Dieu dans la France du XVIIIe siècle.* Paris: Hachette, 1978.

Radushev, Evgeni. "The Spread of Islam in the Ottoman Balkans: Revisiting Bulliet's Method on Religious Conversion." *Oriental Archive* 78 (2010): 363–84.

Rady, Martyn. "Hungarian Procedural Law and Part Two of the Tripartitum." In *Custom and Law in Central Europe*, edited by Martyn Rady and Bak M. János, 47–70. Cambridge: Centre for European Legal Studies, 2003.

Rady, Martyn. "Justice Delayed? Litigation and Dispute Settlement in Fifteenth-Century Hungary." *Central Europe* 2 (2004): 3–14.

Ramminger, Johann. *Neulateinische Wortliste*, accessed June 16, 2016, www.neulatein.de/words/3/015247.htm.

Redfield, Robert. *Peasant Society and Culture: An Anthropological Approach to Civilization*. Chicago: Chicago University Press, 1956.

Rehberg, Andreas. "L'affluenza di ordinandi a Roma alla vigilia della riforma luterana." In *La papauté à la Renaissance*, edited by Florence Alazard and Frank La Brasca, 167–249. Paris: Champion, 2007.

Reinhard, Wolfgang. "Kirche als Mobilitätskanal der frühneuzeitlichen Gesellschaft." In *Ständische Gesellschaft und soziale Mobilität*, edited by Winfried Schulze, 333–52. Munich: De Gruyter, 1988.

Reizner, János. "A Császár-féle felső-magyarországi 1631–1632-ik évi pórlázadás okmánytára: 1. közlemény" [The documents of the peasant revolt led by Császár in 1631–1632 Upper-Hungary: First part]. *Történelmi Tár* 11, no. 1 (1888): 120–39.

Reizner, János. *Szeged története*. [History of Szeged]. Vol. 1. Szeged: Szeged Város Közönsége, 1899.

Riis, Ole and Linda Woodhead. *A Sociology of Religious Emotion*. Oxford: Oxford University Press, 2010.

Ritoókné Szalay, Ágnes. *"Nympha Super Ripam Danubii": Tanulmányok a XV–XVI. századi magyarországi művelődés köréből* ["Nymph on the bank of the Danube": Studies on the literate culture of Hungary in the fifteenth and sixteenth centuries]. Budapest: Balassi, 2002.

RMNY = *Régi Magyarországi Nyomtatványok (1473–1670)* [Old Prints in Hungary]. 4 vols. Budapest: MTA–OSZK, 1971–2012.

Roest, Bert, ed. *Religious Orders and Religious Identity Formation, ca. 1420–1620*. Leiden: Brill, 2016.

Roper, Lyndal. *Oedipus and the Devil: Witchcraft, Sexuality and Religion in Early Modern Europe*. London: Routledge, 1994.

Rosenwein, Barbara H. *Introduction to Emotional Communities in the Early Middle Ages*, edited by Barbara H. Rosenwein, I–XXXI. Ithaca and London: Cornell University Press, 2006.

Rothman, Natalie. *Brokering Empire: Trans-Imperial Subjects between Venice and Istanbul*. Ithaca: Cornell University Press, 2012.

Rott, Jean, ed. *Correspondance de Martin Bucer*, vol. 1. Leiden: Brill, 1979.

Rubin, Miri. *Corpus Christi. The Eucharist in Late Medieval Culture*. Cambridge: Cambridge University Press, 1991.

Rüttgardt, Antje. *Klosteraustritte in der frühen Reformation: Studien zu Flugschriften der Jahre 1522 bis 1524*. Gütersloh: Gütersloher Verlagshaus, 2007.

Sack, Hilmar. *Der Krieg in den Köpfen. Die Erinnerung and den Dreißigjährigen Krieg in der deutschen Krisenerfahrung zwischen Julirevolution und deutschem Krieg*. Berlin: Duncker & Humblot, 2008.

Salonen, Kirsi and Jussi Hanska. *Entering a Clerical Career at the Roman Curia, 1458–1471*. Farnham: Ashgate, 2013.

Salonen, Kirsi and Ludwig Schmugge. *A Sip from the Well of Grace: Medieval Texts from the Apostolic Penitentiary*. Washington: Catholic University of America Press, 2009.

Sarbak, Gábor, ed. *Decus solitudinis: pálos évszázadok* [Decus solitudinis: Pauline centuries]. Piliscsaba: Művelődéstörténeti műhely—Rendtörténeti konferenciák, 2007.

Sarbak, Gábor. "Die 'Devotio moderna' in Ungarn." In *Die 'Neue Frömmigkeit' in Europa im Spätmittelalter*, edited by Marek Dervich and Martial Staub, 249–66. Göttingen: Vandenhoeck & Ruprecht, 2004.

Sarbak, Gábor. "Gyöngyösi, Gregor." In *Biographisch-bibliographisches Kirchenlexikon*, edited by Friedrich Wilhelm Bautz and Traugott Bautz, 571–74. Herzberg: Traugott Bautz, 2012.

Sarbak, Gábor, ed. *Der Paulinerorden: Geschichte—Geist—Kultur*. Budapest: Szent István Társulat, 2010.

Schilling, Heinz. "Reformation-Umbruch oder Gipfelpunkt eines Tempts des Réformes." In *Die frühe Reformation in Deutschland als Umbruch. Wissenschafltiches Symposiumdes Vereins für Reformationsgeschichte 1996*, edited by Bernd Moeller and Stephen E. Buckwalter, 13–34. Gütersloh, 1998.

Schilling, Johannes. *Gewesene Mönche. Lebensgeschichte in der Reformation*. Munich: Stiftung Historisches Kolleg, 1990.

Schindler, Norbert. "Guardians of Disorder: Rituals of Youthful Culture at the Dawn of the Modern Age." In *A History of Young People in the West, vol. 1. Ancient and Medieval Rites of Passage*, edited by Giovanni Levi and Jean Claude Schmitt, 240–82 and 364–77. Cambridge–London: Belknap Press of Harvard University Press, 1997.

Schindler, Norbert. "Karneval, Kirche und verkehrte Welt. Zur Funktion der Lachkultur im 16. Jahrhundert." In idem, *Widerspenstige Leute. Studien zur Volkskultur in der fruhen Neuzeit*. 121–74. Frankfurt/M: Fischer Taschenbuch Verlag, 1992.

Schindler, Norbert. "Nocturnal Disturbances: On the Social History of the Night in the Early Modern Period." In idem *Rebellion, Community and Custom in Early Modern Germany*, 225–35. Cambridge: Cambridge University Press, 2002.

Schindler, Norbert. *Rebellion, Community and Custom in Early Modern Germany*. Cambridge: Cambridge University Press, 2002.

Schmidt, Fr. Wilh. Val., ed. *Petri Alfonsi Disciplina Clericalis*. Berlin: T.C.F: Enslin, 1827.

Schwerhoff, Blauert and Gert Schwerhoff, eds. *Kriminalitätsgeschichte: Beiträge zur social- und Kulturgeschichte der Vormoderne*, Konflikte und Kultur: Historische Perspektiven, 1. Konstanz: UVK Universitätsverlag, 2000.

Schwerhoff, Gerd. "Zivilisationsprozess und Geschichtswissenschaft. Norbert Elias' Forschungsparadigma in historischer Sicht." *Historische Zeitschrift* 266 (1998): 561–606.

Scribner, Robert W. and Tom Scott, eds. *The German Peasants' War: A History in Documents.* London-New Jersey: Humanities Press International, 1991.

Scribner, Robert W. *The German Reformation.* London: Macmillan, 1986.

Scribner, Robert W. *Popular Culture and Popular Movements in Reformation Germany.* London: Hambledon Press, 1987.

Sheffley, David L. *Schools and Schooling in Late Medieval Germany, Regensburg 1250–1500.* Leiden and Boston: Brill, 2008.

Smail, Lord Daniel. *The Consumption of Justice: Emotions, Publicity, and Legal Culture in Marseille, 1264–1423.* Ithaca and London: Cornell University Press, 2003.

Smith, Preserved. *Erasmus: A Study of His Life, Ideals, and Place in History.* London: Harper and Brothers Publishers, 1923.

Smith, William F. *Rabelais in his Writings.* Cambridge: Cambridge University Press, 1918.

Solymosi, László. "A veszprémi székesegyházi könyvtár és kölcsönzői a középkor végén" [The borrowers of the Veszprém Cathedral Library at the end of the Middle Ages]. *Veszprémi Szemle* 3 (1995): 3–15.

Sontag, Susan. *Regarding the Pain of the Others.* New York: St Martins Press, 2003.

Spufford, Margaret. "First Steps in Literacy: The Reading and Writing Experiences of the Humblest Seventeenth-Century Spiritual Autobiographers." *Social History* 4 (1979): 407–35.

Stoler, Ann Laura. "Intimidation of Empire: Predicaments of the Tactile and Unseen." In idem *Haunted by Empire: Geographies of Intimacy in North American History,* 1–22. Durham and London: Duke University Press, 2006.

Stone, Lawrence. "The Educational Revolution in England." *Past and Present* 28 (1964): 41–80.

Stone, Lawrence. *The Family, Sex and Marriage in England 1500–1800.* New York: Harper&Row, 1977.

Suad, Joseph, ed. *Methodologies, Paradigms and Sources.* Vol. 1. of *Encyclopedia of Women and Islamic Cultures.* Leiden: Brill, 2003.

Svec Goetschi, Milena. *Klosterflucht und Bittgang. Apostasie und Monastische Mobilität im 15. Jahrhundert.* Vienna, Cologne, Weimar: Böhlau, 2015.

Swanson, Robert N. "Before the Protestant Clergy: The Construction and Deconstruction of Medieval Priesthood" In *The Protestant Clergy of Early Modern Europe,* edited by C. Scott Dixon and Luise Schorn-Schütte, 39–59. New York: Palgrave Macmillan, 2003.

Sz. Simon, Éva. "Flight or Submission: Changing Identities in the Ottoman–Hungarian Borderlands. The County of Zala in the 1570s." In *Osmanischer Orient und Ostmitteleuropa,* edited by Robert Born and Andreas Puth, 33–46. Stuttgart: Franz Steiner Verlag, 2014.

Szabó, István. "A jobbágynevek kialakulása" [The development of serf names]. In *Jobbágyok-parasztok: Értekezések a magyar parasztság történetéből* [Serfs and peasants: Essays on the history of the Hungarian peasantry], edited by András Mező, 223–36. Budapest: Akadémiai Kiadó, 1976.

Szabó, István. *A középkori magyar falu* [The medieval village in Hungary]. Budapest: Akadémiai Kiadó, 1969.

Szakály, Ferenc. *Magyar adóztatás a török hódoltságban* [Hungarian taxation in Ottoman Hungary]. Budapest: Akadémiai Kiadó, 1981.

Szakály, Ferenc. "Magyar diplomaták, utazók, rabok és renegátok a 16. századi Isztambulban" [Hungarian diplomats, travelers, prisoners and renegades in sixteenth-century Istanbul]. In idem *Szigetvári Csöbör Balázs török miniatúrái (1570)* [Turkish Miniatures of Balázs Csöbör of Szigetvár (1570)], 45–46. Budapest: Európa, 1983.

Szakály, Ferenc. *Mezőváros és reformáció: Tanulmányok a korai magyar polgárosodás történetéhez* [Market town and Reformation: Studies on the early phase of the rise of the Burgess class in Hungary]. Budapest: Balassi Kiadó, 1995.

Szakály, Ferenc. "Remargues sur l'armée de Jovan Tcherni." *Acta Historica* (1978): 59–63.

Szende, Katalin. "A soproni középkori végrendeletek egyház- és tárgytörténeti tanulságai" [The lessons with regard to church history and the history of material culture of the medieval testaments of Sopron]. *Soproni Szemle* 44 (1990): 268–72.

Szilády, Áron. *Temesvári Pelbárt élete és munkái* [The life and works of Pelbárt Temesvári]. Budapest: MTA Irodalomtörténeti Bizottsága, 1880.

Szűcs, Jenő. "A ferences obszervancia és az 1514. évi parasztháború. Egy kódex tanúsága." [Franciscan Observants and the peasant war of 1514: Testimony of a codex.] *Levéltári Közlemények* 43 (1972): 213–63.

Szűcs, Jenő. "Ferences ellenzéki áramlat a magyar parasztháború és reformáció hátterében" [Franciscan opposition movement in the background of the Hungarian peasant revolt and the Reformation]. *Irodalomtörténeti Közlemények* 78 (1974): 409–35.

Szűcs, Jenő. "Die Ideologie des Bauernkrieges." In *Aus der Geschichte der Ostmitteleuropäischen Bauernbewegungen im 16.–17. Jahrhundert*, edited by Heckenast Gusztáv, 157–88. Budapest: Akadémiai Kiadó, 1977.

Takáts, Sándor. *Rajzok a török világból* [Images from the Turkish world]. 2 vols. Budapest: MTA, 1915–1917.

Tarnai, Andor. *'A magyar nyelvet írni kezdik': Irodalmi gondolkodás a középkori Magyarországon* ["They start to write the Hungarian language": Literary thinking in medieval Hungary]. Budapest: Akadémiai Kiadó, 1984.

Thompson, Edward P. "Time, Work-Discipline and Industrial Capitalism." *Past and Present* 38 (1967): 56–97.

Tonk, Sándor. *Erdélyiek egyetemjárása a középkorban* [The peregrinatio academica of Transylvanians in the Middle Ages]. Bucharest: Kriterion, 1979.

Tönnies, Ferdinand. *Gemeinschaft und Gesellschaft.* Leipzig: Fues's Verlag, 1887.

Tóth, Péter G. "A fájdalom metaforái: A testi fájdalom, a kegyetlenség és a vértanúság látványa a kora újkori Magyarországon" [Metaphors of pain: The scene of bodily pain, brutality and martyrdom in early modern Hungary]. In *Mikrokozmosz-makrokozmosz: Vallásetnológiai fogalmak tudományközi megközelítésben* [Microcosm-macrocosm: Interdisciplinary approach to concepts of ethnography of religion], edited by Pócs Éva, 319–72. Budapest: Balassi Kiadó, 2001.

Tóth, Péter G. "A lator teste és a lator test: A bűnösség kultúrája a kora újkori Magyarországon és a büntetés-emlékeztetés problémája (vázlat)" [The body of the rouge and the rouge body: The culture of sin in early modern Hungary and punishments as rites of memory. A draft]. *Korall* 4, no. 5–6 (2001): 141–62.

Trexler, Richard C. "The Feast of St. John and Other Friends." In *Public Life in Renaissance Florence.* 240–262. Edited by Richard C. Trexler. Ithaka and London: Cornell University Press, 1991.

Trexler, Richard C. *Public Life in Renaissance Florence* New York: Academic Press, 1980.

Tringli, István. "Az 1481. évi szlavóniai közgyűlés" [The Slavonian General Assembly in 1481]. In *Tanulmányok Borsa Iván tiszteletére* [Essays in honor of Iván Borsa], edited by Csukovits Enikő, 291–318. Budapest: Magyar Országos Levéltár, 1998.

Tringli, István. "Fehde und Gewalttätigkeit: Vergleich eines germanischen und ungarischen Rechtsinstituts." In *Legal Transitions: Development of Law in Formerly Socialist States and the Challenges of the European Union—Rechtsentwicklung in den ehemealigen sozialistischen Staten und die Hearusforderung der Europäischen Union*, edited by Balogh Elemér, Hegedüs Andrea, Mezei Péter, Szomora Zsolt and Traser Julianna Sára, 281–6. Szeged: Pólya E. Alapítvány, 2007.

Tringli, István. "Jagelló-kori levelesítő jegyzék Zalából" [A list of proscribed criminals from the County of Zala in the Jagiełło era]. *Levéltári Közlemények* 69 (1998): 3–30.

Tringli, István. "Pest megye a későközépkorban" [Pest County in the Late Middle Ages]. In *Pest megye monográfiája, 1/2. A honfoglalástól 1686-ig* [A monograph on Pest County from the Conquest until 1686], edited by Zsoldos Attila, 75–194. Budapest: Pest Megye Monográfia Közalapítvány, 2001.

Trusen, Winfried. "Zur Bedeutung des geistlichen Forum internum und externum für die spätmittelalterliche Gesellschaft." *Zeitschrift der Savigny-Stiftung der Rechtsgeschichte 107, Kanonistische Abteilung* 76 (1990): 254–85.

Tüskés, Anna. *Magyarországi diákok a bécsi egyetemen* [Students from Hungary at the University of Vienna]. Magyarországi diákok a középkori egyetemeken 1. Budapest: ELTE Lvt., 2008.

V. Kovács, Sándor. *Eszmetörténet és régi magyar irodalom* [Intellectual history and Old Hungarian literature]. Budapest: Magvető, 1987.

V. Kovács, Sándor. "Kolostori műveltség és magyar kódexirodalom" [Cloister Culture and Hungarian codex literature]. In idem *Eszmetörténet és régi magyar irodalom:*

Tanulmányok [Intellectual history and Old Hungarian literature: Essays], 133–184. Budapest: Magvető, 1987.

Valter, Ilona. "Falusi és mezővárosi iskolák a középkorban" [Village and market town schools in the Middle Ages]. In *A magyar iskola első évszázadai* [The first centuries of Hungarian schools], edited by Szende Katalin, 61–7. The Győr exhibition and catalogue of the 1000 Years of Hungarian Schools National Program. Győr: Xántus Múzeum, 1996.

van Dülmen, Richard. *Das Haus und seine Menschen.* Kultur und Alltag in der Frühen Neuzeit. Munich: C.H. Beck, 2005.

van Dülmen, Richard. *Theatre of Horror: Crime and Punishment in Early Modern Germany*. Cambridge: Polity Press, 1990.

Vargas, Michael A. *Taming a Brood of Vipers: Medieval and Early Modern Medieval World.* Leiden: Brill, 2011.

Virágh, Jenő. *Dr. Luther Márton önmagáról* [Dr. Martin Luther on himself]. Budapest: Ordass Lajos Baráti Kör, 1991.

Weinrich, Lorenz. *Hungarici monasterii ordinis sancti Pauli primi heremitae de Urbe Roma instrumenta et priorum registra.* Budapest and Roma: METEM, 1999.

Weinrich, Lorenz. *Das ungarische Paulinerkloster Santo Stefano Rotondo in Rom, 1404–1579.* Berlin: Duncker&Humblot GmbH, 1998.

Wendehorts, Alfred. "Wer konnte im Mittelalter lesen und schreiben?" In *Schulen und Studium im sozialen Wandel des hohen und späten Mittelalters*, edited by Johannes Fried, 11–33. Sigmaringen: Jan Thorbecke Verlag, 1986.

Worstbrock, Franz Josef, ed. *Deutscher Humanismus 1480–1520. Verfasserlexikon.* Vol 1. Berlin–New York: De Gruyter, 2008.

Zarinebaf-Shahr, Fariba. "Women, Law and Imperial Justice in Ottoman Istanbul in the Late Seventeenth Century." In *Women, the Family and Divorce Laws in Islamic History*, edited by Amira El Azhary Sonbol, 81–95. Syracuse: Syracuse University Press, 1996.

Zoványi, Jenő. *A reformáczió Magyarországon 1565-ig* [The Reformation in Hungary until 1565]. Budapest: ÁKV, 1986.

Index

www.ingramcontent.com/pod-product-compliance
Lightning Source LLC
LaVergne TN
LVHW010641300926
849161LV00005B/1017

* 9 7 8 9 0 0 4 3 6 1 1 5 7 *